CHICKEN, MULES AND TWO OLD FOOLS

NEW YORK TIMES BESTSELLING AUTHOR

VICTORIA TWEAD

Copyright © 2010 Victoria Twead

Published by Ant Press - www.antpress.org

Hardback ISBN: 978-1-922476-30-2

Paperback ISBN: 978-1-922476-07-4

Large Print Paperback: 978-1-922476-17-3

Also available in digital editions.

All rights reserved.

No part of this book may be reproduced in any form or by any electronic or mechanical means, including information storage and retrieval systems, without written permission from the author, except for the use of brief quotations in a book review.

CONTENTS

The Old Fools Series	v
FREE Photo Book	vi
1. THE FIVE YEAR PLAN	1
Grumpy's Garlic Mushrooms	8
2. JUDITH, MOTHER AND KURT	11
Spicy Mediterranean Dip	17
3. SIGNED AND SEALED	19
Bethina's Ham, Tomato & Garlic Toasts	26
4. PACO AND BETHINA	27
Crispy Potatoes in Spicy Tomato Sauce	33
5. THE DYNAMIC DUO	35
Spanish Spinach	41
6. BEWARE THE MAN WITH THE VAN	43
Spanish Potato Salad	50
7. AUGUST	53
Vegetable Kebabs	61
8. SATELLITES AND PARTIES	63
Paco's Sangria	70
9. GRAPES AND DOCTORS	71
Carmen-Bethina's Poor Man's potatoes	78
10. THE ECO-WARRIORS	81
Barbecued Sardines	87
11. MULES AND STORMS	89
Summer Pork with Sherry	96
12. ¡FIESTA!	99
Asparagus Salad	107
13. PROCESSIONS AND PUDDINGS	109
The Winning Rice Pudding Recipe	116
14. CHICKENS	119
Paco's Rabbit Stew	126
15. AND MORE CHICKENS	129
Chicken and Prawn Paella	137
16. Eggs	139
Salted Almonds	147

17. THE EQUATORS	149
Beef in Fruit Sauce (Ecuadorian Recipe)	156
18. COLIN HELPS OUT	159
Colin's Spanish Omelette	165
19. COCKY	167
Chickpea and Chorizo Soup	174
20. THE COMMUNE	177
Spanish Cauliflower and Paprika	186
21. DEATHS AND PANCHO PINOCHET	189
Summer Baked Potatoes	197
22. SUPPORTING PANCHO	199
Creamy Pork and Paprika	206
23. AWAY-DAYS AND ANIMALS	209
Gazpacho (Cold Tomato Soup) from Andalucía	216
24. JELLYFISH AND CHICKENS	219
Marinated Anchovy Tapa	227
25. THE NEW HOUSES	229
Spanish Meatballs	236
26. GIFTS	239
Tuna with a Spicy Sauce	246
27. AND MORE GIFTS	247
Scrambled Eggs with Ham	253
28. THE JEEP	255
Spinach and Mackerel Toasts	261
29. DOCTOR'S ORDERS	263
Warming Winter's Brunch	271
30. HOUSE SWAP	273
Sticky Toffee Pudding a la Glennys	281
31. EPILOGUE	283
A request…	287
So what happened next?	289
BOOKCLUB Discussion Questions	292
The Old Fools series	295
The Sixpenny Cross series	297
More books by Victoria Twead…	298
Contacts and Links	300
Ant Press Online	307

THE OLD FOOLS SERIES
AVAILABLE IN PAPERBACK, LARGE PRINT AND EBOOK EDITIONS

Chickens, Mules and Two Old Fools is the first book in the *Old Fools* series by New York Times and Wall Street Journal bestselling author, Victoria Twead.

Chickens, Mules and Two Old Fools
Two Old Fools ~ Olé!
Two Old Fools on a Camel
Two Old Fools in Spain Again
Two Old Fools in Turmoil
Two Old Fools Down Under

Prequels
One Young Fool in Dorset
One Young Fool in South Africa

FREE PHOTO BOOK
TO BROWSE OR DOWNLOAD

For photographs and additional unpublished material to accompany this book, browse or download the

FREE PHOTO BOOK
from
www.victoriatwead.com/free-stuff

To the villagers of El Hoyo, young and old, whose warm welcome, patience and generosity was astonishing.
I thank them all from the bottom of my heart.

And to Juliet and Sue, the Gin Twins.
May their bottle never run dry.

1

THE FIVE YEAR PLAN

"Hello?"

"This is Kurt."

"Oh! Hello, Kurt. How are you?"

"I am vell. The papers you vill sign now. I haf made an appointment vith the Notary for you May 23rd, 12 o'clock."

"Right, I'll check the flights and…" but he had already hung up.

Kurt, our German estate agent, was the type of person one obeyed without question. So, on May 23rd, we found ourselves back in Spain, seated round a huge polished table in the Notary's office. Beside us sat our bank manager holding a briefcase stuffed with bank notes.

Nine months earlier, we had never met Kurt. Nine months earlier, Joe and I lived in an ordinary house, in an ordinary Sussex town. Nine months earlier we had ordinary jobs and expected an ordinary future.

Then, one dismal Sunday, I decided to change all that.

"**…heavy showers are expected to last through the Bank Holiday weekend and into next week. Temperatures are struggling to reach 14 degrees…**"

August, and the weather-girl was wearing a coat, sheltering under an umbrella. June had been wet, July wetter. I sighed, stabbing the 'off' button on the remote control before she could depress me further. Agh! Typical British weather.

My depression changed to frustration. The private thoughts that had been tormenting me so long returned. Why should we put up with it? Why not move? Why not live in my beloved Spain where the sun always shines?

I walked to the window. Raindrops like slug trails trickled down the windowpane. Steely clouds hung low, heavy with more rain, smothering the town. Sodden litter sat drowning in the gutter.

"Joe?" He was dozing, stretched out on the sofa, mouth slightly open. "Joe, I want to talk to you about something."

Poor Joe, my long-suffering husband. His gangly frame was sprawled out, newspaper slipping from his fingers. He was utterly relaxed, blissfully unaware that our lives were about to change course.

How different he looked in scruffy jeans compared with his usual crisp uniform. But to me, whatever he wore, he was always the same, an officer and a gentleman. Nearing retirement from the Forces, I knew he was looking forward to a tension-free future, but the television weather-girl had galvanised me into action. The metaphorical bee in my bonnet would not be stilled. It buzzed and grew until it became a hornet demanding attention.

"Huh? What's the matter?" His words were blurred with sleep, his eyes still closed. Rain beat a tattoo on the window pane.

"Joe? Are you listening?"

"Uhuh…"

"When you retire, I want us to sell up and buy a house in Spain." Deep breath.

There. The bomb was dropped. I had finally admitted my longing. I wanted to abandon England with its ceaseless rain. I wanted to move permanently to Spain.

Sleep forgotten, Joe pulled himself upright, confusion in his blue eyes as he tried to read my expression.

"Vicky, what did you say just then?" he asked, squinting at me.

"I want to go and live in Spain."

"You can't be serious."

"Yes, I am."

Of course it wasn't just the rain. I had plenty of reasons, some vague, some more solid.

I presented my pitch carefully. Our children, adults now, were scattered round the world; Scotland, Australia and London. No grandchildren yet on the horizon and Joe only had a year before he retired. Then we would be free as birds to nest where we pleased.

And the cost of living in Spain would be so much lower. Council tax a fraction of what we usually paid, cheaper food, cheaper houses… The list went on.

Joe listened closely and I watched his reactions. Usually, *he* is the impetuous one, not me. But I was well aware that his retirement fantasy was being threatened. His dream of lounging all day in his dressing-gown, writing his book and diverting himself with the odd mathematical problem was being exploded.

"Hang on, Vicky, I thought we had it all planned? I thought you would do a few days of supply teaching if you wanted, while I start writing my book." Joe absentmindedly scratched his nether regions. For once I ignored his infuriating habit; I was in full flow.

"But imagine writing in Spain! Imagine sitting outside in the shade of a grapevine and writing your masterpiece."

Outside, windscreen wipers slapped as cars swept past, tyres sending up plumes of filthy water. Joe glanced out of the window at the driving rain and I sensed I had scored an important point.

"Why don't you write one of your famous lists?" he suggested, only half joking.

I am well known for my lists and records. Inheriting the record-keeping gene from my father, I can't help myself. I make a note of the weather every day, the temperature, the first snowdrop, the day the ants fly, the exchange rate of the euro, everything. I make shopping lists, separate ones for each shop. I make To Do lists and 'Joe, will you please' lists. I make packing lists before holidays. I even make lists of lists. My nickname at work was Schindler.

So I set to work and composed what I considered to be a killer pitch:

Sunny weather
Cheap houses
Live in the country
Ridiculously low council tax
Friendly people
Less crime
No heating bills
Cheap petrol
Wonderful Spanish food
Cheap wine and beer
Could get satellite TV so you won't miss English football
Much more laid-back life style
Could afford house big enough for family and visitors to stay
No TV licence
Only short flight to UK
Might live longer because Mediterranean diet is healthiest in the world

When I ran dry, I handed the list to Joe. He glanced at it and snorted.

"I'm going to make a coffee," he said, but he took my list with him. He was in the kitchen a long time.

When he came out, I looked up at him expectantly. He ignored me, snatched a pen and scribbled on the bottom of the list. Satisfied, he threw it on the table and left the room. I grabbed it and read his additions. He'd pressed so hard with the pen that he'd nearly gone through the paper.

Joe had written:

CAN'T SPEAK SPANISH!
TOO MANY FLIES!
MOVING HOUSE IS THE PITS!

For weeks we debated, bouncing arguments for and against like a game of ping pong. Even when we weren't discussing it, the subject hung in the air between us, almost tangible. Then one day, (was it a coincidence that it was raining yet again?) Joe surprised me.

"Vicky, why don't you book us a holiday over Christmas, and we could just take a look."

The hug I gave him nearly crushed his ribs.

"Hang on!" he said, detaching himself and holding me at arm's length. "What I'm trying to say is, well, I'm willing to compromise."

"What do you mean, 'compromise'?"

"How about if we look on it as a five year plan? We don't sell this house, just rent it out. Okay, we could move to Spain, but not necessarily for ever. At the end of five years, we can make up our minds whether to come back to England or stay out there. I'm happy to try it for five years. What do you think?"

I turned it over in my mind. Move to Spain, but look on it as a sort of project? Actually, it seemed rather a good idea. In fact, a perfect compromise.

Joe was watching me. "Well? Agreed?"

"Agreed…" It was a victory of sorts. A Five Year Plan. Yes, I saw the sense in that. Anything could happen in five years.

"Well, go on, then. Book a holiday over Christmas and we'll take it from there."

So I logged onto the Internet and booked a two week holiday in Almería.

Why Almería? Well, we already knew the area quite well as this would be our fourth visit. And I considered this part of Andalucía to be perfect. Only two and a half hours flight from London, guaranteed sunshine, friendly people and jaw-dropping views. It ticked all my boxes. Joe agreed cautiously that the area could be ideal.

So the destination was decided, but what type of home in Spain would we want? Our budget was reduced because we weren't going to sell our English house. We'd have to find something cheap.

On previous visits, I'd hated all the houses we'd noticed in the resorts. Mass produced boxes on legoland estates, each identical, each characterless and overlooking the next. No, I knew what I really wanted: a house we could fix up, with views and space, preferably in an unspoiled Spanish village.

Unlike Joe, I've always been obsessed with houses. I was the driving force and it was the hard climb up the English property ladder that allowed us even to contemplate moving abroad. In the past few years, we had bought a derelict house, improved and sold it, making a good profit. So we bought another and repeated the process. It was gruelling work. We both had other careers, but it was well worth the effort. Now we could afford to rent out our home in England and still buy a modest house in Spain.

"If we do decide to move out there," said Joe, "and we buy an old place to do up, it's not going to be like doing up houses in England. Everything's going to be different there."

How right he was.

Like a child, I yearned for that Christmas to come. I couldn't wait to set foot on Spanish soil again. We arrived, and although Christmas lights decorated the airport, it was warm enough to remove our jackets. Before long, we had found our hotel and settled in.

The next morning, we hired a little car. Joe, having finally accepted the inevitable, was happy to drive into the mountains in search of The House. We had two weeks to find it.

Yet again the mountains seduced us. The endless blue sky where birds of prey wheeled lazily. The neat orchards splashed with bright oranges and lemons. The secret, sleepy villages nestled into valleys. Even the roads, narrow, treacherous and winding, couldn't break the spell that Andalucía cast over us.

Daily, we drove through whitewashed villages where little old ladies dressed in black stopped sweeping their doorsteps to watch us pass. We waved at farmers working in their fields, the dry dust swirling in irritated clouds from their labours. We paused to allow goat-herds to pass with their flocks, the lead goat's bell clanging bossily as the herd followed, snatching mouthfuls of vegetation on the run.

Although we hadn't yet found The House, we were positive we'd found the area we wanted to live in.

One day we drove into a village that clung to the steep mountainside by its fingernails. We entered a bar that was buzzing with activity. It was busy and the air heavy with smoke. The white-aproned bartender looked us up and down and jerked his head in greeting. No smile, just a nod.

Joe found a rocky wooden table by the window with panoramic views and we settled ourselves, soaking in the atmosphere. Four old men played cards at the next table. A heated debate was taking place between another group. I caught the words 'Barcelona' and 'Real Madrid'. Most of the bar's customers were male.

Grumpy, the bartender, wiped his hands on his apron and approached our table, flicking off imaginary crumbs from the surface with the back of his hand. He had a splendid moustache which concealed any expression he may have had, and made communication difficult.

"Could we see the menu, please?" asked Joe in his best phrase book Spanish.

Grumpy shook his head and snorted. It seemed there was no menu.

"No *importa*," said Joe. "It doesn't matter."

Using a combination of sign language and impatient grunts, Grumpy took our order but our meal was destined to be a surprise. A basket of bread was slammed onto the table, followed by two plates of food. Garlic mushrooms - delicious. We cleaned our plates and leaned back, digesting our food and the surroundings. In typical Spanish fashion, the drinkers at the bar bellowed at each other as though every individual had profound hearing problems.

"We're running out of time," said Joe. "We can carry on gallivanting around the countryside, but we aren't going to find anything. I very much doubt we'll find a house this holiday."

Suddenly, clear as cut crystal, the English words, "Oh, bugger! Where are my keys?" floated above the Spanish hubbub.

GRUMPY'S GARLIC MUSHROOMS
CHAMPIÑONES AL AJILLO

Tapa means 'lid' or 'cover' in Spanish. It's thought that the name originally came from the practice of placing slices of meat on top of a sherry glass, to keep out flies. The meat, often ham or chorizo, was characteristically salty, inducing thirst. Bartenders saw this and began serving a variety of tapas which increased alcohol sales. Thus a new tradition was born.

Ingredients (serves 4)

- 50ml (2 fl oz) extra virgin olive oil
- 250g (8oz) fresh mushrooms (sliced)
- 4-6 cloves of garlic (chopped or sliced)
- 3 tablespoons dry Spanish sherry
- 2 tablespoons lemon juice
- Large pinch of dried chili flakes
- Large pinch of paprika
- Salt, freshly ground pepper
- Chopped parsley to garnish

Method

- Heat the oil in a frying pan and fry the mushrooms over a high heat for 2 or 3 minutes. Stir constantly.
- Lower the heat and add the garlic, lemon juice, sherry, salt and pepper.
- For a milder flavour you can leave it at that if you like. But if

you like a few 'fireworks', now is the time to add the dried chili and paprika as well.
- Cook for another 5 minutes or so until the garlic and mushrooms have softened, then remove from the heat.
- Sprinkle with chopped parsley and divide up into pre-heated little dishes.
- Serve with plenty of fresh, crusty bread to mop up the seriously garlicky juices.

2

JUDITH, MOTHER AND KURT

We swung round, just as the owner of the voice found her keys and rattled them in the air triumphantly. She finished her good-byes to her drinking companions in perfect Spanish, loud and fluent.

This opportunity was just too good to pass. As she strode past our table, I smiled and said, "Hello, you're English, aren't you?" Unoriginal, I admit, but it had the desired affect. She applied the brakes.

"I'm Vicky, and this is Joe," I said. "We just love this area. Have you lived here long?"

Judith was unique. Stout, in her sixties, she had a thick plait snaking down her back. She was dressed in English country tweeds and sensible walking shoes.

We shook hands and she sank heavily into the chair Joe pulled out for her.

"Twenty-five years," she said. "Good Lord, where does the time go?"

"Well, you're obviously very settled here," said Joe.

"Bloody nice place to be," she said, leaning forward, knees apart, hands toying with her bunch of keys. "Climate's much kinder to Mother's rheumatism, don't you know."

Judith's voice was cultured although often punctuated by colourful expletives. Although looking and behaving like an eccentric English aristocrat, she seemed entirely at home in this remote corner of Spain. And judging by her interaction with the people at the bar, she was accepted and respected by the villagers. To us, she was friendly and informative, answering all our tentative questions in her strident voice.

"Awfully laid back, the Spanish," she said. "Our cleaner, Ana, needs a stick of dynamite under her before she gets going."

"Do you ever think of going back to England?" I asked, feeling rather sorry for poor Ana.

"Good heavens, dear!" she said, eyes bulging. "Not on your Nellie! Don't miss Old Blighty one bit!"

Eventually, she looked at the man's watch on her wrist.

"Bloody hell!" she said. "Look at the time! Mother will be wondering where I am. Come back to my house, why don't you, and meet Mother?" Joe and I agreed, hastily paid Grumpy and followed her out into the bright sunlight.

"Where are you, you little bastards?" she called when we were outside. Joe looked shocked and I froze on the spot. Several dogs slid out of the shadows and loped towards her, and we realised that it was not us she was addressing.

"How many dogs do you have?" I asked, knee deep in panting canines.

"Nine," Judith replied shortly. "And that one over there is called 'Half'."

I must have looked blank.

"He's the latest. We always said we'd never have ten dogs so when he joined us, we called him 'Half'. So now we only have nine and a Half. Bloody Spaniards, don't know how to look after animals!"

Judith's house was just down the street from Grumpy's. Huge double doors were unlocked by an outsize key and we were ushered into the darkness beyond. Our eyes adjusted and we saw we were standing in an Aladdin's cave. The living room was crammed with huge solid pieces of antique English furniture, gleaming with age and history. Vast mirrors hung on the walls. Every surface was cluttered with knick-knacks and valuable bric-a-brac. Looking closer, the enormous sideboard and mahogany table legs were pale and splintered in places where the dogs had chewed them.

Shelves bowed with dusty figurines and piles of books. Occasionally, dark shapes shifted and we could distinguish cats sleeping on every level. One cat draped itself along the mantelpiece, another on the grand piano. A shaft of light sliced through a crack in the wooden shutter, spotlighting dancing motes of dust and cat fur.

"Let me introduce you to Mother," shouted Judith, clicking on a Tiffany table lamp. A figure uncoiled itself from the ornate chaise longue, dislodging an orange cat that spilled to the floor. "Then we'll have a little drinky-poo."

We were mesmerised by Mother. She must have been eighty-five years of age but was draped in a lacy, diaphanous dress, low cut to reveal maximum cleavage and totally transparent against the light. She lay poised like a sex kitten, exuding glamour and wafting Chanel No.5.

"Pleased to meet you," said the old lady, extending manicured fingers for us to shake.

Joe and I spent a wine-soaked hour or so with these welcoming ladies, perched on the antique sofa, wedged between cats and dogs.

"Got a dispensation from my Bishop in England," boomed Judith. "Have to attend their church here, don't you know. Bloody Catholics couldn't organise a piss-up in a brewery. Soon put the priest right, didn't I, Mother?"

The village church-bells rang on cue, as if in agreement. Mother was admiring her nails and not listening. A small hairy dog resembling a floor mop began humping a cushion on the floor.

"Well, m'dears. If you're serious about moving here, I suggest you have a chin-wag with Kurt," said Judith, scribbling a telephone number on the back of a church newsletter. "Don't go to any of the bloody estate agents in town. Crooks, all of 'em. Let me know how you get on."

Eventually, we thanked Judith and said good-bye to Mother. We staggered out into the street plastered, both by red wine and pet hair, clutching Kurt's telephone number.

With Judith's voice ringing in our ears, *"Straight as a bloody die, don't you know,"* we contacted Kurt the next day. He was an unofficial estate agent to foreigners and very German. He spoke excellent Spanish, rather quaint English and was married to Paula, a Spanish solicitor. Also, his business partner, Marco, was on the local council. An irresistible package. We were confident he was the right person to help us find The House.

We met at the appointed time in the square of Judith's village, outside the Town Hall. Several elderly Spanish men sat on benches and ceased their conversations to eye us. A group of women, all dressed in black, inspected us like curious crows. When we introduced ourselves, Kurt's handshake exuded efficiency. Tall, fit and utterly Teutonic, his curly blond hair flopped when he talked as though punctuating his sentences.

"I haf three houses for you to look," he said. "So I hope you are full of the beans." He marched off down the street.

His muscular legs covered distances in long, swinging strides while we panted pathetically behind him. Desperately trying to anticipate his next move, we concentrated on his retreating back. Frequently he made unexpected left or right turns, resulting in Joe and me crashing heavily into each other in the frantic effort to keep up. It must have looked like some silly Laurel and Hardy scene.

The first house had no roof.

"Is this it?" Joe muttered to me from the corner of his mouth. I rolled my eyes, but didn't reply. Kurt ignored our dismayed expressions and unlocked the front door with a flourish.

"This is a good house," he said. "All the rooms are very big."

Well, that was true. All the rooms were light and airy, too, as expected from a house with no roof. In the kitchen, clumps of weeds sprouted from between the cracked floor tiles. We halted in a bedroom and looked up at the sky above.

"It's, er, very nice," I said, "but actually I think we might prefer a house with a roof."

Kurt's flaxen eyebrows shot up in surprise, as though we had asked for an indoor sauna, or home cinema.

"*Ja*, but I think you vill like the next house. It has a roof."

Relieved, we were taken over the mountain to the next house. It stood alone in scrub land, a single ragged palm tree standing guard.

"This is also a good house. It has a roof and a palm tree." Kurt's blue eyes challenged us to find fault *this* time.

To be fair, the front of the house looked quite impressive, but neglected. Joe disappeared around the corner of the building while Kurt fumbled the key into the lock.

Yes, it had a roof. And a palm tree. I couldn't help feeling quite excited. Kurt finally unlocked the door and tried to push it open. The door resisted, so he shouldered it. Still it stood firm, forcing him to give it a hefty Germanic kick. Success. The door swung open and Kurt and I both jumped in surprise. There, in the middle of the room in front of us, stood Joe.

"How did you get in?" I asked, astonished.

"It's got no walls at the back. Or down one side."

"No valls, but this is a good house. It has a roof and a palm tree," said Kurt, recovering, clearly confident that we could overlook this minor flaw. Was there a glimmer of humour in those blue eyes?

We continued the tour. Joe was right, several walls had caved in, rocks lying where they had fallen. Birds flew out shrieking as we disturbed them in the kitchen. Soft rabbit and goat droppings squelched underfoot. Two feral cats burst out from a corner and slunk away over the hillside. A cold wind blew more debris into the house, depositing it on the mound that had already accumulated over time.

"I think we need a house that has a roof and walls," said Joe firmly, and I nodded.

Kurt did not seem discouraged. We exited and he locked the door behind us again.

"What's the point of locking the door when the house has no walls?" I asked, curious.

"Insurance," he said, flicking the forelock from his eyes. "Now, I haf one house more. It is a very good house. It has valls, and a roof, but no palm tree. You vill follow me." We climbed back into the car.

Perhaps just a kilometre away as the quail flies, but a good eight kilometres by road, was the next village, El Hoyo. The road was empty as Kurt steered the car up, ever up and crested the mountain. Without warning, he swung off onto a single track road that threatened to drop off the edge of a precipice. Fir trees clung to the mountainsides in deep green knots. Olive trees were planted in military rows on terraces excavated by farmers generations ago. Almond trees displayed their white blossoms.

Kurt slowed the car so we could take in the scene below. We peered down and were rewarded with our first glimpse of El Hoyo. That day it was shrouded in mist which cleared as the wind chased the wispy clouds away. A typical Moorish whitewashed village, El Hoyo was much smaller than Judith's village. Deep in the fold of the valley, the village houses huddled together, protected on all sides by the ancient slopes. It was just a cluster of houses, most very old, many derelict. Narrow streets separated the rows of houses. In the centre was the square, boasting shade-trees, seats and a fountain. The church was imposing and astonishingly pink. On the outskirts of the village stood a few modern houses.

I found I was holding my breath, captivated by the painting below. Kurt revved the car up and we started to descend in a white-knuckle ride of twists and turns.

He parked the car by the square and we all got out. There was no sign of life apart from a couple of bored dogs and a feather of smoke curling from one chimney.

"It's so quiet," I breathed. A cock crowed somewhere.

"Ja, you haf plenty of quiet and peace. No person vill molest you." He turned up a side street with Joe and me close on his heels, then halted suddenly causing us to crash into him from behind.

Alonso, the owner of the house for sale, stood beaming on the doorstep. Small of stature but strong and gnarled as an olive log, he greeted us. Joe and Kurt shook his proffered hand but I was seized and kissed on the cheeks, one, two, Spanish style.

Squeezed in the middle of a row of terraced houses, this house appeared unpromising from the outside. It looked tiny and cramped, as though it was trying to shoulder its neighbours aside for more space. The frontage was only as wide as the front door and a small window. Alonso and Kurt stepped aside and we entered.

SPICY MEDITERRANEAN DIP

A mildly spicy, smooth, light dip perfect for an aperitif or buffet.

Ingredients

- 1 large jar of chickpeas (not dried)
- 175 ml (6 fl oz) olive oil
- Salt
- 1 teaspoon pepper
- 2 tablespoons cumin
- 2 teaspoons hot paprika

Method

- Place the chickpeas and the olive oil into a large bowl and blend into a smooth puree.
- Add the salt and pepper and the cumin and blend again. It's important to taste as you go, adding more cumin as necessary.
- Pour into a dish, sprinkling the top with a little more cumin and the hot paprika.
- Place in the freezer for about 10 minutes to set slightly.
- Serve with slices of raw carrot, cucumber, peppers and celery.

3

SIGNED AND SEALED

Standing in the living room, Joe and I looked around.

"It smells damp," said Joe, wrinkling his nose.

"And it's so dark," I said. "Even with the lights on."

"Well, at least it has walls and a roof." Joe's attempt at humour did not amuse me.

Kurt and Alonso had followed us in, still chatting. A hideous plastic chandelier hung from the low ceiling just above Kurt's head, like a crazy Ascot hat. The fireplace was ugly and small, caked with old grease. On one wall a sinister looking crack zigzagged from floor to ceiling, like a lightning bolt.

"What's that?" asked Joe, pointing.

"Terremoto," said Alonso cheerfully.

"The earthquake made the crack," said Kurt.

Joe and I exchanged glances. What? Earthquakes hadn't even crossed our minds. Could it happen again? Was this house unsafe?

Alonso rattled away to Kurt, who occasionally interpreted for us. "He says he vill present you the television. It is German," said Kurt. We tried hard to look excited at owning the ancient dust-covered television squatting malevolently in the corner.

We left Alonso and Kurt downstairs and climbed the stairs, holding onto the flimsy metal pole screwed into the wall which served as a handrail. The cement steps were cracked and filthy. Upstairs there were three rooms, each with a tiny, shuttered, barred window. Dust-laden cobwebs spanned every corner and alcove like tattered Victorian lace. Rusty bedsteads with mildewed mattresses sheltered more beetles and spiders' nests.

"It's awful," said Joe. "Whoever takes this on has got to be mad. It would cost a fortune to put right."

"I agree," I said. "It's horrible. I wouldn't touch it with a barge-pole."

We went back downstairs where Kurt and Alonso were still jabbering away in the living room. We carried on exploring. The living room opened onto another room, then another, and another. We lost count. It was a rabbit warren.

One room appeared to have been hewn out of the mountainside. It was a cave room, dark and windowless.

"This would make a good bedroom for someone," said Joe. "Bet it stays really cool in summer."

"Maybe, but not for us." I said. Joe didn't reply, and there was a peculiar look on his face which I couldn't quite read.

Like most old Spanish houses, this one was a veritable Tardis. Joe had to stoop frequently as the doorways were built for people much shorter than ourselves. Dried hams and rusty agricultural tools hung from the ceilings. Sacks of potatoes leaned against crumbling walls.

The only bathroom was downstairs. It boasted a miniature green bath complete with plastic curtain and a chipped sink propped up at a crazy angle by bits of wood. An antiquated toilet with high cistern reminded me of my early schooldays in the sixties. Joe pulled the chain to test it, and it came away in his hand. Quickly, he kicked it behind the toilet to hide it.

"Well, at least it's got a shower," he said and drew the plastic curtain aside. The whole curtain, plus rail, clattered to the floor.

"Don't touch anything else!" I hissed. This house was clearly a disaster. We returned to the living room where Alonso and Kurt were still deep in conversation.

"Where's the kitchen?" I whispered to Joe, and Kurt heard me.

"The wife of Alonso cooks here," explained Kurt, flapping his hand at the open fireplace. Really? I was full of admiration.

The tour was not over; there was much more to see. Alonso showed us more rooms that we hadn't noticed before. Another door opened onto an overgrown walled garden. He showed us two workshops and a fairly decent garage. Still there was more; a ruined building and a plot of fenced land planted with fruit trees – bizarrely on the other side of the street. Everything was run down and neglected, but in spite of myself, I was beginning to be charmed.

The tour had ended and Kurt turned to us, his blond eyebrows and shoulders raised in question.

"We love it! We'll take it," said Joe.

I swung round and gaped at him, open-mouthed with horror.

When it comes to shopping, even for houses, Joe is impetuous. I am far more cautious. I need to make lists. I need time to think, to weigh things up, to decide.

Buy *this* house? Was he *crazy?* I tried to protest but no sound came out.

I couldn't speak because there was an unexpected battle going on in my head. Heart was fighting with Common Sense. It was a funny thing, but without warning, the house was growing on me. I found my mind churning with ideas for rooms. How to create a kitchen opening onto that walled garden. Perhaps have roof terraces to take in the stunning mountain views.

"Think of the work!" said Common Sense. *"The place is a disaster!"*

"Yes, but imagine how it could be... Imagine being part of this little village. Look at those views..." said Heart.

"We're looking for a project," said Joe. "I think we could do wonders with this cottage. And perhaps we could build a couple of houses in the orchard over the road. It's just an overgrown eye-sore at the moment, and the old ruin up there is positively dangerous."

"Permission from the council vill not be a problem," said Kurt.

Common Sense gave up the fight. It didn't matter about frayed electric cables sticking out of walls like discarded spaghetti. Never mind the heaps of grit like dusty molehills in every room where the walls were forever disintegrating in avalanches.

Yes, I could see past all the decay. I could visualise this place as our home and project for the next five years, maybe longer. My heart hammered.

So that was it. We had found The House.

If Kurt was delighted at our decision to buy the house, he didn't show it. However, he wasted no time. We drove straight back down the mountain to the city.

"We must make all things lawful," he said. "It is lucky. The paperverk is correct. Alonso already has an *escritura* for the house."

I had read about *escrituras*, or deeds to houses. Very few owners bothered with them as most houses were passed down from generation to generation. Buying an old Spanish house with its paperwork already in order was a rarity.

Kurt marched us into the bank in Almería to open bank accounts and pay a deposit. The bank was large and airy. There were comfortable easy chairs, sweets in bowls, free coffee, ashtrays and magazines laid out on coffee tables for those waiting. I mentally compared it with the grim, unwelcoming banks I was familiar with in England. I knew which I preferred.

We were introduced to our new bank manager, Lola. Another surprise. Could this really be our bank manager? Lola was lovely; sable haired and sultry. When she spoke (in flawless English) her husky voice was like dark treacle running through sugar cane. I caught Joe gaping and kicked him under the table.

There were no formalities, we were on first name terms immediately. Efficient as well as beguiling, Lola beckoned seductively over her shoulder, led us to her office, then helped us sign on the dotted lines. I recalled the stuffy suited bank managers I had met in England. West Sussex suddenly seemed a long way away.

Joe stopped drooling long enough to hand over a credit card to pay the deposit, and that was it. The die was cast. We were going to live in a tumbledown cottage in a quirky little village in the Alpujarra mountains.

We were given four months to pay Alonso the balance for the house. Meanwhile, the papers would be prepared ready for the official completion of sale. Nothing more to do now except return to England.

"I can't believe we've done it!" I said outside the bank. "We've paid a deposit on a house here in Spain! I wish we didn't have to go back to England. I wish we could just stay here for ever."

"Well, we can't," said Joe. "And don't forget, when we do move out, life's not going to be a picnic. We need to get that house up to scratch if we're going to make a good profit in five years."

"But if we love it, we might stay permanently," I said, clinging to my dream.

Joe snorted. "We'll see," he said.

The holiday was over. Back to England to plan and wait for the paperwork to be completed. Time to exchange sapphire skies for steel.

Back in England we began preparations. We found a letting agent to handle the rental of our house. We transferred money through cyber space to Luscious Lola at the Spanish bank. We took crash courses in Spanish. We waited while winter melted into spring. And then, at long last, the phone rang.

"Hello?"

"This is Kurt."

"Oh! Hello, Kurt. How are you?"

"I am vell. The papers you vill sign now. I haf made an appointment vith the Notary for you May 23rd, 12 o'clock."

"Right, I'll check the flights and…" but the line was already dead.

Which was why, on May 23rd we found ourselves in the Notary's office. Venetian blinds cut out the sunlight and bright fluorescent strip-lighting flickered above. We all sat round a huge oval polished table. The Notary presided in an important looking upholstered chair. The rest of us sat in red plastic ones. Besides ourselves, there was Kurt, his business partner Marco, Luscious Lola and Kurt's solicitor wife Paula. Opposite us and dressed in their best clothes, all in a row like swallows on a telegraph wire, sat Alonso and his wife, his three grown up sons and their wives, his daughter and son-in-law.

The Notary straightened the stack of papers in front of him and raised one finger for silence. Alonso's family stopped twittering instantly and sat still. Order restored to his satisfaction, the Notary began. Slowly, he read aloud the deeds of the estate, all sixteen pages of it. He may as well have been reading instructions on how to split the atom; we understood nothing. I entertained myself by watching the others. Kurt sat straight and tall, staring directly ahead, occasionally twitching the blond forelock from his eyes. His solicitor wife Paula nodded wisely every few moments. Marco looked bored and kept clearing his throat. Alonso beamed but was clearly out of his depth. His wife and daughter held hands and glanced at each other frequently. Only the son-in-law listened intently, head on one side, eyes furtively flicking from the Notary back to us.

Eventually, papers were signed and Luscious Lola produced several piles of banknotes from her briefcase. These were pushed over to Alonso. Before he could reach them, the son-in-law's hand shot out like a trap-door spider, and intercepted the piles. More papers were read aloud to the accompaniment of 'flip,flip,flip,' as the son-in-law counted the banknotes. Paula and the Notary finalised a few small points and still the 'flip,flip,flip,' continued.

We didn't notice who finally pocketed the money, but at last we were presented with a huge bunch of keys. This acted like a signal, and the atmosphere changed dramatically. The transaction was complete and celebratory smiles wreathed every face. Chairs scraped as everyone sprang to life. A fest of handshaking and back clapping commenced. All the women were seized, embraced and kissed.

Kurt and Marco were the last to leave.

"Thank you, Kurt," I said. "Thank you for sorting out everything so efficiently."

"It is no problem," he said. "I haf arranged the electricity and the vater, also." We shook hands yet again, and Kurt and Marco walked away.

No going back, we'd done it, we now owned a house in a tiny Spanish village. I tightened my grip on the bunch of keys then danced a little jig on the pavement.

"We're moving to Spain! We're moving to Spain! No more England! No more rain!"

Passers-by looked amused, Joe just shook his head.

"Don't use up all your energy," he said. "Remember what work we've got to do this week."

As it was the school half-term break in England, we had allowed ourselves a week in Spain. Now we had the house keys, our week was going to be busy. We wanted to move in the summer and planned to clear the house now, in readiness, but with only a week, it was a tall order.

First thing - buy a wheelbarrow in the shopping mall. All wheelbarrows in Spain seemed to be bright yellow with green handles. I took a photo of Joe wheeling it through the shopping centre but we were never to see that photo, or any of the others we took that week.

Our hotel room was on the third floor with a balcony overlooking the gardens. I was the first to wake one morning, and couldn't find my handbag.

"Joe? Have you seen my bag? I thought I left it on the armchair, but I can't seem to find it."

"No, haven't seen it. Wish someone would give me a euro for every time you've lost your bag! Huh! I'd be a rich man. Can't be far. Have you been out on the balcony this morning?"

"No, why?"

"Well, the sliding door is slightly ajar." Joe opened it further and stepped out onto the balcony. At exactly the same moment, the man from the room next door stepped out onto his balcony.

"Morning," said Joe, stretching.

"Oh, hello, there," said the man. "Just escaping the missus. She's lost her bloomin' handbag again."

"You're joking!" said Joe, amused. "So's mine! She's looking for it now."

It took a couple of seconds for the penny to drop, then they both stared at each other, wide-eyed.

BETHINA'S HAM, TOMATO & GARLIC TOASTS

JAMÓN, TOMATE Y AJO CON PAN

Perfect as a breakfast, lunch or late night snack.

Ingredients

- Slices of bread (baguette, cut diagonally)
- 1 clove garlic, cut in half
- 1 very ripe tomato
- Slices of *jamon serrano* or ham of your choice
- Extra virgin olive oil

Method

- Preheat the grill.
- Toast the bread and, while still warm, rub with the halved garlic to flavour the slices.
- Rub the bread with the halved tomato. Squeeze in as much of the flesh as you can.
- Sprinkle with a pinch of salt and freshly-ground pepper.
- Drizzle with some extra virgin olive oil and top it off with the ham.

4

PACO AND BETHINA

Simultaneously, Joe and our next door neighbour gripped the handrail and peered down over the balcony. There were clear black scuff marks on the white wall below. Someone had scaled the side of the building in the night, using the balcony railings to hold onto.

Joe and the man stared at the shoe scuff marks, then at each other.

"Was your sliding door open this morning?" asked the man.

"It was," said Joe. "I think we've been burgled."

And so we had. My handbag containing mobile phone and camera were stolen. My purse had gone. Joe went and had a look outside and made a discovery. The thieves, probably kids, had hung the looted handbag on some railings outside, along with our neighbour's bag. I suppose we were lucky; they hadn't taken my address book, passport or return airline tickets, but it was still a blow. And such a waste of time as we had to wait for fingerprints to be taken from our room, and give statements down at the Police Station. Time much better spent clearing the house.

"So much for Spain having less crime," grunted Joe as we left the Police Station. Of course the burglars were never found.

Every day we drove up the mountain to our new house. It smelled damp and neglected. House martins had built nests in the porch above the front door. Inside, cockroaches scuttled back into dark corners. Cobwebs draped from the ceiling. Each room was still stuffed with Alonso's abandoned clutter. The weeds in the garden, celebrating Alonso's absence, had grown to waist level. Like explorers in an Amazon jungle, we hacked a path through the garden from the back gate to the future kitchen door.

The wheelbarrow was well used. We crammed it full of clutter from the house: old pictures, rotten cupboards, wasps' nests, weird tools, cages, mildewed mattresses and a chipped china statue of the Last Supper. We transported the junk to the orchard above. Then came the bigger furniture pieces. Dismantling the rusty iron beds wasn't too bad, neither was shifting the broken tables and chairs. (The promised German television was nowhere to be seen - probably snaffled by the son-in-law.) But the yellow vinyl sofa was much more of a challenge.

The only way to dispose of it was to lug it out of the front door, along the street, up into the next street, and so to the orchard. The sun was hot, the sofa heavy and the street uphill. Sweating and panting, we rested halfway. Joe returned to the house and brought back drinks. Sitting on the sofa in the middle of the street, we refreshed ourselves with cans of Coke. Leaning back, we slowly regained our breath and admired the view. I fiddled with a decrepit transistor radio we were also dumping and, surprisingly, it crackled into life. Tinny music filled the air.

"This is the life!" said Joe, basking in the sun, sipping from his can.

I nodded, eyes closed, enjoying the break and the sun's warm rays. I swung my legs off the ground and put my feet in Joe's lap, stretching luxuriously, wriggling my toes.

And that was how we first met Paco.

About our age, short, dressed in working clothes, Paco rounded the corner and stopped in astonishment. Then his swarthy face split into a huge grin. We jumped up off the sofa, silenced the radio and shook hands.

"*Los Ingleses!*" he shouted, pumping our hands, slapping us on the backs and roaring with laughter. Next around the corner came his wife, apron-clad, round as a Teletubby, rosy-cheeked and smiling. More handshaking and Spanish kisses.

"*Soy Paco,*" he announced, pointing at himself with a horny finger. Then, poking his wife, "*Bethina!*"

We introduced ourselves likewise.

"Ah, Joe and Veeky," repeated Paco.

In case he thought English people usually relaxed on sofas in the middle of the street listening to music, we explained using a mixture of bad Spanish and hand signals. Our Spanish lessons hadn't prepared us for situations like this. Paco seemed to grasp that we were carrying the sofa to the orchard to be dumped. He nodded but cut us short.

"Come with me," he said, and dismissed Alonso's sofa with a wave of his hand.

The sofa was abandoned in the middle of the road. Joe was frog-marched back down the street while Bethina and I followed, my arm clamped in a vice-like grip.

Just before we reached our house, they stopped and pushed open the front door beside ours. It became clear that these were our next door neighbours, and we were herded into their little house. What a contrast! Where our house was dusty and damp, their house smelled of herbs and the white walls gleamed. Framed family photographs hung in neat rows and a vase of wild flowers stood on the table.

"You will have something to eat and drink, no?" said Paco and pressed us into chairs. "Here, I have something for you to try."

"Thank you…" we said, watching him wrestle with an unlabelled bottle. He puffed and blew until the cork surrendered with a satisfying pop.

"Home-made," he said, smacking his lips. "Taste the Andalucían grapes, taste the sun!"

"*Delicioso,*" I said, taking a sip. "This is delicious!" And it was.

"Last year was a very good year. Plenty of rain in spring, then a long hot summer. In September, I will show you how we make the wine, *no?* You will come with us to my *cortijo,* you will see how wine should be made."

"Thank you, that will be lovely."

"And now you must try this one, too." His face turned red from the effort as he uncorked bottle Number Two. "This is from the year before, also a very good year."

We quickly drained our glasses and held them out to be refilled. I couldn't taste the difference, but it was very nice.

"Aha! Now you must taste this one! Tell me what you think..."

He battled with a third bottle and finally won. Joe and I obediently drained our second glass and waited. Paco, still breathless from effort, splashed the red wine Number Three into our glasses. We tasted it and nodded at Paco.

"*Delicioso*," I said again. It tasted the same as the other two.

"*¿Delicioso?*" said Paco, outraged. "*¿Delicioso?* This is the wine of my friend, Juan Pedro. It is rubbish wine! See how clear my wine is, then look at Juan Pedro's wine! His wine is cloudy, *no?*"

Alarmed, Joe and I stared at the three bottles, comparing them. They all looked identical.

"Pah!" His fist slammed down on the table making me jump and the glasses rattle. "That Juan Pedro has no idea! He should take a lesson from me! I try to teach him how to make good wine, but does he listen? No!"

"Yes, I can see the difference," said Joe, betraying me utterly. "Your wine is much clearer, and tastes much better."

Paco beamed again, his outrage forgotten.

"Women!" he said, putting his arm round Joe's shoulders. "What do they know about good wine?"

Bethina clattered around her tiny kitchen while the red wine flowed freely. She put plates of smoked ham, tomato, cheese and bread on the plastic tablecloth then joined us to sit at the table. A goodly amount of her body spilled over the edges of her chair.

And so our first serious Spanish lesson began. Although we understood most of what was being said to us, it was hard constructing sentences ourselves. I was grateful that the burglars had left me my Spanish/English dictionary, now ever present in my pocket.

Paco and Bethina were fascinated by us. They asked about our jobs in England, why we were moving to Spain and about our children.

"*Nuestros niños*," said Bethina, "these are our children." Dimples appeared in her round cheeks. She was pointing to three framed photos on the wall. "This one is Diego, he is thirty-two. He grows tomatoes, the best in Andalucía! Diego's tomatoes are sent all over the world, even England! These tomatoes we are eating now were grown by my son, Diego."

"They're very good," I said.

Joe and Paco were talking about cars. I heard them discussing Range Rovers, both nodding and agreeing that Range Rovers were excellent cars.

"And this photo is Sofía," continued Bethina. She paused and shook her head sadly. "Sofía is twenty-eight, and does not have a husband."

Sofía's face smiled down at us from the wall. She was very beautiful. High cheek bones, big expressive eyes and glossy dark hair.

"She's not married?" I asked, surprised.

"Pah!" yelled Paco, thumping his fist on the table again. Range Rovers were forgotten as he fumed over his wayward daughter. "She should be married by now! But always there is something wrong with every boy she meets."

"*Claro*," nodded Bethina sadly, "that's true."

"The boy is too thin, or too fat, or wears the wrong clothes… No boy is good enough!" Paco clearly felt strongly about this subject. "Many times she meets a very nice boy, but never does she want him for a husband!"

Bethina inclined her head. "*Claro*," she said.

"And the third photo?" I asked, trying to change the subject. "The little boy?"

"Ah," said Bethina, softening.

She stopped herself and giggled coyly, stealing a look at her husband. Paco's black mood instantly fell away. He beamed proudly and puffed out his chest.

"Our little surprise, our gift from God," he said. "That's Little Paco, he's only eight."

On cue, Little Paco came hurtling into the house. Dark skinned, dark haired, he had the same mischievous eyes as his father. Scarcely noticing us, he excitedly plonked his latest treasure on the tablecloth.

"Mama! Papa! See what I caught!"

It was a large, juicy green cricket. For just a moment, everyone stopped and stared, including the cricket. Then the poor creature sensed freedom, gathered itself and hopped sideways onto a plate of sliced ham. Bethina squealed in fright and leaped to her feet, knocking her chair backwards. The cricket glared balefully at us and tensed for its next launch.

Paco moved like lightning, seizing the cricket in one capable hand and his son's ear in the other.

"Pacito! What do you think you are doing? We have visitors!"

Both cricket and small boy were evicted, protesting, from the house and into the street.

Bethina was not pleased with her son. She followed, standing in the doorway, blocking the light and scolding her son outside. Our grasp of the language was weak, but Bethina's meaning was clear. No entry. Small boys with crickets not welcome.

We learned much that day. We learned that most of the houses were only occupied at weekends and in the heat of the summer. That Paco was a lorry driver and related to most of the villagers in some way. That there were only three telephones in the village - luckily we had one. That the village Fiesta every October was unmissable.

Another fact that became obvious was that Paco's wine glasses possessed magical properties. As fast as we drank, they were mysteriously refilled. Never did the level drop more than a centimetre from the top. This may explain why I didn't remember the drive back down the mountain. I did remember the hugs and Spanish kisses when we left. I vaguely remembered dumping the yellow sofa in the orchard as planned. But the journey back to the hotel remains a blur.

And so back again to England for the very last time. Two frantic months of teaching, packing, arranging the removals, selling unwanted stuff on eBay. For me, it was rather like being pregnant. Outwardly you carry on with normal life, but inwardly you are secretly, deliciously obsessed with that new life inside. I could think of nothing but our new life in Spain.

CRISPY POTATOES IN SPICY TOMATO SAUCE
PATATAS BRAVAS

Nobody can resist this classic *tapas* dish. Wonderful chunks of potato in a spicy tomato sauce.

Ingredients (serves 4)

- 1 kg (2lb) potatoes, peeled, and cut into 2cm (1in) inch cubes
- 1 small onion, finely chopped
- 2 cloves garlic, crushed
- Salt and freshly ground black pepper
- 500g (1lb) tomatoes
- 3 teaspoons (paprika)
- ¼ teaspoon cayenne pepper
- ¼ teaspoon chopped fresh thyme
- 1 teaspoon tomato puree
- Olive oil, for frying
- Chopped parsley to garnish

Method

- Par-boil the potatoes for 5 to 10 minutes.
- Drain the water.
- Let the steam evaporate for a minute or so and then give the

pan a good shake. This roughs up the outsides nicely. Set aside.
- Prepare the tomatoes by cutting a cross in the base and plunging them into boiling water for 10 to 15 seconds. Plunge into cold water and the skin should peel away easily. Chop the tomatoes.
- Fry the onion until soft. Add the garlic, paprika, thyme and cayenne pepper, then cook for another couple of minutes.
- Add the chopped tomato and puree and cook, uncovered, until the sauce thickens, about 20 minutes.
- During cooking, add the salt and pepper to taste. If the sauce seems too dry, add a little water.
- Meanwhile, re-heat the frying oil and fry the potatoes until golden brown. This gives them a crisp coating and prevents the sauce from soaking in too much. They should be beautifully crisp outside and soft and fluffy inside.
- To serve, place the potatoes in a serving bowl, then cover with the spicy sauce.
- Sprinkle with chopped parsley.

5
THE DYNAMIC DUO

At last July came, and the end of the school summer term. The assembly hall was hot and airless. Flies buzzed and bumped angrily against the windows. Little boys picked at their scabby knees. Girls, lanky in their outgrown school uniform dresses, played with their hair or with the hair of the girl in front.

"And so I'd like to ask Mrs Twead to come up to the front. She's been filling in as a supply teacher for a number of years now and is leaving us to live in Spain..." The Head Teacher finished and waited as I picked my way between the lines of cross-legged children.

This was a sad day. I was only a lowly supply teacher but most of my time had been spent in this school. I knew every child's name and the staff were close friends.

I reached the front and cleared my throat. I fear public speaking along with hairy spiders and quadratic equations.

"Thank you," I said, taking a deep breath. "Thank you, and I will miss you all. This school is very special and I have really enjoyed working here and being part of it. Thank you for making me so welcome." I meant it.

"However," I added, pointing to my name badge pinned on my blouse above 'Supply Teacher' and the school crest, "I won't throw this

badge away just yet. You never know, I might be back and need it..."
Below me, the sea of little upturned faces smiled back.

Silently I prayed to whoever was up on high that this would never be the case. I so wanted our Five Year Plan to be a huge success. I wanted Joe to love Spain as much as I did, to agree to live there even after our five years were completed.

That evening, relaxed with glass in hand at the end-of-term Staff Barbecue, I allowed my eyes to roam round the garden. I tried to freeze-frame the memory to be pulled out and cherished later, sometime in my new life. The young American teacher who deserved a Nobel Peace Prize for her ability to inspire seven year olds. The 'in' jokes and the teachers who'd made me laugh in the staff room until my ribs ached. The friends who'd joined me at belly dancing evening classes.... And not just the people; the very English flowers in the beds, the lush trees, the unmistakably English feel of it all...

I was exchanging all of it for strangers speaking a foreign language in a country whose customs I didn't understand. Andalucían landscapes as different from West Sussex as hedgehogs are to bluebells. (Did they have hedgehogs in Spain? Or bluebells?) I was swapping a comfortable house and well-paid job with a derelict cottage and hard manual labour.

You bet I was ready to swap, and I couldn't wait! No more endless grey, no more early morning telephone calls from schools inviting me to replace a sick teacher, no more traffic fumes, no more queues in Tesco. Bring it on!

The Staff Barbecue was in full swing and I drifted between groups. Conversations that evening followed roughly the same script:

"Hello, Vicky, you lucky thing! You must be so excited! When do you leave?"

"Sunday." The boxes were packed, the ferry booked.

"So, do you know lots of people out there already?"

"Well, no, not really."

"Well, you'll soon make friends. And is your house nice?"

"We love it."

True, but I didn't add that it had no kitchen. The toilet didn't work and the bath was only big enough for a gnome. The floors were cracked cement or earth. The walls were a metre thick, made of rubble and disintegrating. The roof beams had woodworm. The electrics were disastrous and the plumbing a joke. Just to name a few little drawbacks.

A pause. "So you speak Spanish?"

"A bit. We've been going to Spanish classes. Enough to get by, and I'm sure we'll pick it up."

"Gosh, good luck to you, Vicky, I think you are very brave." Privately, I agreed.

A shout came from somewhere in the garden behind me. One of my closest friends, Juliet, gin and tonic welded to her hand, yelled, "We'll come and visit you, won't we, Sue?"

Juliet and Sue, the 'Gin Twins' I called them. I was going to miss them.

"Of course we'll visit!" Sue was slurring just a little. "Get on the Internet tomorrow, Jules. Book a flight for October, half-term."

I smiled to myself. They were more than welcome but had they forgotten our new house had no kitchen or working bathroom? I assumed it was the gin talking and forgot all about it. I was wrong.

Later that night I was presented with armfuls of leaving gifts. I unwrapped drawing pads, charcoal, pastels, tubes of paint, everything required for a hobby artist with plenty of leisure time. My lovely friends had obviously pictured me seated quietly on the mountainside, sombrero shading my eyes, painting Andalucían landscapes. I knew better. It would take years of intensive labour and stretching of our DIY skills to merely make our house habitable. I was far more likely to be mixing cement than delicately daubing paint on canvas. However, I promised myself that one day, when it was all done, I would indeed sit and paint the mountain scenery.

Meanwhile, one thousand five hundred miles away, in a tiny village in the Alpujarra mountains, a crumbling cottage waited for us, empty and decaying.

They say that moving house is equally as stressful as divorce and only marginally less traumatic than bereavement. With this in mind, I can give you some advice; never hire a Man with a Van. No, splash out - have it all done professionally. Choose a reputable company, sit back and let them get on with it. Hindsight is a wonderful thing.

It started off well enough. I got removal quotes from three separate companies, then suffered an attack of the vapours when I read the figures on the bottom line.

"Have you thought about asking Matthew's father, Dick Smithers?" asked someone in the staff-room. I wish I could remember who first made that suggestion so that I could stick pins in her effigy.

"Dick Smithers! That's a good idea," said someone else. "He's driven lorries taking charity stuff to the Eastern Block loads of times. You know, humanitarian supplies for orphanages. Why don't you ask him? I bet he'd do the move for you."

"I know Dick," I said. "He comes into school sometimes to help out, doesn't he?"

"Yes, that's him. I don't think he's got his own lorry, but you could hire one."

"Good idea," I said. "I'll ask him if he's interested."

So I asked him the very next time I saw him. He seemed ideal, and he was enthusiastic.

"No problem at all," Dick said. "You hire the truck, and put me down as 'main driver'. I've got a mate who'll come along to help."

"That sounds brilliant!" I was delighted.

"You pack everything up in boxes in advance, we'll load up, and Bob's your uncle!" he said cheerfully.

"Right!"

"Then me and my mate'll go in the truck, and you can follow behind in your car. No problem."

"Excellent! That sounds perfect!" I couldn't wait to tell Joe. We settled on a price; a huge saving compared with the professional quotes.

Joe was based at an Army barracks in the north of England and only came home at weekends leaving me with most of the packing. I didn't mind, I was very organised. I made lists to my heart's content. Gradually, all our possessions were packed. Boxes containing breakables were labelled 'FRAGILE' in huge red letters.

Of course, on moving day it poured with rain. Dick turned up but his mate did not. We let Dick take charge, assuming that his experience in packing lorries was far superior to ours. I suppose that's when the warning lights should have started flashing.

Dick's modus operandi was to load boxes and furniture as swiftly as possible, regardless of shape or size. Very soon, the lorry was in danger of being full and Dick was using my washing line to tie things down. To cram more in, we had to scramble like monkeys over chests of drawers and chairs to fill spaces towards the back. The load was precarious and frequently shifted, reminding me of Steptoe and Son's cart. For me, as self-proclaimed Queen of lists and organisation, it was purgatory.

Then Dick's mate turned up. Dressed in a fetching yellow tracksuit, Dale was an out-of-work actor from Brighton. An actor he may have been, a manual labourer he was not. While Joe and Dick strained, muscles knotted in effort, Dale skipped from box to box, always picking the lightest to carry. His half-hearted efforts were accompanied by "Oops-a-daisy!" or little girlish squeals until I could sense Joe's blood pressure and temper rising at equal rates. Mercifully, Dale had to leave early to do his pizza delivery shift. He was not missed.

Dick chose that time to make a public announcement. "Can't hang about in Spain," he said. "Got another job. Gotta be back in the UK by Tuesday."

Joe stared at him. "What do you mean? Are you seriously expecting to drive all the way across France and Spain, unload the lorry, drive back again, all by Tuesday?"

"Yeah, should be able to do it if we don't hang around." Dick was defensive.

"That's ridiculous!"

"Nah, we just do it in one hit, no overnight stops."

"You must be joking!" Joe was nearly speechless.

I agreed. Both Joe and I drive like geriatric tortoises. We are every young person's nightmare; we never exceed the speed limit and stay glued to the slow lane on motorways. Our vision of tootling slowly across the Continent with the roof down on the jeep vapourised instantly. Gone was the plan to enjoy the scenery. No pausing awhile to take in the views. No leisurely meals in some French or Spanish bar. No nights spent in quirky hotels. Now we were destined to hare across France and Spain in the wake of the rattling, overstuffed lorry with a demented Michael Schumacher wannabe at the wheel.

"Right," said Dick, impervious to Joe's wrath. "I'm off then. I'll pick Dale up in the morning, and we'll see you on the ferry."

That night Joe's temper continued simmering just below boiling point. Our nerves were frayed and we turned on each other like cornered animals. We slept on an inflatable mattress (the bed was packed) in the living room, scarcely speaking. In the morning we locked up, packed the last of our possessions, and headed towards Portsmouth. I checked my list for the last time. All present and correct. Until the last item…

"Oh, no!" I wailed. "We've forgotten Great Aunt Elsa!"

SPANISH SPINACH
ESPINACAS A LA ESPAÑA

A very simple, tasty side dish. A sprinkling of crumbled blue cheese or feta is a delicious variation.

Ingredients (serves 2 as a side dish)

- 500g (18oz) fresh spinach leaves
- 4 cloves garlic
- Extra virgin olive oil
- Salt

Method

- Trim the stems of the spinach and wash the leaves by rinsing under running water to remove any dirt. Drain the spinach and pat the leaves dry with kitchen paper.
- Peel and slice the garlic and then heat the oil in a large frying pan.
- Add the sliced garlic and sauté for a few minutes until it begins to brown.
- Add the spinach to the pan, pressing down with your hand to get it all in, then turn the spinach a few times to coat it all with garlic and olive oil.
- Cover and reduce the heat and cook for a minute or so.
- Turn the spinach over and cook for another minute until the

spinach is nicely wilted.
- Drain any excess liquid and serve immediately with an extra drizzle of olive oil and a little salt to season.

6

BEWARE THE MAN WITH THE VAN

Forgotten Great Aunt Elsa? Joe's forehead creased. We were a couple of miles into our journey and this was not good news.

"We'll have to go back and get her," I said. "We can't leave her in England."

Joe knew better than to argue. Great Aunt Elsa had been with me since I was a child. Not Great Aunt Elsa herself, of course, but the oil painting of her. Painted in 1897, she had stood the test of time. Still in her original frame, she smiled serenely down at me from every wall I hung her on over the years. She'd watched me grow, marry, raise children. She was part of my life. If I was leaving the country, so was she. And not in the removal lorry, either. She was coming with us, where I could keep an eye on her.

So we turned back, collected Great Aunt Elsa, wrapped her tenderly in a blanket and set off again. We still reached Portsmouth in good time, boarded the ferry and waved good-bye to England's grey receding shores.

As we stood on deck, I tried to analyse my feelings. Now that moving was a reality, was it a wrench to leave England behind? Perhaps I was unusual, but I felt only excitement, no regret. What would I miss? I could think of nothing except Marmite and Heinz baked beans. What about friends? Well, they were welcome to visit us and we were bound to make new friends in Spain. And the Internet ensured easy contact with all our family.

I recalled the neat modern house we'd left behind. Well, we would work hard and soon make our Spanish house into a home. I was fifty, Joe fifty-three, but we weren't ready for Zimmer frames yet. I caught my breath, overwhelmed by the excitement of it all. Joe misread my sigh and his big warm hand closed over mine on the rail.

"Don't worry," he said. "If it all goes wrong we can always come back. Don't forget, it's a Five Year Plan."

But I was sure we had made the right decision. I knew it wouldn't be easy, but I was utterly positive we were doing the right thing. And in five years time, I would try to convince Joe we should stay.

The ferry crossing was uneventful except that we avoided Dick and Dale at all costs. We ducked behind bulkheads, dived into rest rooms, anything rather than being forced to sit and chat with them. Joe insisted that we didn't need to drive in convoy. After all, we had the Google route directions and could keep in touch by mobile phone when necessary. Dick had Kurt's number just in case.

"Dick by name, Dick by nature," Joe growled. "Dick and Dale - sounds like a bloody double act. I'm not going to break my neck trying to keep up with that pair of clowns. Huh! We'll go as fast as we comfortably can, but that's it!"

We were much more optimistic when we arrived in France. We didn't see Dick's lorry disembark, but we had the Google directions so we knew we weren't far behind. However, I'd clearly overestimated my own navigation skills.

We were lost even before we left Le Havre. The Google directions were hurled out of the window amidst curses unbecoming to a lady. At the first service station we bought a map that covered both France and Spain, and chose the route we thought shortest. Mile after mile we drove, through rustic towns, past acres of vineyards, alongside fields of sunflowers and up into the mountains. On and on and on. By nightfall we were exhausted but had still not quite reached the Spanish border.

"This is ridiculous," muttered Joe for the fiftieth time. "I've had enough! We're stopping, and that's all there is to it."

"Perhaps we're ahead of them?" I said as we pulled into a particularly grotty service station that offered overnight accommodation. "My! This place looks awful!"

"You're right, it's horrendous, but it'll have to do. I can't drive anymore tonight."

"Do you think they have a star system in France, like in Britain? You know, Five Stars for the best…"

"Judging by the outside, I'd say this is a Minus Five. Come on, let's get Great Aunt Elsa in, have a wash and go to bed."

We didn't complain anymore, we were too bone-tired. Joe, Great Aunt Elsa and I put up with the grimy decor and moth-eaten carpets. In spite of the grey sheets, Joe and I slept the sleep of the truly exhausted.

Morning arrived too soon. Another day of solid driving. At least the jeep's roof was folded back now and we could bask in the heat. It was a bit of a shock when we reached the edge of the map and realised that we were still four hundred miles away from Almería.

And then the mobile shrilled.

"This is Kurt."

"Oh, hello…"

"Here is Dick and Dale." The signal was weak, the voice faint.

"Kurt? Kurt? Where is Dick and Dale? I mean, where exactly are they?" It sounded like a comedy sketch.

"…unfortunate event…" The signal died.

"Kurt? Kurt! What unfortunate event? I can't hear you! Damn!"

But the mobile refused to connect us. Unfortunate event? Had they driven off the mountain road in their haste? Was the lorry upside down in the bottom of a valley, wheels spinning in the air, our worldly possessions strewn through olive groves?

"They beat us," Joe said glumly. "They got there first."

The rest of the journey was a game of 'Guess the Accident'. It was nightfall when we reached the village but, being July, the village was packed. Children played in the square, people sat chatting on the benches. Everybody froze and heads swivelled to watch us pass. I smiled and waved, feeling like the Queen on a drive-past. Hearts racing, we pulled up outside our house, behind the lorry. It seemed intact, until Joe silently pointed. It had a huge dent in one side and heavy black scrape marks. No sign of the Dynamic Duo.

Then Kurt's car pulled up and Dick and Dale leaped out, looking fresh and immaculate.

"What kept you?" said Dick. "We got here at lunchtime. Phoned your bloke Kurt. He showed us where to come and took us back to Almería. Booked in one of them 'hostal' places - had a meal and a bit of a siesta. So where you been?"

"Just driving," I said. Why did I feel guilty? We had got there as fast as we could.

"And where did he get that tan?" accused Dale pointing at Joe. Joe's face and bald head shone like a red pepper, burned by the sun through the jeep's roof.

"Well, we gotta get this job done quickly," said Dick and exaggeratedly rolled up his sleeves in readiness.

I unlocked the front door and turned back to speak to Kurt and thank him for directing the Dynamic Duo, but he and his car had vanished. It was then that I registered the lamp-post. Like an inebriate outside a pub at closing time, it leaned precariously, the lamp lolling loosely like a drunken man's head. That explained the 'unfortunate event' and the damage to the truck. I was mortified. This was not how I wanted to make an entrance to the village.

So began a night of work unloading the lorry. Dick and Dale exercised as much delicacy and care for our possessions as a pair of particularly bad-tempered airport baggage handlers. Boxes clearly marked 'FRAGILE' were crashed down. The washing machine was dropped. Drawers spilled out of chests and trails of debris began to mark the path from house to lorry. Dale got away with doing as little as possible. Dick checked his watch every few minutes. Joe was totally exhausted and pale under his sunburn.

Unlike us, Great Aunt Elsa had travelled well. She still looked as fresh and serene as she did in 1897. I carried her carefully to a safe, quiet place, away from the mayhem. I chose the bathroom.

Paco appeared from next door.

"Pah!" he said, thumping a box marked 'Fragile' and making the contents rattle. "We will soon finish moving these." The only cheerful one of the group, he threw himself into the task and lifted boxes as though they contained feathers. We were overcome by his kindness and gratefully accepted his help.

"Veeky, do you have glasses?" he asked, hours later.

"Yes, but I don't know which box they're in."

Paco disappeared for a few moments, then reappeared with a bottle of whiskey and glasses. Joe looked at Paco's smiling face, then at the whiskey bottle. I witnessed his pallor change from pale to green as he bolted to the bathroom, his hand clamped to his mouth. Joe made it to the bathroom, but unfortunately Dale was relieving himself at the time. He was singularly unimpressed by the contents of Joe's stomach being sprayed forcefully all over his designer tracksuit.

Even more unfortunately, Joe's outburst also drenched Great Aunt Elsa.

Mercifully, the lorry was finally empty. Manoeuvering it into the village had been no picnic, hence the lamp-post casualty, but getting it out was going to be worse. The streets were narrow, barely the width of the lorry. The corners were right angles, and at three in the morning, it was pitch dark. Paco took charge, and waved and signalled as Dick reversed. Apart from giving the poor suffering lamp-post another swipe, all went well until they reached the square.

Paco was doing a sterling job of directing but something important was lost in translation. With a sickening crunch, Dick backed the lorry into the village fountain. We could only gaze dumbly as the previously proud little spout of water wilted and became a trickle that puddled inkily at our feet.

Paco seemed unconcerned and went off to bed. Dick and Dale drove away and out of our lives for ever. I gently sponged Great Aunt Elsa, restoring her to her former glory.

Joe and I spent the first night of our new life on the inflatable mattress on the dirt floor of the cave bedroom, watched over by towers of swaying boxes.

I awoke that first morning and lay still for a few minutes. Utter silence, apart from Joe's rhythmic breathing beside me. No traffic noise, not even birdsong. I cracked my eyelids open but could see nothing. I sat up and looked around the room, but it was absolute blackness. Never in my life had I experienced such complete enveloping blackness. In England, even at midnight, there were always streetlights, and dim light showing the rectangle of the window, even with curtains drawn. But here, in our cave bedroom, I felt as though my eyes were still closed.

Such a feeling of exhilaration washed over me that I had to catch my breath. We'd done it! We were in our new home, in an obscure tiny village in Spain! I left Joe sleeping and, arms outstretched like a blind woman, felt for the doorway.

Fumbling for unfamiliar light switches, I made my way between boxes to the back door. I pushed it open and stepped into the garden.

It was a brand new day. The sun still hung low over the mountain tops, but was climbing slowly, heavily. Shadows were long and deep, throwing the gullies and crags into sharp relief. The olive groves were bathed in golden light. A hairdryer breeze ruffled the leaves of our vine. A cock crowed, answered by another on the other side of the valley.

I inhaled deeply, savouring the pure mountain air. I was filled with such happiness and excitement that I found my fists were clenched.

"A brand new day, and a brand new life," said Joe who had materialised beside me. He voiced my thoughts exactly.

We ate our breakfast alfresco. It was a poor affair of leftover motorway services sandwiches, but eaten alfresco it was ambrosia, food of the gods. Eventually the heat and our need to get sorted drove us back inside, but we never forgot that first breakfast.

We put aside the problem of the damaged lamp-post and destroyed fountain. We'd ask Kurt what to do about that. And we hoped that the insurance would cover the damage to the truck. For now, one of our first jobs was to set up a kitchen of sorts.

Bizarrely, at the foot of the stairs there was a sink with running water. We brought in a cupboard for crockery, a kettle and the microwave, and so a temporary kitchen was created. The microwave functioned perfectly, but the novelty of Spanish electricity proved too much for it. Mysteriously, the numbers vanished from the digital display, never to be seen again. We could cook but had to count the number of times we pressed the button to set the minutes required. A minor inconvenience we soon accepted.

Provisions arrived daily in small white vans which wended their way down into the valley. They announced their arrival to the villagers by hooting furiously during their entire descent into the valley, ceasing only when they reached the square. Bethina, starched apron crackling, marched me along to introduce me to the delights of buying from the back of these vans. Bread, fish, vegetables and fruit, all fresh, all local. On Sundays, delicious cakes came with the bread.

One afternoon we were taking a siesta when we were woken by urgent loudspeaker announcements. Joe leaped out of bed in terror.

"It's an earthquake warning!" he gasped. "Quick, get the valuables, we may have to move fast!"

SPANISH POTATO SALAD
ENSALADILLA

Spanish potato salad is a popular *tapa* dish that goes particularly well with beer, so highly recommended at a barbecue.

Ingredients

- 3 medium potatoes
- 150g (5oz) fresh or frozen peas
- 120g (4oz) green beans
- 1 large carrot
- 1 small onion
- 1 small red pepper
- 2 tablespoons green olives
- 2 hard boiled eggs
- 1 medium tomato
- 1 tablespoon capers

The Dressing:

- 200ml (7 fl oz) mayonnaise
- 1 teaspoon French mustard
- 1 tablespoon lemon juice

Method

- Peel and dice the carrot and potato. Boil the potato and carrot in water until just tender.
- Add the peas and green beans and cook for a further 5 minutes until all the vegetables are cooked.
- Drain and place in a large bowl or serving dish.
- Peel and finely chop the onion, chop the pepper and tomato and slice the hard boiled eggs.
- Add the pepper, onion, eggs, capers, tomato and olives to the other vegetables and mix together.
- In a separate bowl, make the dressing by mixing together the mayonnaise, mustard and lemon juice.
- Slowly spoon the dressing onto the salad and mix together without smothering the salad.
- Garnish with chopped parsley and freshly ground black pepper.

7
AUGUST

An earthquake? I sat up in alarm as he pulled on his shorts (inside out) and raced towards the square and the source of the commotion.

Valuables? What valuables? Fuzzy from sleep, I couldn't think clearly. What did one do in an earthquake? Drive away from it? Head for high ground? I didn't know. I dressed quickly, grabbed Great Aunt Elsa, and was heading for the front door when Joe returned. He was looking rueful and carrying a crate.

"What was it?" I asked, still clutching Great Aunt Elsa.

"A van. Selling peaches."

"Not an earthquake warning?"

"No."

"Oh. What's in the crate?"

"Peaches."

"Peaches? A whole crate? How ever many did you get?"

"Four euros' worth. That's all I had in my shorts pocket."

"But there must be 40 peaches in there! How are we going to eat so many peaches?"

"Don't know. But when I ran into the square, everybody thought I was desperate for peaches. They all stood aside in the queue and let me go first. So I had to buy some."

"But why buy a whole crate?"

"I showed him my four euros, and that's what he gave me."

We feasted on peaches for days, but couldn't finish them. The fruit flies soon attacked, and we had to throw the rest away.

El Hoyo boasted one shop, or perhaps that was too optimistic a term to describe it. Years ago it was not only a shop, but a thriving restaurant. In those days, the village was home to lead miners and their families, but the mine now stood idle and the workers had departed. The shop remained but now stocked very little. The owners, Marcia and Old Sancho, were in their eighties and too old to be bothered much with it.

Marcia was a tiny sprightly lady, dressed in black and with eyes as sharp as a little bird's. She smelt faintly of almonds and her white hair was scraped back into a bun held in place by countless silver hairpins. These hairpins frequently slid out when she shook her head, which she did often.

Old Sancho was much more relaxed. Most days he sat outside the shop grinning vacantly to anyone who spoke to him. His mind was obviously deteriorating, but his kind, simple eyes hinted of great wisdom in the past. Each evening he strolled around the village with his black cat. It was a familiar sight, the old man in his slippers and walking stick, the black cat scampering at his heels. We grew to recognise the sound of the tapping stick and Old Sancho's ever-present flatulence as he passed our house. 'Tap, tap, paaarp! Tap, tap, paaarp!'

Buying food was no problem, but there is a limit to what one can microwave or barbecue. Paco and Bethina treated us like impoverished relatives and we often ate in their house, squeezed round their table alongside cousins, in-laws, friends and relations. Wine flowed freely. The food was always fresh, heavily laced with garlic but very strange to our British palates. Once we were served little roast birds not much bigger than sparrows. They lay upside down on our plates with their tiny feet in the air.

One Spanish delicacy we dreaded was pigs' trotters. The Spanish don't object if their food is cold, so by the time we were served, a trotter complete with knuckle sat on our plates in a pool of congealed fat and gravy.

"Thank you so much," I said, "but I'm full already. I don't think I could manage that."

Bethina looked disappointed but took my trotter away. The spotlight was on Joe and the atmosphere was electric with anticipation. Bethina stood poised, smoothing her apron, waiting expectantly. Paco refilled our wine glasses. Silence fell as the cousins and relations stopped everything to watch him taste.

Joe was brave. He seized the trotter as he had seen Paco do, and pulled off a piece of cold fat with his teeth. He chewed courageously and smiled at Bethina who beamed with pleasure and turned back to her cooking. Paco clapped Joe on the back and refilled everyone's glasses again. The cousins cheered in approval and all started talking at once. Joe masticated valiantly, using the wine to wash down the rubbery lumps of fat. At last the plate was clear and Joe leaned back in relief.

Bethina appeared again with saucepan and ladle. "*¿Te gustó?* Did you like it?" she asked.

I couldn't resist. "He loved it!" I piped up. "He said he'd like some more." There was murder in Joe's eyes as yet again the ladle descended to his plate.

With Kurt's help, we wrote a letter of apology to the Mayor. We offered to pay for the repair of the lamp-post and fountain. We never received a reply.

It was the end of July and the clock was ticking. In four weeks' time Joe would fly back to England to complete his time in the army. August was going to be a frantic month of preparation before he left me, all on my own in Spain.

And August was an awesome month. The blue sky stretched to eternity punctuated only by swallows cavorting like Spitfires. Each morning the sun rose and bathed our world in warmth and the extraordinary light unique to Spain. Minute by minute the sun grew fiercer, forcing folk to take cover in the coolness of their houses. Until evening, the streets stayed deserted and silent except for the panting of dogs under cars. The mountain ranges, once so lush, now reclined, hot, dry and yellow, like lions resting in the midday sun. The olive trees stood bowed, silvery leaves shimmering listlessly in the heat haze.

"I know we hate talking about it," said Joe, one day, "but at the end of August, I'll be gone. There's no way round it. I have to finish my last four months in the Army."

"I know."

"Well, you don't have to stay here on your own. You could come back with me, and stay with someone in England until Christmas. Perhaps Juliet? Or you could stay with your sister, or Grace and Paul on their boat? Then we'll come back to Spain together."

"No."

"Are you absolutely sure you'll be okay on your own?"

"I'll be fine. I want to stay here. I can get lots of stuff done on the house in four months."

"But you'll be all on your own."

"I don't mind."

"But you've got no kitchen, or proper bathroom yet."

"I don't mind. I'll manage."

"Paco said it's going to get much colder."

"We're in southern Spain! It's not going to get as cold as Britain, is it?"

"Paco said they have frost sometimes."

"Well, we'll have to get that wood-burning stove we saw. If we put that in, I'll be absolutely fine."

Joe gave up. He had one month's leave left, so we would have to use that time as profitably as possible. In the searing heat of August we had to prepare for winter. The clock kept ticking.

Top priority was acquiring the wood-burning stove. We chose a big black monster which the shop kindly loaded onto our long-suffering jeep with a fork lift truck. The poor little jeep sank visibly under the massive weight and we set off gingerly up the mountain road, back to the village. Shifting it up the garden path to its final destination in the living room took a whole day. Inch by inch we heaved the colossal lump of cast iron. The length of our small garden seemed to have grown to several kilometres. And connecting the metal tubes and pushing them up the chimney proved testing. The only way to do it was for Joe to climb up into the chimney to make the adjustments.

"We're about a bloody metre short," echoed his disembodied voice down the chimney. He clambered out, like a creature from a horror film, spitting soot and swearing. Fifty years of soot and grease plastered his profusely sweating body. Only his eyes were distinguishable, red rimmed and shiny.

"I'll have to drive back down the mountain and pick up another length of tube." Joe was not happy.

"Do you have to?"

"No choice. Only way to finish the job. Hell, why do the shops have to be so far away?" Living half an hour away from a big town was sometimes a distinct disadvantage. "Wouldn't have to do this if we lived in Britain." He grabbed the car keys.

"You can't go like that!" I protested. "You'll frighten small children."

"Just watch me. It's not worth washing or getting changed because I've got to go up that bloody chimney again." He had a point. I helped him throw some covers over the car seats and he departed, growling.

I kept checking my watch, and the church-bells marked every hour, reminding me how long he was gone. I knew the journey down took about half an hour, allow fifteen minutes for buying the tube in the shop, half an hour back. So why wasn't he home after three hours? At long last he returned, tube in hand.

"What happened? What took you so long? I was getting worried…"

"Huh! I was halfway down the mountain when I got a puncture."

"Oh, no! What did you do?"

"Pulled over, of course, and started changing it. Then this posh car came along. You know the sort - flashy sports car type of thing. There was this young bloke in it. Anyway, he got out of his car and came over."

"Did he offer to help?"

"Yes, that's the funny thing. He was dressed in a smart business suit ... and you can see what I looked like." Joe pointed at his black face and sooty clothes.

"How d'you mean, 'funny thing'? D'you mean because he was dressed in a business suit?"

"Well, yes, but I mean - would you offer to help someone looking like me?"

I shook my head. He was right.

"I was really taken aback. I know how I must have looked, and I was sweating and swearing..."

I thought about it. How kind of this young man to offer help, regardless of soiling his smart expensive clothes. Of course Joe refused, but we never forgot the generosity extended, just one example of many we were to experience.

Armed with the final length of tube, the wood-burning stove was at last installed to Joe's satisfaction. Only one chore left to do ... test it. Even though the temperature was already in the 40s, we lit the fire and the room became an inferno of heat. The villagers looked at the smoke pouring from our chimney with bemused expressions. Crazy English!

Another important job was renovating the bathroom, but this was doomed to failure. It was possible take a shower standing in the midget bath, so that was okay. The chipped old sink was fine for the moment, so long as you didn't lean on it. But the toilet cistern leaked so badly the floor was perpetually wet. We blocked off the water flow feeding the cistern and resorted to flushing the toilet with a bucket of water. Completely renovating the bathroom would take time and planning. We didn't have the time as the end of August was looming, and we couldn't plan because we didn't know where the soil pipe was leading. To plan and relocate a new toilet and bathroom suite, we would need to know exactly where our cesspit was.

Sewage is a subject I had never troubled myself with before, but living in a Spanish village, sewage (euphemistically called *'aguas negras'* - black water) was something Joe and I discussed daily. When we bought the house, it never occurred to us that we were not on mains drainage. So where was our cesspit located?

"We'll have to search every inch of the ground floor. It must be somewhere..." I started pacing, eyes downcast, searching for a clue.

"Stamp your feet, see if it sounds hollow anywhere."

"All sounds solid to me. Where can it be?"

"Dunno. But if it's not in the house, it must be in the garden." We continued our stamping dance outside.

Paco saw us, removed his hat and scratched his head, bemused.

"What are you doing, English?"

"Trying to find our cesspit. Do you know where it is?"

Paco screwed up his face in thought. "No, I don't know where it is. Every house is different, no?" He shook his head and began walking away. Then he stopped and called over his shoulder, "If it smells, you must throw a dead chicken down the toilet."

"Oh, right. Why?"

"That will start the bacteria working again."

Helpful advice, but we still hadn't located the wretched cesspit.

"Let's ask Marcia at the shop," I suggested. "She might know, and if she doesn't know, Geronimo might be there. We could ask him, too." So we strolled down to the shop.

Marcia knew everybody and everything about the village, she was the obvious person to ask.

"No," she said, shaking her head. A hairpin escaped and bounced on the counter. "I don't know where it is. Ask Geronimo. He might know."

We'd met Geronimo many times and liked him very much. In his forties, periwinkle blue eyes, long curly hair flowing past his shoulders like an ageing rock star, Geronimo was probably Marcia's best customer. Several times a day he would pop into the shop, and despite Marcia's reluctance and severe scolding, would exit bearing bottles of beer. He worked for the council and resurfaced streets, cleared roads, whatever was needed to keep the village running smoothly. He was always accompanied by his three dogs and plenty of liquid refreshment. In his spare time, he helped fellow villagers, particularly the elderly. Nothing was too much trouble for him. He would fix roofs, chop firewood, whitewash houses, anything. He flatly refused payment, unless of course it came in a bottle.

Geronimo was always easy to find. If he wasn't working round the village, he would be sitting companionably with Marcia's husband,

Old Sancho, and his black cat outside the shop. Old Sancho would doze and smile while Geronimo, bottle in hand and dogs at his feet, extolled the virtues of his beloved football team, Real Madrid.

Yes, Geronimo was the one to consult. We found him halfway up a ladder outside the church.

"*Buenos dias,* Geronimo," we said. "How are you?"

"*Mal,*" he said as usual. "Bad." He reversed down the ladder, his three dogs watching with interest.

"Geronimo, do you know where Alonso's cesspit is? We can't find it."

Geronimo stood with his head on one side, deep in thought, then took a swig from his beer.

"Follow me," he said after another swig.

VEGETABLE KEBABS
BROCHETAS DE VERDURAS

These easy-to-make vegetable kebabs are a great accompaniment to any barbecue. Use any combination of your favourite vegetables, these ingredients are just suggestions.

Ingredients (serves 4)

- 1 aubergine
- 8 - 10 cherry tomatoes
- 1 medium red pepper
- 1 medium green pepper
- 1 medium onion
- 8-10 mushrooms
- Fresh or dried thyme
- Olive oil

Method

- Cut all vegetables into bite sized slices.
- Peel the onion and slice.
- Create the kebabs by alternating.
- Pour a generous amount of olive oil into a large shallow dish, adding plenty of thyme.
- Lay the kebabs in the oil and allow to marinade for about 2 hours. Turn occasionally.

- Add the kebabs and allow to marinade in the oil turning now and then for an hour or so.
- Cook on a barbecue or grill until ready.
- Serve with barbecued meat and crusty bread.

8
SATELLITES AND PARTIES

The three dogs, Joe and I trailed after Geronimo back to our house. In the street outside our garden gate, he stopped.

"I don't know where your cesspit is," he said, shaking his long hair from side to side. "But this is yours."

His toe was tapping the manhole in the road. Setting his bottle down, he knelt and lifted the cover. In a circle, we all peered solemnly down into the darkness: Geronimo, Joe, myself and the three dogs.

"It's brand new," observed Joe, his voice echoing down the hole. "It's never been used."

"*Sí, señor,*" agreed Geronimo. "It is new."

With much arm-waving and body language, he explained that the sewage system was all in place for the village, but not yet connected.

"When will it be connected?" I asked.

Geronimo shrugged, palms upward. "*Pronto,* soon. When the Mayor is ready."

"Why is there no pipe running from our house to the manhole?" asked Joe.

"You must do that," said Geronimo, pointing at us. "You must put a pipe in and join it here, at the manhole."

"What, everybody has to put in their own tubes?"

"*Sí.*"

"But we don't know where our cesspit is..." We were back to square one.

Geronimo shrugged some more, and took another thoughtful pull from his bottle.

"Thank you for showing us the manhole, Geronimo," I said. "Would you like to come in for a drink?"

"A drink?" Geronimo looked shocked. "This early? *¡Madre Mia!* I couldn't possibly! Well, perhaps a small drink, but nothing alcoholic, you understand."

"That's fine. A coffee, maybe? Or a Coke? Or juice?"

"Well, perhaps one small brandy..."

So we sat in our overgrown garden watching the level on the brandy bottle descend. I noticed that Geronimo's power of speech declined in exact proportion with the amount of brandy left in the bottle.

"Real Madrid...never has a team played with such skill, such beauty..." His eyes were moist with passion.

Then later: "... every kick ... poetry ... just poetry ..." Another swallow. "Such grace, such..." He sighed deeply, then shook his head, hair flailing. Fat tears squeezed from his eyes. "Ah, Real Madrid..." he whispered, overcome.

He drained his glass, words having now entirely deserted him. Dumbly, he waved his arms, tears running down his cheeks as he tried to convey to us the magic that was Real Madrid.

The brandy bottle stood empty, so he left us, shoulders still shaking with emotion. The three dogs loped behind, heads hung low in sympathy.

We were grateful to Geronimo but still did not have an answer to our question. So, as a last resort, we phoned Kurt. Kurt contacted Alonso, the previous owner, telling him we had some questions about the house.

Two days later, Alonso appeared on our doorstep and we invited him in. He was exactly as I remembered; weather-beaten and gnarled. Twisting his cloth cap in his hands, he was clearly ill at ease. We were very pleased to see him, but his Andalucían dialect was so strong that we had more problems than usual communicating. Our questions baffled him and he didn't understand what we wanted to know. At a loss, I phoned Judith.

"Judith?"

"Yes, m'dear? How can I help?"

"Judith, we've got Alonso with us. We're still trying to find our cesspit. We've looked everywhere and we can't find it. Alonso can't understand us, and we can't understand him. Can you talk to him, please?"

"Bloody Spanish drains!" Judith shouted. "Don't you fret, dear. Pass the receiver over to Alonso, I'll soon find out what is bloody what!"

Alonso took the proffered receiver and held it to his ear, then jerked it away again as though it had stung him. Judith was in full flow and although we couldn't make out the words, we could appreciate the volume. Alonso listened quietly, receiver now held several safe inches from his ear, merely interrupting Judith's tirade with the occasional, "*Tranquilo, tranquilo.*"

Phone call completed, Alonso beckoned us and trotted off to the workshop. In one corner, he exaggeratedly mimed pulling his trousers down and squatting.

"*¡Caca!*" he explained, pointing to the ground beneath his feet.

Great! So now we knew where the cesspit was. But there was no point in creating a luxury bathroom if at some later date we would have to dig it all up again to connect to mains drainage. Reluctantly, we let well alone and left the bathroom as it was, bucket of water, midget bath, cesspit and all.

The next job Joe wanted to tackle was satellite television. Judith suggested an excellent hardware shop that supplied dishes, so off we went to buy one. The dish seemed enormous, but we assembled and fixed it. Printed instructions are things to be ignored, according to Joe, so it wasn't until we'd wasted a day on it that we realised we needed an even bigger dish. This one was too small.

Back to the hardware shop. Luckily they took it back and ordered us the bigger dish. This one was a colossus. We could barely wedge it into the back of the jeep and we felt like a ship in full sail as we drove home back up the mountain.

Paco helped Joe fix it to the roof, but however hard we tried, we couldn't get a picture. Joe was not pleased; he was desperate to watch the Olympics.

"Ask Judith if she knows any satellite companies," he called down. "I give up with this thing."

In a fit of pique, he took the dish down again and laid it on the roof.

I did as asked and called Judith. She recommended Satellite Installers Inc. who kindly agreed to come that same afternoon. Joe paced the floor impatiently waiting for them to arrive.

Suddenly, from nowhere, a freak gust of wind blasted through the valley, causing our shutters and doors to bang. Something crashed outside and the look of horror on Joe's face must have mirrored my own. We knew exactly what had happened.

We charged outside but it was too late. The wind had caught the giant satellite dish and dashed it to the road below. To our dismay, the dish now sported a sizeable dent. Alas, its former perfect symmetry was damaged beyond repair.

Satellite Installers Inc. arrived. They turned out to be a British father and son team, very earnest and utterly dedicated to the fascinating art of satellite installation. They had driven a long way so I plied them with cold drinks and tried unsuccessfully to engage them in small talk. Only when satellite dishes were mentioned did they become animated, their eyes brightening as they warmed to their favourite subject.

Joe led them upstairs and onto the roof, ruefully explaining the unfortunate calamity that the dish had suffered earlier. Father and son exchanged looks. There was a simultaneous sharp intake of breath. Both heads shook in unison.

"Gawd! There's no way that dish will pick up anything," declared the father.

"Not a chance," said the son. "Not with a dent like that."

"Can't we just try?" begged Joe. "The Olympics are on…"

Father and son shook their heads grimly like doctors pronouncing death at a hospital bedside, but took pity on Joe.

"Aye, we'll give it a go, but that dish is ruined, you mark my words," said the father.

Twenty minutes later, the dish was erected and orientated and the son was fiddling half-heartedly with our television controls. Suddenly, his eyes blazed and his whole demeanour exuded intense excitement. Scientists discovering the cure for the common cold could not have been more enthralled or jubilant.

"Dad! DAD! Where are you? Here, quick! Come and have a look at this! You are never going to believe this!"

The father joined his son at the television. "Well, I'm blowed!" he breathed, naked wonder on his face.

We had a perfect picture. And we could scroll through all the channels without a hitch. Father and son stood shoulder to shoulder, mouths hanging open, hypnotised by the screen.

"Look at that! They can even get Channel 4!" gasped the son at last, eyes bulging. "We can't even get Channel 4 ourselves - back home at our house!"

"Well, bless me, I've never seen anything like it!" The father slapped his thigh gleefully. "I thought that dish had had it! That dish had a whopping great dent in it! Just wait 'til we get home and tell everybody! We're gonna dine out on this story for years!"

We thanked and paid the elated pair who left, almost skipping, ecstatically reliving the extraordinary moment when a picture had appeared on our TV. Everybody was happy. Joe was thrilled that he could watch the Olympics. Me? I was just glad I'd never have to attend one of their dinner parties.

Two other events stick in my mind about that first August, each equally delightful, unsophisticated and charming.

One hot night we heard unfamiliar noises coming from the square, cheering and clapping. We strolled down to investigate. At one end of the square a huge screen had been erected and Geronimo had taken the role of projectionist. Laid on by the town council, a Walt Disney type film was being shown. Untidy rows of small children sat cross-legged on the ground, spellbound. Mothers sat on benches, chatting quietly and jiggling pushchairs containing sleeping infants. Gangly teenagers lounged about, coiled round lamp-posts, poking and teasing each other, pretending to have no interest in the film. The elderly had brought knitting and their own seats, a colourful assortment of dining room and kitchen chairs grouped in clusters. A scops owl hooted in the distance somewhere, answered by another, then a third on the other side of the valley.

It was a perfect village scene. I wished I was a talented artist and could capture that moment in time on canvas forever.

On yet another sultry evening, Paco pounded on our front door in his usual deafening fashion.

"English! Come out and join the party!"

To our surprise, the street was full of people. A long table laden down with food had been set up outside our front door, stretching down past Paco's. In the centre was a cake with candles. The table occupied the whole space of the narrow street. Any vehicle rounding the corner would have to stop, reverse and find another way. People could barely squeeze past.

"It's Little Paco's birthday, *no?*" said Paco and thrust glasses of wine into our hands.

Of course it made perfect sense; there wasn't space inside Paco's house. They didn't have a garden, so the street was the obvious place for a party. Bethina made heroic attempts to keep order as kids scrambled into their places, noise level rising to a crescendo. Little Paco grinned broadly. Nine years old and the centre of attention.

"But we're filthy! We've been cementing."

"Pah!" said Paco, thumping the door frame with his fist. "*No importa.* It doesn't matter! Have a drink and forget work for today."

Nobody cared that Joe and I were covered in dust and grit from working on the house, we were welcome anyway. We stood with the other adults watching the kids having a great time. Having eaten enough, they left the table to romp and run wild through the village as Spanish children can safely do. The abandoned table looked as though a plague of soldier ants had marched through. Bethina, best apron flapping, assisted by Sofía and various female relations, cleared it all up, then dumped more plates of food on the table.

It was the adults' turn. Three hours later we were still sitting in the street, under the stars, drink in hand, work forgotten. Just enjoying the moment - thoroughly content with our new life. I so hoped that these special moments would outweigh the hard labour and difficulties that living in Spain threw at us. I hoped Joe would forget chimneys, sewage and dented satellite dishes and grow to love Spain as much as I already did.

Too soon, August softened into September. The fierce sun had become a little more friendly. The grapes on our vine blushed purple. Swallows perched chattering in long lines on the telephone wires, probably discussing the long journey ahead. The Spanish school term started again and families holidaying in the village went back to their city jobs below.

"You must not worry! We will take care of her!" bellowed Paco, clapping Joe on the back with such force that he choked.

"Thank you," said Joe, "and I'll see you in December."

It was hard saying good-bye to Joe at the airport. However, I reminded myself that I had plenty to occupy myself with, and the time would soon pass. I was intending to keep busy by whitewashing walls and laying floor tiles in our bedroom. But it was not to be. Thanks to Paco and some lively visitors, I would have very little time to myself.

PACO'S SANGRIA
SANGRIA DE PACO

Sangria is enjoyed all year round, but is particularly pleasant in the hot summer months. Also, there are many fruits in season to choose from. There are hundreds of different sangria recipes in existence, including ones using white wine instead of red. The one rule seems to be; the better the wine, the better the sangria.

In Paco's opinion, the name 'sangria' derives from 'sangre' meaning 'blood'. Paco explained that blood is red and thick, essential for life. Sangria, he argued, is equally precious and resembles blood.

Ingredients (serves 4-6)

- 1 bottle of medium to good quality red wine - chilled
- Half teacup sugar
- 1 can of fizzy lemon drink
- 1 can of fizzy orange drink
- Fruit cut in wedges, not peeled - choose from apples, kiwis, oranges, melon or peaches
- Ice cubes

Method

- Pour the wine into a large jug.
- Stir in the sugar with a wooden spoon.
- Add the fizzy drinks, fruit and ice cubes.
- Stir well and serve.

9

GRAPES AND DOCTORS

Although I badly missed Joe, I settled into life without him surprisingly easily. There were so many jobs I wanted to carry out in the house. My intention was to do as much as possible before his return in December.

Paco, Bethina and the family arrived next door, without fail, every Friday night amid much hooting and cheering, tumbling chaotically out of their Range Rover like a litter of exuberant puppies. So that was the weekends taken care of. I was given no choice. I was hauled out of my house, fed and entertained until, exhausted but honoured to be so accepted, I waved them good-bye every Sunday night.

I began to understand much more about their way of life. During the week they lived in their beautiful big house down in the city. Paco worked long hours lorry driving and Little Paco went to school. Big brother Diego ran his greenhouse empire growing tomatoes and big sister Sofía worked in a shop in the mall. And Bethina looked after them all.

Until Friday. Then they would pack up the Range Rover with supplies and charge up the mountain to their beloved village house. Over the weekend, they would catch up with all their friends and relations. Every evening, at five o'clock, all the villagers would take a constitutional up the steep mountain road. Even the most ancient folk walked up the hill daily. This was another chance to greet acquaintances, admire new babies and generally exchange news.

Later, the men watched football or argued politics over copious amounts of beer and home-made wine, always separate from the women.

"Can I help wash up?" Joe had asked once, weeks ago. His question was met with utter disbelief and horror by the women, and derision by the men.

"That's women's work!" said Paco. "Men do not help in the house. Do you ever help in the house, Fausto?"

"¡Madre mia! Never!" said his brother-in-law. "And we have been married 25 years. What about you, Gabriel? Pedro? Miguel?"

"No, never!" All the men were in agreement.

"Do men do women's work in England?" Paco asked.

"Of course, all the time. Most husbands help their wives."

The men shook their heads, fascinated, digesting this extraordinary piece of information. The women were equally fascinated. They were open-mouthed, clearly shocked at the very idea.

"Veeky, is that true? English men do housework?"

"Yes, and cooking. And helping with the children."

"¡Madre mia!" said Bethina at last. "Can you imagine that? Men washing the dishes? England must be a very strange country."

All the women were nodding in agreement. In rural Spain, men worked and played hard while the women's role was to look after their men. They rarely strayed from the kitchen. It was like going back fifty years in time.

In the evenings, the women stayed together in the kitchen, joking and hooting with laughter. They played cards gambling with dried beans, roasted nuts on the fire and waited on the men. The men ate, drank and exchanged views in the next room.

Meanwhile, regardless of the dark or time, the children ran free, shouting, yelling, darting from house to house, playing ball in the streets or hide-and-seek in the square.

In addition to the town house and village house, Paco had a *cortijo* or smallholding, high in the mountain overlooking the village. Here he grew olives, grapes, almonds, potatoes, garlic and other vegetables, as well as raising quails and chickens.

One Saturday morning in September, there was much activity outside, then the familiar pounding of Paco's fist on my door. I opened up to see a convoy. At the head of the procession was Paco's old van, engine running, trailer in tow. The trailer was crammed with family members, boxes and bags. The cars lined up behind were equally stuffed with friends, relations and provisions.

"Veeky! Come on!" yelled Paco. "We're off to the *cortijo!*"

"But I've got work to do…"

"Pah!" said Paco, giving Bethina's ample rump a hefty slap as she passed by, laden with bags. "Forget working in the house today. Come on, you don't need to bring anything. Work? We'll show you work! Today we are pressing grapes."

A space in the van opened up for me, and we set off up the mountain. The road soon became a dirt track and I stopped enjoying the views when I saw the perilous drops. The van barely clung to the track and I thought we would surely go over the edge, especially at the speed Paco was driving. I was sweating, partly from terror, and partly because I was wedged in so tightly between Bethina and Uncle Felix, with Little Paco on my lap.

Several times Paco jumped out to push gates open. These gates were artful affairs constructed from bedsprings, not pretty, but very serviceable. At some points the track had eroded away completely or was obstructed by rock slides. Then all the passengers were disgorged until the cars had negotiated the assault course safely, whereupon we all climbed in again and continued up.

At long last, we were at the top of the mountain. We all piled out beside Paco's *cortijo*.

"It's beautiful up here!" I said. It was a magnificent spot.

"This land has been in our family for generations," said Paco. "Look down there."

Looking down, our village looked like a toy town nestling snugly in the valley. The mountains stretched in every direction and the sea beyond shimmered deep blue, the horizon straight as a ruler.

Paco's *cortijo* was about the size of a double garage, but it was not the *cortijo* that drew my eye. It was the pyramids of purple grapes, stacked in crates, tall as a man, piled up all around. Each bunch of grapes, plump and perfect, waiting. I'd never seen so many grapes in one place and was blissfully unaware that, by the end of the day, I'd be sick of the sight of them.

The grapes were ignored and everyone burst into the cool and dark of the *cortijo*. A wonderful aroma pervaded from the bunches of herbs strung from the ceiling. Paco gave me a guided tour which didn't take long. The room was dominated by a huge fireplace, complete with neatly stacked logs. In the centre stood a long table with mismatched chairs placed around. In one corner was a sink, supplied by water from a rainwater tank, a couple of kitchen wall cupboards and a gas burner. Evidently there was no electricity or mains water. I wondered how and where anyone answered the call of nature.

In another corner near the entrance was a built-in Heath Robinson affair which I couldn't identify. It consisted of a large vat with reservoir below, and weights standing by. Another gadget stood nearby. It was a kind of metal barrel on its side, on wheels. It had a huge handle that turned a horizontal corkscrew.

All was to be revealed later, but for now the women were on autopilot and a delicious meal of *patatas a lo pobre* (poor man's potatoes) was conjured up and set on the table. The meal was not rushed, but eventually the women cleared away, while the men wheeled out the barrel contraption and set it up with buckets placed under. Next, the first crates of grapes were hauled in. Time to begin work.

"Veeky, watch me," said Bethina.

All the women were crowded round the barrel and I carefully copied Bethina's actions. She grabbed a bunch of grapes, checked them over, then stripped the grapes in fistfuls, throwing them into the barrel. The big stems were discarded. That's not too hard, I thought, and imitated her movements.

Juice ran down my arms, dripped off my elbows. Grape skins wedged under my fingernails. Half an hour later I felt like a zombie, sticky, hands already stained black, fingers aching, back sore from stooping. My movements became mechanical - grab, strip, chuck, drip.

It was relentless, hour after hour, the heaps of waiting grapes diminishing oh, so slowly. The flies tormented, never ceasing. The women laughed and chattered without pause and I became too tired to try to work out what they were talking about. I felt deeply ashamed for being such a namby-pamby weakling while these strong women just took the task in their stride.

Every now and then someone would seize the handle and turn the corkscrew device that crushed the grapes and separated more sticks from the pulp. The juicy pulp splattered into the bucket below, splashing our legs and soaking our feet with syrupy goo.

When the bucket filled, the men lugged it away and emptied it into the vat. Sinews straining, they heaved the massive weights on top, then turned a wheel to lower them and crush the pulp. A steady stream of pure clear grape juice poured from the reservoir into plastic buckets, which was transferred to barrels. Paco filled a cup for me to sample. It was like a taste of heaven.

At one point, Bethina stopped. She dipped her hands into a bucket of water to rinse them, then beckoned.

"Veeky, follow me."

Off she trotted, into the bright sunshine outside, to the back of the quail pens, with me two steps behind. The children were giving the chickens a hard time, chasing them through the olive trees. First chickens, then children galloped past in clouds of dust, too immersed in their own pursuits to notice us.

"Veeky, this is the place."

She pointed down at the spot of ground we were standing on.

"Here?"

"*Claro.*" She was nodding furiously and looking at me expectantly.

I had absolutely no idea what Bethina was trying to show me. I bent down low, examining the soil closely. Was she trying to show me a seedling? Or was the earth special here in some way? I looked up at her blankly. She sighed, exasperated, then flipped up her apron, hauled down her voluminous white bloomers, squatted, and relieved herself on the dusty ground. Now I got it. I averted my eyes and thanked her, assuring her I didn't need to do likewise just now.

Back to work. More grapes, more flies, more purple sludge. It all ended at eight o'clock when it grew too dark to see what we were doing. I was numb with tiredness. Every bone ached and I felt as dirty and sticky as though I'd been dipped in honey and rolled in grit.

My shower at home that night was blissful and the water ran pink with juice, grape skins clogging the drain hole. Gradually, my back stopped aching and I could flex my fingers without discomfort.

Judith phoned many times, usually just to check if all was well. And there was always some drama or crisis in her life to relate.

"Vicky! It's Judith!" Dogs barked loudly in the background.

"Hello, Judith!"

"How are you coping on your own?" Bethina next door could have heard her through the metre thick wall.

"Fine, thank you. Everything's fine," I replied. "How are you and Mother?"

"I'm top hole. Couldn't be better, m'dear. But poor Mother's been through the bloody wars lately."

"Oh, I'm sorry to hear that. What happened?"

"Fell over one of the bloody cats, dear! Nasty fall. Lucky she didn't break anything. Ghastly bruises, though. Really shook her up. Called the bloody Spanish doctor in to check her over, and would you believe it? He was off on some bloody conference and we had to make do with the locum!"

"Oh dear, was he no good?"

"Turned out to be a bloody woman, dear! Said Mother was fine, just shaken and bruised. Said regular glasses of red wine would help, and gave her a spliff!"

"A what?"

"A spliff, dear. A joint! Bloody marijuana!"

"You're joking!"

"Nope! A bloody spliff!"

"So what did you do?"

"Well, Mother tried it and said it sorted her out a treat. Said she felt very relaxed. Cheered her up no end. Surprised me, though, I can tell you! Fancy the locum being a bloody woman!"

So that was okay then. Another crisis averted.

Telephone calls with Judith were never boring, and often very enlightening. The next call from her would leave me squirming and pink with embarrassment.

CARMEN-BETHINA'S POOR MAN'S POTATOES
PATATAS A LO POBRE

This must be one of Spain's most iconic dishes. The ingredients are cheap, but filling and utterly delicious.

Ingredients (serves 4)

- 15 tbsp olive oil
- 1 kg (2lb) potatoes - peeled, cut into chunks
- 3 large onions
- 3 green peppers - seeded, roughly chopped
- Large handful mushrooms - wiped, roughly chopped
- 5 cloves garlic - roughly chopped
- 4 fresh bay leaves
- Salt and freshly ground black pepper to taste

Method

- Heat 5 tablespoons of oil in a large saucepan.
- Add the onion and pinch of salt.
- Cook slowly on a lowish to medium heat for 20 - 30 minutes.
- Stir frequently until onion is golden brown and soft.
- Add the peppers, garlic and bay leaves.
- Cook for another 15 minutes.
- Meanwhile, chop the potatoes and salt lightly.

- When the peppers are soft, add the remaining oil.
- Ensure the oil is hot before adding the potato chunks.
- Simmer gently for 20-30 minutes, stirring occasionally, until the potatoes are soft.
- Drain using a slotted spoon or colander.
- Serve with fresh crusty bread, or as an accompaniment with roast pork or lamb.

10

THE ECO-WARRIORS

"Bloody Hoover's packed up, dear," Judith lamented. "And we've got visitors coming over from England on Wednesday. Our charlady, Ana, is in a real tizz. Get DOWN, Tyson. Curly, be quiet!"

"Well, why don't you borrow my Dyson?" I said. "I'm in all day if you want to pick it up."

Secretly I sympathised with Ana. Cleaning that house must have been an uphill task.

"Marvelous idea! Mother? MOTHER! Vicky's going to lend us her Dyson!" Her shout set the dogs barking again. "I'll pop round later and get it. Tyson! Leave Fluffy alone - she's not interested. Now, m'dear, what have you been doing since Joe went back to England?"

"Oh, just stuff on the house. And Paco and Bethina took me up to their *cortijo* for grape pressing."

"God's teeth, Tyson, STOP IT! Fluffy doesn't want to do that... Sorry, Vicky, were you talking about Paco and *Carmen?*" She sounded puzzled.

"Paco and his wife, Bethina," I repeated.

"Your next door neighbours, Paco and his wife Carmen, with Sofía and Little Paco?" Judith knew everyone in both villages, so I was confused.

"Oh," I said, "we call her 'Bethina'. Paco introduced her as Bethina when we first met, ages ago. Has she got two names?"

There was a short silence as she thought about that, then a huge guffaw erupted, setting the dogs off again.

"Vicky! Are you sure he didn't say *'vecina'?*" she roared, choking on more laughter. She explained that in Andalucía, 'v' is pronounced 'b' and that a 'c' in the middle of a word is said with a lisp, sounding like 'th'. Thus *'vecina'*, meaning neighbour, became Bethina. Understanding dawned. That first day, Paco had said, pointing to himself, *"Soy Paco."* (I am Paco) and when he had introduced Carmen, he had pointed at her and described her as *'vecina'* (neighbour). I was mortified. We had been calling Carmen 'neighbour' for many months. Joe sometimes even called her Beth, or Betty for short.

I couldn't apologise enough to Carmen when I saw her next.

"No pasa nada," she said, round cheeks dimpling. "It doesn't matter. I thought that is how people call each other in England."

Judith borrowed the Dyson and returned it the next day after Ana, her cleaner, had finished with it. It was stuffed full with enough animal hair to reconstitute a decent sized dog, but at least her house was ready for the expected visitors.

The Dyson had done a very thorough job. When I emptied it, several odd things fell out. A dog tag, a black lace garter, a guitar plectrum and a small but important looking key.

I phoned Judith to report the key find. I didn't mention the black lace garter.

"Good Lord, Vicky. Awfully well done, m'dear! We've been looking everywhere for that wretched key!"

"Oh, is it important?"

"Important, dear? It's bloody vital! It's the key to the drinks cabinet. We were just trying to pick the lock with Mother's nail file when you phoned."

September brought my first visitors. Knowing they were coming sent me into a flurry of preparation and panic. I frantically sorted out a bedroom. I assembled the double bed, found suitable furniture, evicted families of geckos and swept the dirt floor until I exploded into sneezing and coughing fits from dust inhalation. The result wasn't too bad. The roof didn't leak in that room and the mountain views (if you could force the ancient shutters open) were magnificent.

Although the bedroom was just about acceptable, there was nothing I could do about the bathroom. Or the fact we had no kitchen. Until Joe returned in December any major renovations were out of the question.

However, I comforted myself that my sister Caroline and her husband Nicholas had spent time in Africa doing voluntary work, and assumed they were probably used to basic accommodation.

Caroline and I look alike, but there the resemblance ends. She is confident and lively. I am quiet and circumspect. She speaks seven languages fluently - including Spanish. I still struggle with Spanish. She is scathing of television and cars (she and Nicholas choose to have neither), whereas I love my TV and couldn't be without a car. They never buy new if they can make do with the old. Any necessary purchase is weighed up and rigorously discussed before the shared purse sees the light of day. I am the opposite; if something breaks down, I usually buy a new one rather than trying to get it fixed. Both Caroline and Nicholas's passion in life is the Environment and Saving the Planet. I try to do my bit but don't get much further than throwing paper and wine bottles into the recycling skip.

In spite of their foibles, they are incredibly thoughtful and generous. They arrived carrying only backpacks and still managed to bring presents for me: books, candles and bread-making flour for my bread-making machine.

I needn't have worried about the house, they slotted into the way of life perfectly. Not even the washing facilities bothered them. In fact, washing became a ritual and masterclass in conservation.

It went like this: Caroline would announce she was having a shower. She would take her shower swiftly, mindful of economising on water, leaving the plug in the bath so every drop was saved. Then Nicholas would use this water to take his bath, even though it was only a few inches deep. Next they would bring their clothes to the bathroom and wash them in the same water. Finally, the now grey water was scooped out and used to water the grapevine. I was filled with wonder.

I had never met a couple who shared so many things. Apart from bath water, they also shared a towel. They refused my offer of big, fluffy bath towels, preferring instead to share a threadbare remnant that I probably wouldn't even use to clean the car. They shared a toothbrush and comb. They shared a tea-bag, then shared it again for a second cup. They shared food from their plates like new lovers, and being small in stature, even sat together in an armchair like Tweedledum and Tweedledee.

Most days they would set out on a trek up the mountains. First they plastered each other with total block sun-cream. Then they donned their sun hats, complete with flap to protect the back of the neck. Their water carrier, which closely resembled a colostomy bag, yellowing and floppy, was filled. Final check - binoculars, compass, camera, glucose sweets. Because of their fascination with all things natural, they avoided tracks and paths. They preferred to scramble up the most rugged terrain in search of rare lichen or indigenous succulents. From our garden, they looked like tiny insects clambering up a compost heap.

When they returned, they proudly showed me the photos they had taken. Frame after frame of close-up studies of plants. Nicholas, usually silent, transformed into an enthusiastic instructor, describing the plant species, using the Latin terms, almost stuttering in his excitement. And there was plenty of flora and fauna for him to study. The geckos I had evicted earlier had returned to the bedroom, much to his delight, and our overgrown garden was another rich vein of botanical discoveries.

One day Nicholas went missing for a couple of hours and I asked Caroline where he was. She merely pointed to the garden. Barely visible, crouched in the scrub, Nicholas was motionless. He was in a world of his own, binoculars trained on a wasps' nest in the garden wall. I am ashamed to admit that a few months later, we interred that same wasps' nest with cement.

On another occasion we had been shopping down in the town. An exhausting business when your companions need to discuss every purchase at length. The longest delay was at the fish counter. There was just too much choice. The display was a work of art, fish of every shape and hue reposing on beds of ice. Caroline and Nicholas tested the poor assistant to distraction, changing their minds about which fish to buy for the evening barbecue.

"We don't need two, we can share one," said Nicholas.

"But will that be enough?" Caroline worried.

"Well, we can choose a big one." Then, to the assistant, "That one, please. No, the one behind it. Oh, that's bigger than I thought - maybe the one on the left, no, perhaps the next one…"

And so it continued until they were both finally satisfied and the weighed, wrapped fish was handed over like a newborn baby. The assistant and I were united in relief. I sped the trolley away before they could change their minds again.

It was a beautiful evening. The swallows overhead were replaced by bats. The cicadas chirped their evening choruses before falling silent. A fox barked some distance away. We felt totally at peace. Nicholas had lit the barbecue and the precious fish, now wrapped in foil, was sizzling appetisingly. Nicholas and Caroline shared salad duties and were engrossed in chopping and slicing. The telephone rang, Joe's daily call from England, and I left the peaceful domestic scene to go inside and answer it.

As I finished the call and put the receiver down, an agonised howl from the garden split the air. I shot outside and was met by chaos. Chairs were overturned, Caroline stood frozen to the spot, mouth hanging open, while Nicholas was shaking with fury, his fist clenched. Then I saw the cause of the debacle.

High on the garden wall sat one of the village cats. She was one of our favourites, part Siamese, part tabby, very beautiful. Although feral, she was slightly tamer than the other cats and often snoozed in our garden. We fed her scraps occasionally but had never named her. Clamped between her teeth was a large hunk of fish, complete with aluminium foil.

Nicholas's love of wildlife seemed to have evaporated. And his eagerness to share was also under question.

"Damn cat! How dare you! That was our bloody supper!"

Caroline was more philosophical. "Well, there's quite a lot left," she said. "If we just cut the end off..."

Nicholas was having none of it, literally. Teeth clenched, he flashed her a glare that nearly turned our wine to vinegar and stomped off to bed refusing any supper, even though it was only nine o'clock.

And the cat? She dined well that night. I later named her Thief Cat and she continued to ornament our garden with her graceful form, dozing, but always with one china blue eye slightly open, no doubt waiting for that perfect opportunity to return.

I was sorry when Caroline and Nicholas left. They were good company. Caroline spoke perfect Spanish and had been a great help to me. Nicholas had taught me how to identify fascinating creatures, like the carpenter bee which, like a huge, harmless, purple torpedo, blundered round the garden in search of rotten wood to build its home. He showed me the busy little shield beetles and identified birdsong.

But, to this day, none of us have ever mentioned the incident of Thief Cat and the stolen fish again.

However, my next set of visitors turned out to be even livelier than the last...

BARBECUED SARDINES

Just three ingredients and a barbecue is all you need for this wonderful summer dish.

Ingredients (serves 4)

- 8 medium to large sardines
- Handful fresh parsley
- Salt to season

Method

- Clean the sardines and remove the heads, then wash under running water.
- Cook on a barbecue or under the grill for a few minutes each side until cooked through.
- Season with salt and garnish with a squeeze of lemon juice and fresh chopped parsley.

11

MULES AND STORMS

By October, there were very few people living in the village during the week. In fact I was shocked to learn that there were but five souls in total. By now I knew them all well. Marcia and Old Sancho at the shop, Geronimo with his three dogs, Paco's ancient Uncle Felix. And me.

I saw Marcia and Old Sancho every day as she set aside a loaf of bread to save me listening out for the bread van's hoot. If I was waiting for a letter I would pop into the shop as Marcia's was also the unofficial Post Office. We had hung a smart new shiny black mailbox outside our house, but it was ignored by the postman. The only thing I ever found in it was dust, and once a dead carpenter bee that must have blundered in by mistake. All village post was dumped at Marcia's for collection.

The weather was still warm enough for Old Sancho and his cat to doze outside the shop, and Geronimo was often there too. I always greeted them with *"¿Qué tal?"* (How's things?) and the reply was always the same. Old Sancho just smiled in his simple way. The cat would arch her back to be stroked. Geronimo would shake his head grimly, long hair swinging, and answer, *"Mal!"* (bad) before taking another swig from his beer.

Sometimes Uncle Felix sat with them. His clothes were as ancient as himself and hung off his wiry frame like a sack thrown over a nail. His flat cap was threadbare and pulled down to shade his eyes. He had only two teeth, one upper, one lower. Uncle Felix had been a shepherd all his life and could neither read nor write. Nor had he ever visited a doctor or dentist, and Paco once whispered to Joe that Uncle Felix had 'never had a woman'.

Paco told us that during the reign of the Spanish dictator, General Franco, Uncle Felix, like all young men, had been conscripted. Never having left the village before, his family pinned a label on his back with his name and destination, and left him at the railway station. Felix served his time, and when his tour of duty ended, the army once again pinned his name and address on his back and put him on a train home.

Uncle Felix lived in a two-roomed cottage in the village. One room was his, and the other was home to his mule and two chickens. The mule was a glossy beauty and clearly adored Uncle Felix. He would tether her on patches of waste ground to graze, but she had only one thing on her mind - Felix. Countless times we saw her trotting through the streets, rope trailing, often still attached to the stake she had managed to wrench from the ground. Ears alert, eyes bright, she was on a mission - find her beloved master.

Her ability to find him was unerring. As she rounded a street corner and caught sight of him, she would break into a canter. She had found him! Whinnying happily, she lovingly nuzzled the object of her affections. It was a never-ending source of amusement to the villagers.

I once patted the mule and asked Uncle Felix what her name was. He looked at me with scorn. "Mule, of course," he replied. Of course. Silly me.

Although our new mailbox was always empty, my inbox was being bombarded with emails. Back in Sussex, my two friends from school, Juliet and Sue, were preparing for their first visit out to me. The Gin Twins were coming for four days during their half term and they were full of questions. What shall we bring? What clothes do we need? Is gin cheap?

I made it as clear as I could how basic their accommodation would be, even sending photographs so that they wouldn't be disappointed. I told them how they needed to bring only shorts and maybe jeans if we went out to eat. No posh clothes, no high heels. And, yes, gin was cheap.

Much as I loved the solitude in the village, it was wonderful to see them. They brimmed with hilarious stories from the staff-room and juicy morsels of gossip from my former life. They brought gifts, like books and bayonet-type light bulbs for my English lamps, as Spanish bulbs are different. For my part, I made sure there was plenty of gin in the cupboard.

A word about my lovely friends. Juliet is blonde, dizzy and a coiled spring. Unable to keep still, she lives off nervous energy, exhausting all around her. However, she was the best teaching assistant I had ever had, the sort that knows what you need even before you do. Juliet is up for everything, including representing England in the International Marbles Tournament.

Sue is very different. She is quiet and thoughtful, musically talented, and reveals a wicked dry sense of humour, particularly after a few gins.

There is nothing quite like a Girls Only holiday. The absence of men makes us loosen up and shrug off our roles as wife/mother/teacher/whatever with delicious abandon.

The weather stayed hot and we could drive with the jeep's roof down. Sue (ever the music teacher) led us in raucous songs which we bellowed out to the mountain goats as the jeep meandered along the dusty roads. We visited other villages, went shopping in the city, sunbathed, did crosswords, played games and generally chilled out. When the sun passed the yardarm (often straight after breakfast) the gin bottle came out.

On their last night, we drove down to the city and ate at our favourite restaurant. The Moroccan waiter took our order but only had eyes for Juliet.

"Salad to start?" he asked, his eyes sliding up and down Juliet's body.

"Yes, please, then a tortilla. And two more gin and tonics, please, and an orange juice."

"Of course, beautiful lady. Anything else?"

"No, thank you, that's all."

"Beautiful lady, you are most welcome..." He backed away reluctantly, delivered our order to the kitchen and returned to the dining room, flicking longing glances at Juliet. Still watching her, he reached for the music system controls and turned the volume up high. He approached our table again and bowed low to Juliet, taking her hand.

"Beautiful lady, would you like to dance?"

Sue and I were smirking, and Juliet played along fuelled by gin and her natural effervescence. She plucked a plastic flower from the vase on the table and gripped it between her teeth. Standing, she gave him an exaggerated curtsey. The waiter slipped his other hand around her waist and off they whirled between the tables.

The clattering of cutlery on crockery ceased as diners leaned back to watch the floor show. The Flamenco music was infectious and Sue started to clap in time to the twang of the Spanish guitars. The whole room took up the clapping. Shouts of encouragement in Spanish, English and German accompanied the pair's spinning path. The waiter, head held arrogantly high, eyes hooded, stamped his heels together one last time and finally delivered his flushed partner back to our table.

"Thank you, beautiful lady," he said, and pressed his lips to Juliet's hand.

With a last lingering glance, the waiter went back to his duties and the diners took up their knives and forks again. At our table, the gin continued to flow. The Gin Twins giggled like teenagers throughout the meal amusing me greatly as the sober designated driver.

When we left, the Moroccan waiter shook hands with Sue and me but kissed Juliet on the cheek. He held onto her for far too long, brown eyes smouldering with intent. She extricated herself with difficulty. More cause for hilarity as we stood outside.

"Wow, the wind's really picked up, hasn't it?" observed Sue at last. She was right. Outside the restaurant was an ornamental fountain and the road was soaking wet from where the wind had blown the water sideways. The palm trees lining the roadsides rustled and bent in the wind.

"Don't worry, it's always windy down here in town. When we get back up into the mountains there won't be any wind."

"Are you sure?"

"Of course - we never get really strong winds in our village." A tumbleweed bowled down the street followed by carrier bags and crisp packets.

We set off and headed home. The Gin Twins were in full singing voice while I concentrated on driving. I was a little concerned. Instead of calming, the wind seemed to be growing in strength. Sharp blasts rocked the jeep and made the Gin Twins squeal. Branches and debris littered the dark road.

At last we turned onto the road that descended to our village. The street lights twinkled below as I carefully negotiated the bends. I drove cautiously, ever mindful of the narrowness of the road, the steepness of the drop down and the sudden gusts of wind.

Suddenly a vast shape loomed in front of us. I braked sharply, spoiling the Gin Twins' rendition of 'Windmill in old Amsterdam'.

"I saw a mouse! WHERE? There on the stair! Where on the... Whassup?"

"There's something big in the road." I tried to peer through the dark.

"Big? Big like an elephant?" Howls of laughter from the Gin Twins.

"No, big like a tree."

"A tree?"

"Yes, there's a fallen tree blocking us."

Silence while they thought about that. A gust of wind rocked the jeep.

Then, "Can you drive round it?"

"No way! The road's much too narrow."

"Oh, come on, let's get out and have a look." Juliet was already opening the car door, fighting the wind.

Talking was almost impossible; the wind forced us to shout. We stood assessing the situation. I'd left the headlights on and the size of the obstacle was spotlighted. The uprooted tree stretched right across the road. Its roots pointed into the night sky on one side, while its crown vanished into the darkness of the precipice on the other. The street lights of the village below flickered invitingly. So near, yet so far.

"Right!" shouted Juliet, the practical one. "If we all pull, I bet we could move it." The three of us got into position, arms round the trunk, tugging. "No! All together! Right, one, two, three, PULL!"

Even when synchronised, we made absolutely no impression. The tree didn't budge an inch. The Gin Twins collapsed laughing while the wind howled and tore at the leaves of the branches.

"Okay, use your mobile, call someone to help," yelled Juliet, recovering.

"Who would I ask to come out?"

"The Mayor?" Juliet shouted, and she had a point. The Mayor lived in Judith's village, but was also in charge of our village.

"Why would I have the Mayor's home phone number? And there's no mobile signal here, anyway."

"PARDON?"

"Oh, never mind. Any ideas, Sue? Sue! You haven't said anything for ages."

Sue put her hand up like a child in class. "Girls," she said, "I've got something important to say. REALLY important."

"WHAT?"

"I... I need the loo. And it's urgent!"

"What?"

"I NEED THE LOO!"

"Well, go on the side of the road. We won't look."

Sue's face was red, even in the car's headlights. "No, I can't. It's not just, er, I mean..."

Juliet was severe. The wind died for a second allowing us to hear her perfectly. Her voice changed and she spoke as though back in the infants' classroom.

"Goodness!" she said, wagging her finger at Sue. "You've chosen a fine time to need the toilet, haven't you? Well, you can't do it now. You'll just have to wait!"

This was too much. Juliet and I were helpless with laughter. Poor Sue clutched at herself, exercising supreme control while tears of laughter ran down her face.

I stirred myself into action. I would try signalling. Back in the driver's seat, I flashed the headlights spelling out S.O.S. (Joe, with his military training would have been proud of me.) Zero response. I tried sounding S.O.S. on the hooter. Again, zero response. I leant on the hooter for a full minute but the noise was snatched away by the wind. Nothing happened for about half an hour. We had almost agreed to abandon the jeep, climb over the tree and walk the two miles down to the village. Sue's evacuation problem had subsided for the moment and she felt able to walk.

Then we saw something. Far below us a single moving light faltered. One second it was there, the next it was gone. But every time it reappeared, it was closer.

"It's not a car, there's only one light. Perhaps it's a motorbike?"

"No, it's moving all wrong, and it's too high off the ground for a motorbike."

"Then what is it?" whispered Sue. "It's moving much too fast for a person, and it's sort of, bouncing."

If it wasn't human, what could it be? Juliet voiced what we were all thinking. A thought that filled three middle-aged, normally sensible ladies with dread.

"It's a ghost…"

The wind howled around us again and we huddled closer together, clutching each other in fear. Sue's previous problem returned with a vengeance. The light continued to float towards us, closer, closer.

I didn't believe in ghosts, never had, but that windy moonless night I was sure I was seeing a ghastly apparition. And it was coming closer.

SUMMER PORK WITH SHERRY

This should serve 4 but it depends on the size of the pork fillets, and how hungry your diners are.

Ingredients

- 6 - 8 thin pork fillets
- 2 onions
- 3 carrots
- 2 bay leaves
- ¼ ltr (8 fl oz) Fino de Jerez or similar dry sherry
- Salt
- Pepper
- Olive oil

Method

- Peel the onions and carrots and chop into small pieces.
- Sprinkle a little salt and pepper over the pork. Then, in a large frying pan, heat a little olive oil and brown off the pork fillets on either side. Remove the pork from the pan and set aside.
- In the same oil as the pork, gently fry the onions and carrots until soft, don't allow them to go brown.
- Return the pork to the pan, adding the bay leaves, sherry, salt and pepper.

- Cover and cook gently for about 40 minutes, adding water if necessary, until the pork is tender and the sauce has reduced.
- Serve with creamy mashed potato, rice or a jacket potato.

12

¡FIESTA!

Gradually I could discern a shape. But not a shape that belonged to our world. An irregular, many humped, black shape. A shape that bounced slightly as it covered the ground between us. It was rounding the last bend, phantom light glimmering through the trees, ever approaching.

"It's horrible..." breathed Sue. "And it's nearly here..."

"I think we should run," whispered Juliet, white-faced and serious. "We've still got time."

But our legs had turned to rubber. I could hear my own heart thumping and Juliet's fingernails were digging into my arm. Sue was rigid, none of us could move. United in terror, we held our breath as the vision revealed itself.

Trotting towards us were Geronimo and Uncle Felix, both astride Uncle Felix's mule. Geronimo's long hair and Real Madrid scarf whipped in the gusts, and Uncle Felix had to hold his flat cap down or lose it. Geronimo held a torch and the ubiquitous beer bottle.

"Ladies!" Geronimo waved his beer bottle in greeting. "Do not worry, just wait there. We will move the tree out of the road."

"Hurrah!" yelled Juliet, jumping up and down, fear forgotten. "We're saved!"

"Thank God," muttered Sue to herself.

The mule, cheerful as ever, halted when she reached the fallen tree. Geronimo and Uncle Felix slid off to the ground. Silently they looped a rope round the trunk and secured it around the mule's neck. The mule scarcely strained as she hauled the tree to the nearest widening of the road. Our ordeal was over.

We climbed back into the jeep and drove over the remaining debris, tyres crunching over the almonds that the tree had shed. I slowed down to thank our rescuers.

"*Muchas gracias,*" I said. "Thank you so much."

"*Muchas gracias,*" chorused the Gin Twins, leaning out of the windows.

Uncle Felix merely nodded, eyes downcast, hands twisting the mule's rope. Looking directly at three women was clearly beyond his capability. Geronimo's face was red, whether from the wind or beer, I couldn't say.

"How did you know we were here?" I asked. But Geronimo was otherwise occupied refreshing himself from his bottle.

"Must have been your expert signalling," said Juliet as we drove away. "Joe'll be really impressed when he hears about this."

Back home, Sue now vastly relieved, the Gin Twins happily renewed their acquaintance with the gin bottle. It had been an eventful night.

When we drove past the fallen tree the next day, the leaves had wilted and the tree looked a fraction of the monster it had appeared the night before. By the following day it had been chopped up into neat lengths for firewood. Only shattered almonds on the road gave any clue to our adventure.

I waved goodbye to the Gin Twins and assumed that the village would remain almost deserted until spring. However, as usual, I was wrong.

Although the village was empty on week days, the population still swelled at weekends as families arrived from the city. But now there was a new sense of urgency in the air. People arrived with purpose, with an agenda. And the reason for this energy and atmosphere of anticipation?

I had forgotten the most important annual event in El Hoyo's calendar. The *Fiesta!*

The streets became a hive of activity. Houses were whitewashed, doors varnished, doorsteps polished. The town council hung terracotta pots bursting with crimson geraniums on the walls.

One weekend I heard a commotion outside. To my surprise, the street was filled with furniture. Tables, chairs, a television, all manner of things were stacked up and standing in the street. Any approaching cars would need to reverse and find another route to avoid flattening the sideboard and three piece suite. Carmen-Bethina and Sofía bustled in and out of their house, absorbed in their task.

"What are you doing?" I asked.

"Cleaning," said Carmen-Bethina, pausing to wipe her hands on her apron. "In two weeks it is the *Fiesta*."

"Mama is hoping this year I will find a husband," said Sofía, her beautiful eyes dancing. "She has been to church every week praying that I will."

"*Claro*," said Carmen-Bethina.

"Pah!" said Paco, staggering out of the house with yet more furniture. "For that we need a miracle."

Neighbours we had never met before materialised. A car drew up beside the little tumbledown house opposite our garden gate and three elderly people got out. They stood surveying their house, hands shielding their eyes from the sun in identical poses.

"We will begin outside," said Brown Shirt. He must have been in his seventies, wrinkled but full of drive and energy.

"*¡Madre mia!* No, it is much too hot. It is better to begin inside," said the lady. She had the same build as her companions, the same way of holding her head to one side like an inquisitive sparrow. I guessed they were siblings; two brothers and a sister.

"Always begin on the roof," said Flat Cap. "Always begin at the top, then work down. *Sí*, that is the best way."

The discussion got more heated, then abated as they unloaded the boot of the car. Buckets of whitewash, brushes, cleaning materials and step ladders all lined up along the street.

"We will have coffee first," said the lady.

"No, we must start," said Flat Cap.

"*Sí*, let's start," agreed Brown Shirt. "And do not put too much water in that whitewash."

And so it went on. Every action was discussed and argued over. Every suggestion became a heated debate. They quarrelled, bickered and squabbled over every tiny thing. However, by the time they left that evening, white-speckled and still arguing, the little house looked smart and refreshed.

Next, I had a visit from two smart ladies selling the *Fiesta* programme. I paid up, accepted the programme and was given a pottery jug with 'Fiestas Patronales El Hoyo' inscribed. The ladies pointed to something in the programme. I nodded politely even though I had absolutely no idea what they were talking about. The ladies looked pleased and added the word 'English' to a list.

I got on the phone and checked with Judith. When the barking of the dogs had subsided, I asked my question.

"Judith, what exactly does, er, '*Concurso Gastronomico: presentación de platos*' mean?"

"Oh, well done, dear! So you've entered the Cookery Contest, have you?"

"I have? Cookery Contest? Oh hell!"

"Main course or dessert?"

"It says '*postre*' here."

"Pudding, dear. They take their cooking and their competitions bloody seriously, don't you know!"

This was not good news. I had no kitchen, no oven, no hot-plates. How could I create a delicious dessert when none of my kitchen utensils was even unpacked? How could I represent Britain under those conditions? I was in danger of betraying my country! My mind wrestled with the problem until I came up with a possible solution. I would call in reinforcements; my ocean-going sister-in-law Grace and her husband Paul. I reached for the phone again.

"Hi, Grace! How are you? How's Paul?"

"Vicky! We're absolutely fine. What a coincidence! We're just entering Almería Marina, and I was going to call you so we could meet up."

So my calculations were correct. I knew they had sailed out of Portuguese waters a week or so ago and I guessed they'd be close by now.

"How long are you mooring for?" I asked.

"Oh, about three weeks."

Aha! Perfect.

"How do you fancy coming to stay for a long weekend? Say, the weekend of the fifteenth?" I asked. My plan was coming together. I held my breath.

"That would be lovely," said Grace. "Are you missing Joe and want company?"

It was time to come clean and expose my ulterior motive. Apart from being nice people, Grace is a fabulous cook. She could produce a veritable banquet even in the tiny galley of their boat. I explained my problem and, bless her, she was amused and promised to provide a dessert. I replaced the receiver and stopped worrying, knowing that Britain's culinary reputation would be safe in Grace's capable hands.

During the week before, Geronimo and some colleagues from Judith's village erected a stage in the square. They hung coloured lights from all the trees and 'Welcome to our Fiesta!' signs across the road coming into the village.

On the Friday, my visitors arrived. Paul lugged their suitcase up the stairs while Grace stowed the precious *postre* ingredients in the fridge. Although we had no kitchen yet, the fridge was an essential item and one of our first purchases.

I gave them the guided tour of our little estate, then we went for a stroll around the village. It was still only midday and the streets were quiet. The church-bells chimed twelve times, then paused for thirty seconds or so and chimed twelve times again.

"Do they always do that?" asked Grace.

"Do what?"

"The church-bells. Do they always ring twice?"

"Yes," I said. I had stopped noticing them. Geronimo had shrugged when I asked him why they always rang twice. Paco and Carmen-Bethina didn't know either. It was just accepted.

"I can't believe you're living here," said Grace. "It's a lovely village, but it's a bit of a culture shock, isn't it? A bit 'third world'. I mean, it's not like Sussex, is it?"

"That's why I like it. It's just so different. The pace of life is so much slower."

"Don't you miss going to the pub, or shopping, or speaking English?"

"No, not really."

"What does Joe think?"

"Well, he likes it too, but probably not as much as I do." I kicked at a pebble. "We have this Five Year Plan, you see."

"What's that?" asked Paul.

"We've given ourselves five years. We want to finish doing up the house, build two houses in the orchard, then decide whether we want to stay in Spain or go back to England."

"What d'you think you'll do?"

"Well, it's early days yet, but I think I'll want to stay. Not sure about Joe, though. He's going to take some convincing."

As we passed the square, Geronimo was fiddling with some coloured lights on the stage.

"¿Qué tal?" I asked, as usual.

"Mal, señora," he replied, tossing back his long hair and continuing to fiddle with the bulbs.

Uncle Felix strolled by and settled himself on a bench. Geronimo hooked the last string of lights into place and disappeared behind the stage. We waved to Uncle Felix and headed home.

Suddenly, a deafening explosion echoed round the valley. Grace, Paul and I jumped and clapped our hands to our ears. Turning back, we saw Geronimo standing in the centre of the square. Hugged to his chest was a huge bundle of fireworks. One by one, he lit the fuses of the rockets, not letting go his hold on the stick until the last split second. One by one the rockets roared into the sky. The blasts shook the village and the air was filled with smoke.

"He doesn't even stick the rocket into the ground!" squeaked Grace, her hands over her ears.

"Imagine what Health and Safety in Britain would say if they saw this!" said Paul.

I was not particularly surprised. I was already accustomed to the Spanish lack of safety precautions. Most of the village roofs were made from asbestos. Nobody wore goggles, gloves or earmuffs when employing a chainsaw. And many times I had seen Geronimo stagger onto his doorstep and launch rockets into the sky after his beloved Real Madrid had won a match.

Back in our garden, we exchanged family news and gossip over the first drinks of the day. Paul, Welsh and bearded, told tales of how the boat had behaved and who they had met on the high seas. It fascinated me how he opened can after can of beer, tipping them down his throat in seconds, but never appearing affected by the alcohol. An old sea dog's skill, I assumed.

I checked the programme of events to see what was happening first. According to the timetable, there was to be 'firing of rockets' at 12.00 midday to open the Fiesta. So that explained the fireworks.

The lack of people at the opening ceremony was no indication of what was to come. That evening, people poured into the village. Headlights blazed as a constant stream of cars headed down into the valley. Cars blocked the streets, people gathered in noisy clusters, dogs barked, children yelled; the village was transformed from ghost town to Bangkok at night.

"You haven't put our names down for the Dancing Contest, have you?" asked Grace, flicking pages in the *Fiesta* programme. "It starts at seven o'clock."

"What?" Paul sat bolt upright, panic in his eyes.

"Calm down, calm down. No, I didn't. Relax, have another beer. We can give the Dancing Contest a miss. The big dance starts at ten o'clock tonight so we've got plenty of time to have a drink and get ready."

We sat in the garden, ate, had a few more drinks, then dressed for the dance. As the bells chimed twenty we were sauntering down to the square.

The band, 'Sparkling Mediterranean', was on stage, but they hadn't even started to twinkle yet. Bunches of children chased each other in circles, enjoying the empty space. Old Sancho still sat outside the shop, smiling and staring at nothing in particular. A few groups of villagers stood deep in conversation, and around the edges, some stall holders were setting out their wares. Cars jammed the narrow streets, parked nose to tail, silent and empty.

"Where is everybody?" asked Grace. "I thought the dance started at 10 o'clock?"

"Probably finishing their suppers," I said. "And getting ready."

"Well, we might as well go back to the house and have another drink," said Paul. So we did.

In fact the dancing didn't begin in earnest until well after midnight. The lead singer of the band cleared his throat and growled a final, *"Uno, dos. Uno, dos,"* into the microphone. The band throbbed into life, the beat as hot and heavy as the night air. Slowly but steadily the houses disgorged, people migrating to the square like exotic parrots flocking to a waterhole.

I looked up to see Paco arriving with his usual entourage of friends and relations and a lady I didn't recognise.

ASPARAGUS SALAD
ENSALADA DE ESPÁRRAGOS

This is the basic Spanish recipe, but you could add different ingredients such as cucumber, red or yellow pepper, olives or apple.

Ingredients

- 150g (6oz) fresh green asparagus
- 2 medium tomatoes
- 2 medium potatoes
- 50g (2oz) sweet corn
- Olive oil
- Salt and pepper to season

Method

- Boil the potatoes for about 8 minutes until cooked but still firm, drain and allow to cool.
- Trim the ends of the asparagus, removing any hard bits then blanch in boiling water for a few minutes until just tender, drain and allow to cool.
- When cool, peel the potatoes and cut into bite sized pieces, then cut the tomatoes into similar sized chunks.
- Arrange the potatoes, tomatoes, sweet corn and asparagus onto a serving dish, drizzle with olive oil and then season.

13

PROCESSIONS AND PUDDINGS

Paco was smartly turned out; polished shoes, pressed trousers, crisp shirt, oiled hair. But the vision on his arm was none other than Carmen-Bethina! Gone was the apron, replaced by the soft folds of an off-the-shoulder evening number that floated around her ample curves. High heeled shoes with matching bag and scarlet lipstick completed the ensemble. I tried hard not to stare. She looked stunning.

Sofía looked wonderful, proud head held high. Little Paco was also dressed smartly. He pulled away from his big sister to run excitedly to a bunch of children.

Uncle Felix had made a big effort with his appearance, too. His flat cap had been left at home and his few strands of remaining hair were plastered to his skull with water. He looked curiously naked without his cap, almost vulnerable. I'd never seen him in smart trousers and neat checked shirt before, either, and couldn't help wondering if his mule would recognise him now.

The live band was in full swing, the valley alive and vibrating with noise. Elderly couples gyrated, upright and dignified, while family groups danced together in circles. Children darted in and out, trailing each other and pestering their parents for small change. The stalls were now set up, mostly manned by dark-skinned Moroccans doing a roaring trade in fire crackers, hot dogs and cheap plastic toys. Around the edge, leather-clad youths leaned nonchalantly against parked motor bikes, eyeing up the girls who danced with their families.

Marcia and Old Sancho sat in straight-backed chairs outside their shop. The black cat was absent, probably inside with its paws over its ears, hiding from the constant explosion of firecrackers set off by small boys. Other more needy village cats lurked around the hot dog stalls, watching hopefully for fallen scraps.

Spanish fiestas never revolve around alcohol. Yes, a couple of bars had been set up and were selling drinks, but they were very low-key affairs. The emphasis was on dancing and family enjoyment. The only drunken rowdy behaviour I ever saw at a *fiesta* was by Brits, never the Spanish.

At about two in the morning Geronimo let off more fireworks into the night sky, to a larger and more appreciative audience this time. The square was a seething mass of colour, the noise tremendous. Everyone cheered and whooped and clutched each other, pointing up at the sky. Even Marcia stood and clapped, dislodging hairpins which glittered to the ground. Old Sancho just smiled in his simple way, enjoying everyone else's pleasure. I reminded myself that he had probably attended more than eighty village fiestas before this one.

Fireworks over, the band struck up again and dancing recommenced. By three o'clock Grace, Paul and I were all danced out and crawled our way, exhausted, to bed. But the locals were tireless. The children still weaved in and out of the dancers and the music continued to pound. And this was only Friday night; the *Fiesta* had hardly begun.

Next morning, Grace and I examined the programme closely to find out the order of events. We soon found the running order rarely followed the programme so we just listened. When noise emanated from the square, we walked down to see what was occurring.

Clowns arrived and put on a show for the children. Five-a-side football games were organised. Flamenco dancers performed. An open air theatre company put on 'Fires of the Orient' including fire eaters. The Saturday night dance was even bigger and louder than Friday's.

What the programme didn't mention were the fireworks going off at unexpected times. Saturday's dance hadn't finished until 4 a.m. and we were sound asleep. At eight o'clock on Sunday morning, the valley exploded into a cacophony of gunshots setting off car alarms and dogs barking. We leapt out of bed in fright and converged in the garden to see what was happening.

"Watch out!" shouted Paul. "Don't look up!" We were forced to take cover as a hail of rocket sticks rained on our heads like arrows in 1066.

And the programme only mentioned one of the many processions. The one advertised began with the church-bells clamouring insanely. This was the call to Sunday Mass. Then again, as though rung by mad Quasimodo, the bells announced the end of Mass. The church doors burst open and spewed out the congregation. The statue of Santa Barbara (patron saint of the village) was to be given her annual airing.

Heading the procession was a marching band, percussion thumping, trumpets wheezing. The Mayor followed accompanied by some military dignitaries in uniform. Then came Santa Barbara, proudly carried aloft on a flower-decked bier by Geronimo, Paco and other villagers. Then came the Smart Ladies I recognised from the programme selling. Finally came the rest of the villagers, their visitors and the village dogs.

We stood on our doorstep and watched. The procession took five minutes to pass, then halted and hushed to allow a small boy on a balcony to read something. Suddenly everyone cheered, flowers were thrown down on the crowd, and the procession continued back to the church. Santa Barbara's annual outing was over, and she was put back on her pedestal in the gloomy church until next year. Geronimo let off a few more fireworks for good measure, and the crowd dispersed.

Unfortunately, a firework had landed in the olive grove above the village, setting the parched scrub alight. At first, just plumes of smoke drifted across the mountainside.

"I don't like the look of that," said Paul, tugging at his beard. "That could spread really quickly." As he spoke, the flames licked at a clump of bushes, turning them orange. Several olive trees burst into flame. Then the wind changed, chasing the smoke in our direction. Now we could smell it and hear the dry brush crackling. We watched in horror as it advanced.

"Has someone called the Fire Brigade, do you think?" asked Grace. Her face was white.

"I wonder where the nearest one is?" I had never seen a Spanish fire engine.

"It's getting worse!" said Grace. "I think we should..." As she spoke, the flames reared up. "Quick! I think we should get ready to run!"

Her panic was infectious. I raced after her into the house and grabbed Great Aunt Elsa and my passport. I stood in the middle of the room looking round. Was our stay in Spain to be cut short already? I loved this house, loved this life. I didn't want to leave, I wasn't ready.

"Come and see this," called Paul from outside.

Grace and I emerged and looked at the mountainside above. The fire still danced and shimmied, but silhouetted against the smoke was a crowd of villagers. We watched as they formed a chain down to the village. Geronimo shouted instructions. Buckets, saucepans and pots of water travelled along the human chain to be hurled at the flames. Other volunteers beat and stamped until the orange disappeared and only smoke rose from the ground. The fire was extinguished.

It hadn't taken long to put out. There was no panic from the villagers. They seemed very organised and accustomed to this kind of event.

"I think you can take Great Aunt Elsa back in now," said Paul. Then, glancing at Grace, "And our suitcase." His words were drowned by the drone of a helicopter which appeared over the crest of the mountain. It circled, seemed satisfied that the job was done and wheeled away. It was comforting to know that Fire Department helicopters were on constant standby.

Another procession attracted our attention that weekend. It snaked its way up the almost vertical road to the little shrine above the village. Leading was a mini tractor driven by Geronimo, but it was the trailer it towed that was remarkable.

The trailer was decorated with intertwined branches and leaves. Pot plants stood on the floor of the trailer. In the centre of this leafy jungle, on a dining room chair, sat Old Sancho. Smiling benignly, he sat with his walking stick gripped between his knees.

"Come on, let's follow it!" I said to Grace and Paul.

The winding road up to the shrine was steep and pitted. We were out of breath and panting when we reached it. Old Sancho's knuckles were white with the effort of holding onto his stick and the side of the trailer, but his gentle smile never wavered. The procession reached the shrine, and the Smart Ladies were there to hand out hot chocolate and cakes. Then Old Sancho was lifted back onto his chair, and we all trudged back down the mountain in a giant multi-coloured alligator.

Two o'clock. Time for the Gastronomic Contest. I was nervous, not knowing what to expect, worried that we wouldn't understand what was going on. I didn't worry about our entry because clever Grace had excelled herself. Her sherry trifle was topped with snowy peaks of whipped cream, the glossy strawberries glinting. How could a judge resist?

Carefully, we carried the dish to the square but there was no-one there. Unless you counted Old Sancho, his cat and Uncle Felix. But the two Smart Ladies appeared from nowhere, accepted our dish and placed it on a wall. Then they busied themselves setting up some trestle tables. We stood nearby, trying to shoo the flies off the trifle and guarding it from hopeful village dogs. White paper tablecloths were thrown over the tables, twitched this way and that until the Smart Ladies were satisfied. All this time, our trifle patiently sat and sweated in the sun. At long last, the ladies remembered our contribution and put it on the table, labelled *'Ingles'* (English).

More contestants drifted in and added their dishes to the display. Women milled around tutting and clucking over each others' entries and making last minute adjustments to their own. The square was now filled with people, many clutching plastic cutlery and empty paper plates provided by the Smart Ladies.

Suddenly the atmosphere changed. The crowd quietened and split apart like the Red Sea to allow the Mayor and uniformed dignitaries access to the presentations. The Smart Ladies were in their element as they herded the crowd away from the tables with outstretched arms. The judges were given silver cutlery and invited to begin.

It was a very serious business. They worked along the tables tasting every dish, pausing and looking thoughtful. Then they made notes on their clipboards. Occasionally they conferred, faces deadpan, heads close together, voices hushed. The village ladies leaned forward, ears cupped, desperately straining to catch the words. The Smart Ladies fluttered round the judges, simpering and moving plates a quarter of a centimetre left or right.

Our magnificent trifle had waited nearly two hours in the relentless Spanish sun and was not faring well. Its proud snowy crests had sunk to milky pools as the whipped cream collapsed and melted. The strawberries floated forlornly in a white scum sea. Poor Grace looked miserable, mouth drooped, shoulders sagged. It was not the best example of British cuisine and we were not hopeful.

When the judges reached our dish, they hesitated, unsure how to tackle it. They dipped into the milky lake and pulled out a spoonful of dripping trifle. They tasted, faces inscrutable. I was aware that I was holding my breath, my expression identical to that of the other village contestants.

At long last the judges were satisfied. The Smart Ladies pulled up a wooden crate and the Mayor stepped up importantly. He drew himself up to his full height of five foot five inches and began to speak.

"It is always a great honour to be invited to judge this prestigious cooking contest. The village of El Hoyo may be small, but rarely have I seen such a wonderful array of delightful and delicious dishes…"

The crowd shuffled their feet and stifled yawns. People began to mutter and some of the older ladies fanned themselves exaggeratedly, although their efforts barely stirred the hot heavy air.

"*Madre mia*, get on with it!" hissed a lady to her companion. Perhaps the Mayor heard her because he stepped up a gear.

"And now the moment has arrived," he announced. "The decision is made. And so, without further ado…" He paused for effect, enjoying the suspense he was creating. The crowd stopped fidgeting and waited with bated breath.

"The winning dessert this year is… The traditional Andalucían rice pudding in the green ceramic bowl!"

There was a brief ripple of applause, then the crowd surged

forward like an advancing army, paper plates and cutlery held like shields and weapons. The Smart Ladies skipped aside and the villagers pounced on the entries.

The poor Mayor was almost knocked off his wooden box in the crush. The crowd reached the tables and battle commenced as they fought over the dishes. Within minutes the culinary display was reduced to a few crumbs and greasy smears on the tablecloth. Even our soggy trifle evaporated. A plague of locusts couldn't have demolished the feast more rapidly or efficiently.

The contest was soon forgotten however, as the next event appeared on the stage. Three figures on stilts, crazily dressed, danced and told jokes which entertained the villagers hugely. They ate fire and juggled with flaming torches. Finally they plucked sweets from hidden pockets and threw them to excited children.

And so the festivities continued and we became almost immune to the explosion of fireworks. Event followed event, procession followed procession. Now I understood why Seville always has a Bank Holiday immediately after its Fiesta. To allow the participants to recover from the festivities.

On Sunday evening the cars began to leave as the villagers locked up their houses and returned to the city. Grace and Paul departed and peace descended on the village. Only the coloured lights, rocket sticks and blowing litter gave any clue to the frenzy of the Fiesta weekend. And by ten o'clock nobody remained, except of course for Marcia, Old Sancho, Geronimo and Uncle Felix. And me.

Dear Reader, please do not be unduly concerned about Britain's culinary reputation. It gives me great pleasure and pride to report that the following two years Britain won the contest. I'd love to say that I created the winning dishes, but no, it was my visitors' efforts both times. So thank you, Linda, (now known as the Pudding Queen) and her assistant, Doug, for the bread and butter pudding. And thanks to you, Glennys, for the sticky toffee pudding. Well done all of you.

THE WINNING RICE PUDDING RECIPE
ARROZ CON LECHE

Spain is well known for its delicious, fragrant rice pudding, and this traditional recipe won the fiesta contest.

Ingredients

- ½ kilo (18oz) white short grain rice
- 1½ ltr (2½ pints) milk
- 300ml (11 fl oz) water
- 100g (3½ oz) sugar
- 1 small cinnamon stick
- Some lemon peel shavings
- Pinch salt
- Ground cinnamon for dusting

Method

- Place the water, cinnamon stick, lemon peel, salt, sugar and rice in a large pan and bring to the boil.
- Cover and cook on a low heat until most of the water has been absorbed.
- Remove the lemon peel and cinnamon and transfer to an oven proof dish.
- Add the milk and cook in a medium oven for around 20

minutes until the rice is really tender and the dessert is rich and creamy.
- Sprinkle generously with cinnamon.

14

CHICKENS

Winter in the mountains takes one by surprise. The air is crisp and clean and icy winds funnel through the valley. In the distance, the sea is electric blue, the horizon clearly defined.

Ripening oranges and lemons are bright daubs of paint on a brown canvas. The swallows deserted months ago. At night the temperature can drop to below freezing and village cats sleep on the rooftops huddled close to working chimneys.

Marcia and Old Sancho felt the cold and warmed their old bones by their perpetually burning stove. The shop doors remained closed. If we needed anything, we would tap softly on the window. Marcia would let us in while Old Sancho dozed, only the tip of his nose visible from the folds of his blanket.

Joe was back in Spain for good now, having completed his time in the Army. We kept warm by working on the house, but at night, we too huddled round our fire before taking hot water bottles to bed.

How we loved that wood-burning stove, and how we hated it! Daily chores now included chopping firewood as we struggled to satisfy its voracious appetite. Joe adopted it and spent much time with his temperamental baby. Every evening he would sit hunched on a low stool, peering hopefully into its stomach, willing it to light. He sang tuneless little songs to it, encouraging it to flare.

> "Come on little fire, tra la la,
> You can burn much higher, tra la la,
> Come on, fire, if you're good,
> I will give you lots more wood..."

And so on, and so on. Shivering, he would hand-feed it until it developed a healthy orange flame. But woe betide if he turned his back on it. Then it would sulk and smoke and fizzle out unless he tempted it back to life with choice pieces of kindling and more songs.

Eventually it would flare up enough for us to place saucepans on the top. Sometimes it would become much too enthusiastic, so hot that we sweated and removed layers of clothes. We began to recognise different types of firewood - which logs would burn slowly, which burned hot and fast. Every evening became a battle to keep the stove happy and fed. We were slaves to its moods and insatiable hunger.

Torrential rain caused us to place buckets strategically where our roof leaked. The drip-drip-drip of water plunking into those buckets that first winter will stay with me forever.

We soon exhausted the supplies of firewood that Alonso, the previous owner, had left behind. Then we burnt his old furniture that we had dumped in the orchard. Next, the fruit trees were chopped down and burnt. Our plans to build two houses in the orchard would mean they would be sacrificed anyway. (Geronimo helped us slice the biggest logs with his outsize chainsaw and stayed drinking brandy for the rest of the day.) Lastly, Joe pulled down the old chicken shed and coop in the orchard, and we burnt that, too.

One weekend in January we were in Paco and Carmen-Bethina's house. The fire blazed and quails in tiny domed cages hung on the walls. Paco explained that they were female quails. In spring their call would lure horny male quails, allowing Paco to shoot them. Of course we wholeheartedly disapproved and threatened to release the poor quails when his back was turned, much to his amusement. He thought we were joking. We weren't.

home shredded chicken. They were unharmed, but it reminded me of the stage magic trick where swords are apparently passed through glamorous assistants.

Back in the orchard, Paco pulled his woolly hat off and scratched his head when he saw Alonso's chicken shed had gone.

"*Qué pasa?*" he asked, reproach in his eyes. "What happened to the chicken shed?"

"We burnt it," said Joe. "We used it for firewood."

"Pah!" said Paco and shook his head in disapproval. But he was not a man to be beaten by a little thing like no chicken shed.

Ever resourceful, he dragged over some old doors and leaned them up under the corrugated asbestos roof that was still supported by uprights. There was plenty of chicken wire lying about which he fashioned into a closed-in run secured by bits of wire. He found a stick and fixed it horizontally as a roosting perch.

Time to release the girls. Without ceremony, he emptied the cardboard box and eight chickens slid out to stand stock still like a bizarre waxwork display, frozen on the spot.

"They've never been outside before," I said quietly. "They've never seen the sky. Or grass. Or earth."

Joe nodded. It was a moving moment. Gradually, life flowed back into the eight chickens and they began to explore their new world. Jerky little steps were taken, the ground unfamiliar between their toes. They found the feeder and fed furiously. They took sips of water, tipping their heads back to allow the water to run down their throats. They tasted the grass and picked at tiny specks on the ground. They flapped their wings and stretched - all new luxuries.

"They won't lay eggs for a couple of months," said Paco. "You will need to give them a box to lay in." He left us to it, amused at our rapture.

All work that day was forgotten. We pulled up the old yellow vinyl sofa from Alonso's rubbish pile and just sat and watched. It was fascinating. All the chicken cliches we had ever heard suddenly came to life. The 'Top Hen' emerged quickly, one of the white chickens. Bolder than the rest, she pecked anyone who annoyed her and the others treated her with great respect. The 'pecking order' was established. We named her Mala Leche, meaning bad milk, a Spanish insult.

'As rare as hen's teeth' became clear when we discovered the girls couldn't manage dry bread. Being 'chicken' became clear, too, observing Mala's conquests. If a sister annoyed her, she would attack mercilessly causing her victim to cower low. The cringing chicken didn't attempt to escape, just crouched and endured her whacking until Mala got bored and strutted away.

When dusk fell, we were still in the orchard, still fascinated. Instincts kicked in and the girls started craning their necks, looking for the highest place to roost. Mala was the first to fly up to Paco's makeshift perch. The others followed gradually, bickering like schoolgirls about who was going to sit next to whom.

The next morning brought a huge surprise. It's strange how you can wake up and sense something is wrong, something is different. Our bedroom was a cave room dug into the hillside with no windows, but when we woke we knew instinctively that something was awry. We gasped when Joe opened the shutters in the living room to a white and silent world.

The chickens! They'd never even set claw outside before yesterday. We'd plucked them from their indoor security and exposed them to the harshness of a snowstorm. Their shelter was makeshift and inadequate. We were desperately worried.

There was no denying that the mountains looked awesome. Like a monstrous dazzling duvet, the snow blanketed every contour, ironing out all familiar landmarks. But there was no time to enjoy the wonderland. Fat flakes of snow were still falling. We didn't know it then, but this was to be the heaviest snowfall for sixty years. Snow was rare in this part of the world, we lived on the edge of Europe's only desert, for goodness sake. Paco had told us that occasionally a light dusting might fall, but never more.

There was no time to lose. Joe dressed himself warmly in army boots and several jumpers topped by a thick jacket. He opened the front door. Or tried to. The snow had banked to chest height and blocked the door completely. Never mind, we could use the back door.

Luckily it faced a different direction and could still be pushed open. Just.

It was bitterly cold. He surveyed the scene outside. "I'm just going outside and may be some time," he said. It wasn't really funny but very apt. Captain Oates would have understood.

The orchard was just a few steps away, the chicken coop a few steps more. But reaching it was tough. The drifts were deep and hid the track. Alonso had used the orchard as a dump and so had we. Obstacles were strewn everywhere. Coils of wire, rubble, the yellow sofa, all smothered and concealed under thick snow. Every footstep was taken warily, like a soldier walking across a minefield.

To Joe's horror, the chicken shelter was one enormous snowdrift.

PACO'S RABBIT STEW
CONEJO CON VERDURAS

Rabbit is rarely eaten by some of us, but this traditional rabbit stew with brandy is often enjoyed by the Spanish and frequently cooked on an open fire.

Ingredients (serves 6)

- 2 onions
- 2 aubergines (eggplants)
- 2 red peppers
- 3 green peppers
- 6 ripe tomatoes
- 1 rabbit (cut into pieces)
- 4 tablespoons olive oil
- 1 bulb garlic
- Medium glass of brandy
- Salt and pepper

Method

- Finely chop all the vegetables and set aside.
- Separate the garlic into cloves.
- Heat the oil in a large shallow pan and add the garlic.
- Fry slowly for 5 minutes, then add the rabbit pieces.
- Cook the rabbit slowly for 10 minutes until sealed and slightly golden.

- Add the brandy, cover the pan and continue cooking slowly for a further 20 minutes.
- Remove from the heat and set aside.
- In another pan, heat a little more oil and add the onion, frying until soft.
- Add the aubergines, peppers and brandy juice and cook for about 10 minutes.
- Add the tomatoes. Simmer gently for about an hour, stirring occasionally. The liquid will reduce and become rich and thick.
- Add the rabbit and garlic to the pan, mixing well.
- Season to taste, cover and continue cooking for 20 minutes.
- Serve hot with crusty bread.

15

AND MORE CHICKENS

Joe approached the snowdrift with a sinking heart. And then he noticed the drift had a dip in the middle. The ends of the perch disappeared into white, but, locked on the perch, soaking wet and huddled miserably together, were all eight chickens. Their body warmth had melted the snow around them.

How do you dry a chicken? We didn't know. We did the only thing we could think of, which was rub them briskly with old towels. Joe cleared as much snow out of the coop as he could, uncovering their food and water. Luckily, it stopped snowing and a watery sun peeped out, providing much needed warmth.

Chickens are amazingly hardy creatures. They can survive the furnace of an Andalucían summer or winter temperatures below freezing. Even snow. Our chickens, young as they were, were absolutely fine.

On that first day, we had no electricity, telephone or water. There was nothing to do but sit in darkness as close to the fire as possible. The village was cut off, no traffic could reach us.

On the second day the water returned. Just as well, as our bottled water supplies were low. Geronimo knocked on our door to check if all was well. He unwound the Real Madrid scarf from around his neck and stayed for a few warming brandies. We were relieved to hear that Marcia and Old Sancho had left before the snow to stay with their daughter in the city. Uncle Felix was warm and cosy with his mule.

On the third day, electricity returned. Hooray! Now we could boil a kettle and use the microwave.

On the fourth day, the council 'snowplough' (mini tractor with improvised scoop) made the hazardous journey down to the village. It pushed the snow into great dirty heaps, making the road passable.

On the fifth day, the hordes descended. Except for the very old, none of the locals had seen proper snow before. They poured into the village, marvelling and wondering at the phenomenon. Judith's village, only a few kilometres away, had hardly suffered at all, and everyone was keen to visit snowbound El Hoyo. Paco, Carmen-Bethina and Little Paco arrived.

Paco banged on our door.

"English! Come out for a snowball fight! Come on, Spain against England!"

He was more of a child than his nine year old son. Spain won.

A week later, the snow was a distant memory. The landscape greened as tight buds unfurled. Wild flowers of all colours turned their faces to the sun. Bright poppies flapped their papery petals in the breeze. The first cuckoo arrived, echoing round the valley like a demented Swiss clock.

The snow had actually done us a favour. The village square, old and not designed for extremes of weather, disintegrated. Huge cracks formed, and slabs of stone fell away. That spring, Geronimo and his colleagues built a spanking new square and to our relief, constructed a new fountain to replace the one we had damaged last summer.

The chickens had settled in well. They had grown in confidence and strutted around the coop happily. We felt they were ready to roam the orchard, so we opened the coop. Mala led the way, followed by Ginger and the No-Name Twins, then the rest. It was more entertaining than T.V.

Chickens are as inquisitive as small children and everything was investigated, even our shoelaces, as we sat on Alonso's yellow vinyl sofa watching our flock. When we brought scraps, they hopped on to our knees and ate from our fingers.

Late in the afternoon we decided it was time to lock them up in the coop for the night. Not an easy job. We herded them and succeeded, a few at the time. But as fast as we caught some, others would escape, squirting back through the wire into the orchard. It took half an hour and left us breathless and panting.

"Can't put up with that every night," said Joe.

"Absolutely not!" I said. "But what choice do we have? If we leave them out at night the foxes will have them."

All the next week we went through the same fiasco. Mala was the most cunning. She would wait until we crept up on her, then she'd bolt flapping and squawking across the orchard. We chased chickens round trees, over old furniture, across piles of rubble ... they ran everywhere except back into the coop.

"Quick! The No-Name Twins are coming your way!" yelled Joe. I hurled myself at the nearest Twin and succeeded in grabbing one small tail feather and a mouthful of grit.

"I've got one!" shouted Joe, triumphantly carrying a protesting, squawking Blanca over to the coop. It was inevitable that an old coil of wire would trip him up. Blanca struggled free and bolted to the far side of the orchard.

"Well, the foxes can bloody well eat you! I don't care!" said Joe to all chickens in general. However, in spite of severe sense of humour loss, we persevered and every last chicken was eventually caught and shut in the coop.

One memorable night we were late. The sun had already dipped behind the mountain and the street-lights had flickered into life. Fully prepared to repeat our usual frenzied chase, we looked for the chickens. There was no sign of a single chicken in the whole orchard.

"Where are they?" said Joe, peering into the twilight gloom.

"The fox has had them," I said, guilt washing over me in painful waves.

The sky was turning inky, pierced with pinpoints of starlight. The village rooftops were mere silhouettes and the trees and bushes blurred shapes. The unearthly bark of a fox ricocheted around the valley.

A chicken coughed and we swung round. In the coop, on the perch, like a row of naughty schoolgirls, sat eight chickens, six brown and two white. The saying 'chickens coming home to roost' became evident. And so it was, as soon as the sun set, the girls would put themselves to bed. No fuss, no chasing. Another chicken cliche nailed.

I never dreamed that chickens were interesting, but I was wrong. Each individual developed her own personality, comical to the extreme. Fraidy was the coward of the bunch, setting off alarm calls if a beetle crossed her path. Shawly (so named because of her darker head and shoulders) was the kleptomaniac. Slowly, stealthily, she would sneak up behind the others and launch a surprise raid, whipping juicy morsels from under their beaks. Then she would dash away like an Oxford Street mugger and gobble her spoils in a hidden corner. Ginger was the boldest and most sociable, the first to greet us at the gate, the one to stay and chat if we sat on the sofa.

We were utterly hooked, these silly birds so delighted us with their funny ways. For example, when we came to the orchard empty handed, we were ignored, except, of course, by Ginger who met us at the gate and told us all her news at great length.

However, if we were carrying the blue plastic treat box containing kitchen scraps, their welcome was very different. Eight chickens charged to the gate, some flying like feathered bricks, some running, heads down, legs pumping like pistons. They would arrive in a heap, disentangle themselves and press against the fence. The excitement was intense. Necks became elongated as they craned up, desperate to see what the treats box contained. They wound round our feet, tripping us up. So we'd throw a few scraps as far as possible and they'd all thunder to the spot like rugby players. If we threw more in a different direction, they'd all abandon the first scraps and career over to the latest offerings. Another rugby scrum, until all scraps were exhausted. If the scraps contained spaghetti, two chickens might grab either end of a strand. They would suck in their end until they finished up eyeball to eyeball - unless Shawly sneaked in and stole the middle section.

Dust baths were another source of amusement. The first time we saw a motionless chicken lying in a scrape in the ground with her feet in the air, we thought she was dead. However, after careful scrutiny, we saw she was not dead, but in some kind of trance.

Chickens take dust baths very seriously. First they find a patch of soft ground and scratch at it until the soil is loose and crumbly. Then they lie in it, using beak, wings and feet to shower themselves with the earth. Somehow, they manage to separate their feathers so that the soil invades every crevice. This continues for maybe half an hour, the chicken resting every few minutes, eyes glazed in ecstasy. They lie on their fronts, sides and backs so that every feather becomes coated in dirt. Finally satisfied, they climb out, and this is when the wise stand back. Like a dog after a swim, chickens shake their bodies and rattle their feathers to dislodge every speck of dirt. The result? One shiny, clean, parasite-free chicken. It was a sight to behold, particularly with the white girls, Mala and Blanca. Before our eyes they transformed from mucky chimney sweeps to snowy angels.

We grew ridiculously fond of our girls. Sometimes we talked about the horrible chicken shop and I suppose it was only a matter of time before we found ourselves there again.

This time, the cages contained some young black chickens and some ravishing grey and speckled ones. As before, the stench and noise was overpowering. It was even more distressing to see the unfortunate chickens packed together in tiny cages now that we understood chicken behaviour so much better.

"*¿Cuantos quieren Ustedes?*" asked the assistant. "How many do you want?"

"Two," said Joe.

"Eight," I said.

And so 'Ello Vera, Little Grey, Speckly, Bugger, Fuck and the others entered our lives. We couldn't wait to get them home. In the jeep, we told them all about their new home and how they would be able to scratch in the dirt and spread their wings. We told them all about the chickens already there. We warned them about Shawly stealing their food, and told them to take no notice of Mala and her bossy ways.

They were quiet in their box so we assumed they were listening carefully to our advice.

In the orchard, the older chickens were consumed with curiosity. They circled the cardboard box, chattering amongst themselves.

"We've brought you some new friends," said Joe, gently upending the box. The new girls slid out, blinking in the sudden light. We were about to learn a huge lesson in chicken politics.

Attack! With squawks of rage, the original girls set about the newcomers. The air turned thick with chicken swear words and insults. The little ones shrieked with terror and cowered as the big girls pounced. Beaks stabbed, feathers were wrenched and became airborne before drifting back to ground. It was World War 3, and then some. The new kids in the flock fled, scattered to all corners of the orchard. Total disaster. Our visions of one big happy chicken family sadly dissolved.

The original eight, now known collectively as 'The Mafia', were relentless. Even gentle Ginger revealed an alter ego we had never suspected. The new girls hid under bushes and behind trees because as soon as they were spotted by the Mafia, they were hammered. Doing great impressions of Road Runner, they fled to escape from their bullies. In Britain, the Mafia would all have been served Antisocial Behaviour Orders.

We were at a complete loss. The new girls were uncatchable, scattered to all points of the compass.

I wondered if the Internet might help, and typed in 'introducing new chickens to an existing flock'. The results were varied.

The first advice page adopted the 'No Nonsense' approach, as follows:

'INTRODUCING NEW HENS TO THE FLOCK

Where new birds are introduced to an existing flock, there are always problems because the natural pecking order is disrupted. A hen spotting a newcomer will utter a single warning croak that alerts the rest of the flock. It then becomes fair game to peck at and chase away the stranger.

If it is absolutely necessary to introduce new birds to an existing flock they should be penned in a temporary area next to the run so that they can be seen but not harmed.

Birds can also be beak-trimmed so that they are less able to do damage to each other. The procedure is to trim the pointed tip of the upper mandible of the beak.

Once the birds are taking each other for granted, they can be amalgamated, but a careful watch needs to be kept for potential problems.'

Well, it was much too late to erect a separate pen and introduce the new ones slowly. And there was no way we were going to catch the Mafia and trim their beaks. Unthinkable. I sighed and pulled up another poultry advice page.

This one was ... well, frankly, ridiculous.

'HOW TO INTRODUCE NEW CHICKENS TO AN EXISTING FLOCK

Allow the new bird to roam around a bit in your kitchen (where the inevitable poop won't be too difficult to clean up) or bathroom while you croon SOFTLY to it and feed it little bits of cheese, lunchmeat, diced grapes, raw corn, etc. Sit down on the floor so you aren't towering over it and give it a good 20 minutes to get to know you, and realize what a TERRIFIC person you are. Pick it up and pet it, talking softly and cooing to it all the while. Keep your voice GENTLE, soothing and quiet. Watch your birds' eyes--you may see the pupil expanding and contracting rapidly. This signals excitement, in a GOOD way, for birds. It means that they REALLY like what you are doing to them. Continue to coo at it and praise it for the good little chicken it is. Chickens LOVE to be talked to in a loving tone.

Pick it up and take it into the yard during the day. Hold it tucked under your arm and call your flock. Continue to hold and PET the new bird as you talk to the flock and walk around the yard a bit, showing the new bird around. Walk in and out of the coop. View the nest boxes. Point out the food and water dishes. Give 'em the two dollar tour.

When everyone is ready, go ahead and put the new bird down slowly and stand next to it. Warn them off with a firm, "NOOO--!" and take a step towards them if need be. You may need to chase off aggressors a bit.

YOU are the TOP HEN! Remember, and what YOU say, GOES! Praise GOOD behavior. After a while, your flock WILL remember they have better things to do, lose interest and wander away. After that it's safe to go back inside the house, leaving the new bird to its own devices.'

Oh, please! Our Spanish neighbours already thought we were insane, sitting on the yellow sofa gazing at our flock, letting them hop onto our laps, talking to them. Even if we could catch the newcomers, taking eight chickens, putting them into the bathroom and whispering sweet nothings into their ears was bordering on complete lunacy.

When night fell, the Mafia went to bed and the little ones regrouped. They found the grain feeder and water and gorged themselves while the coast was clear. Finally, they too went to bed, on the floor under the Mafia's perch. It was an uneasy truce.

CHICKEN AND PRAWN PAELLA
PAELLA MIXTA

There are numerous paella recipes which makes choosing just one difficult. This is a particularly delicious one, with chicken breasts and prawns.

Ingredients (serves 8 - 10)

- 2 skinless boneless chicken breasts
- 500g (18oz) uncooked prawns
- 3 tablespoons olive oil
- 1 medium onion
- 2 cloves garlic
- 1 medium red pepper
- 1 medium green pepper
- 2 large tomatoes
- 150g (5oz) fresh frozen garden peas
- 500g (18oz) paella rice
- 1 ltr (2 pints) chicken stock
- ¼ teaspoon saffron
- Salt and pepper

Method

- Peel and clean the prawns and cut the chicken into bite-sized pieces.
- Peel and chop the onion and garlic, chop the peppers and

tomatoes.
- Heat the olive oil in a medium paella pan, add the garlic and onion and cook gently until soft then add the chicken and cook until browned on all sides.
- Add the peppers and cook for 5 minutes.
- Meanwhile, heat the chicken stock.
- Add the tomatoes and cook for 5 minutes.
- Add the rice using a soup ladle, counting as you go (you need to add 3 parts water to one part rice) and cook for 5 minutes.
- Add the chicken stock again ladle by ladle, season and bring to the boil. (Do not stir).
- Reduce the heat, cover and simmer for 15 minutes or so.
- Then add the prawns, peas and the saffron and continue cooking for a further 10 - 15 minutes until the liquid has been absorbed.
- Turn off the heat, cover and leave to rest for 5 minutes before serving.
- Garnish with fresh chopped parsley.

16

EGGS

For the next couple of weeks work on the house suffered. The punch-ups were so severe that we felt obliged to go into the orchard on 'playground duty'. At least that way we could break up some of the fights. But I suppose we were lucky as the orchard was big and had plenty of hiding places. No chicken was ever badly wounded. And as the little ones grew in size and confidence the confrontations dwindled.

Weeks drifted by and we had still not seen an egg. All the girls now had handsome red combs and had grown considerably.

Bugger and Fuck, the two black girls, were particularly beautiful. When the sun caught their feathers they shimmered blue, green and purple. I should explain that their names were unfortunate, not intended, but just kind of stuck because they were the most inquisitive pair. They got under our feet, and were convinced that Joe's shoelaces were worms. He was forever tripping over them and turning the air blue with his curses.

Little Grey, once the smallest, had grown into a huge chicken, towering over the others. She became bad tempered and rose in the pecking order. We renamed her Attila the Hen.

The Internet advised us to provide a dark, quiet box for laying.

They suggested we place some golf balls inside to give the chickens the right idea. Joe found an old discarded wooden trunk and cut an entrance in the front. The girls explored it thoroughly but no eggs were forthcoming. Every day we lifted the lid of the trunk hopefully and every day we were disappointed. Perhaps they were hiding their eggs around the orchard? We bribed Little Paco and the village children, a euro for every egg found. Still no eggs.

One day we entered the orchard, with treat box, and were mobbed as usual. All seemed fine except that Ginger was behaving in a very strange fashion. She was agitated, nervous, obviously troubled by something. We sat down on the sofa, and Ginger hopped onto Joe's lap and buried her head under his arm. Then she tried to get herself inside his jacket, it was most peculiar.

"Do you think she's ill?" I asked.

"I think she might want to lay an egg," Joe said.

He carried her tenderly over to the wooden trunk and popped her in, blocking off the exit. She scrabbled about at first, then went completely quiet. Half an hour ticked past, then the scrabblings started again.

"I'll let her out," said Joe, and unblocked the entrance hole of the trunk.

Ginger came out, blinked and stood still. Then she stretched herself very tall, pointed her beak to the sky, and sang. Well, perhaps not everybody would call it 'singing', chickens not being the most tuneful of creatures. But it was a song of sorts, a 'bok bok bok bok BOKKKKKKK!' sort of song which later became very familiar to us. It was the triumphant Egg Song.

And sure enough, snug in the straw, still warm, so precious, was a perfect little egg.

We were inordinately proud of Ginger and her first egg. I shot off emails to all my friends and family, headed 'We are grandparents!'. I took our little egg next door to show Paco and Carmen-Bethina. They admired it politely, but rolled their eyes when they thought our backs were turned.

The Egg Song was heard increasingly as the No-Name Twins, Mala,

Blanca and the others followed Ginger's example and started laying. We discovered that brown hens lay brown eggs and white hens lay white. Obvious really. We wondered what colour eggs Speckly and Attila the Hen would produce. When their time came, a few weeks later, they laid pinkish eggs. Attila the Hen's were huge and often double yolkers. Bugger and Fuck, the two black hens, laid darker brown eggs.

It became a daily pleasure to lift the lid of the trunk and reveal that clutch of perfect eggs, like finding treasure in a pirate's chest.

The trouble was, we hadn't done our sums. A quick session with the calculator revealed that sixteen chickens, laying one egg each per day, lay a total of one hundred and twelve eggs a week. That's four hundred and forty eggs a month. Let's be fair, and allow the chickens a day off every few days. That still amounts to about four hundred eggs a month. An awesome amount of eggs.

Joe took a dozen eggs with him to Marcia's shop to give away. It was the weekend and the bread van happened to be there surrounded by village ladies.

"Would anyone like some eggs?" he asked. He was almost trampled in the rush. The eggs were snatched out of his hands, and orders were placed for more. One of the Smart Ladies advised Joe to charge 70 cents for half a dozen in future, and so our unplanned business was born.

Joe put up a ship's bell outside our garden gate and our customers rang it constantly. It was good that there was a regular demand for the eggs and that the income paid for the girls' grain. And it was pleasant to chat with the village ladies and practice our Spanish. We got to know our regulars quite well as they'd often stay for a natter. They'd always begin by saying how fresh and tasty the eggs were, then tell us their family news and village gossip.

My favourite 'Egg Lady' was Pepa, a buxom elderly lady with dyed red hair and naughty crinkled eyes. She would ring the bell, then pant her way up the garden path and collapse in a chair under the vine while I fetched the eggs. Then we'd both agree how fresh and tasty the eggs were. Formalities over, she would lean forward conspiratorially and tell me what was going on in the village. I didn't understand everything she said, but I gleaned some juicy snippets worthy of a soap opera.

"Have you met Antonio, your neighbour?" she asked, her face inches from mine across the table. She kept her voice low as though there may be people listening.

"Yes, he seems like a nice man," I said.

"Well! *Sí,* he is my second cousin and you're right, he is a nice man," she said, chins wobbling as she nodded agreement. "But do you know his history?"

I shook my head, curious now. I liked Antonio. He was a small, dapper gentleman who rarely smiled but always greeted us if we passed in the street.

"Antonio used to be a taxi driver in Almería," she began. "A real hard worker. He specialised in taking people across on the ferry to Morocco. Our family was very proud of him because he soon sold his taxi and bought a lorry. Soon after, he bought another lorry. In no time at all he had a whole fleet of lorries!" Dramatic pause which I felt I needed to fill.

"He was doing really well, then?"

Pepa's eyebrows twitched into her red hairline. "Doing well? Very well! Too well!" she said. "Our family was amazed at how well he was doing. He bought a smart house in Almería and married a Moroccan lady. Not that we ever met her, she stayed in Morocco." She paused for effect and I sensed the punch line was coming. I wasn't disappointed.

"He was arrested!" she said. "*¡Madre mia!* He'd been smuggling drugs from Morocco for years. The police had been watching him, and then they caught him." She sat back, deflated, shaking her head sadly, setting the double chins wobbling again. "Seven years in prison he got, seven years… Lost his house in Almería, lost his fleet of lorries, lost everything. All he's got left is his house in the village. He had to go back to working for a company, driving a lorry all over Europe."

Quiet, courteous Antonio an ex-drug smuggler and convict? I was fascinated. I began to look forward to Pepa's visits and her colourful stories.

"The elections for the new Mayor are going to be held in a few months," she said one day.

"Oh, really? Who are the candidates? Who do you think will win?" I asked.

"Well…" she said, shaking her head and pursing her lips. "There is that Angelo Covas Sanchez. But he doesn't stand a chance. He was caught in a broom cupboard with the cleaner at the Town Hall and his wife is threatening to leave him."

"Oh dear. Who else is in the running?"

"Well, Manuel Gomez. He's a member of my family."

"Is he popular?"

"Manuel Gomez? Goodness, no. He made a terrible mess of the water rights for the village. And anyway, he married his first cousin."

"Oh," I said. "But what about Pancho Marcos Martinez? He's the Mayor at the moment, isn't he? Do you think he'll win the election again?"

"*¡Madre mia!* Not a chance! They call him Pancho Pinochet. He'll never get voted for Mayor again with that attitude."

"How many candidates are there?" I asked.

"Just three."

The mayoral elections were going to be interesting. I made a mental note to follow them closely when the time came.

But selling eggs was a mixed blessing. However much entertainment the sales brought, it also caused problems we had not envisaged. The ship's bell would clang at all hours of the day, a constant interruption. Many a barrow of plaster or cement was ruined, abandoned while we served and chatted with an egg customer. Sometimes the bell would ring at eleven o'clock at night. Joe was not pleased.

And woe betide if I had no eggs left. "But it's for the children!" the lady would wail as though I was a hard hearted witch to deprive them.

Sometimes the egg sales even caused fights outside our gate when two customers arrived at the same time. I could hear their conversation from inside.

"Oh, Maria! How are you?"

"Not bad, not bad. And you?"

"Fine, I'm just getting my eggs from the English."

"Yes, me too. I need them for a cake."

"I need them for the children."

"Well, I was here first. The English know I always come on Sunday mornings."

"No, Maria. I already told the English I was baking a cake today."

The voices would be growing in volume and I'd nervously check our egg supplies. Then I'd go down and open the gate and let them both in. Their faces would be wreathed in smiles belying the fact that they'd nearly come to blows in the street. We'd all agree that the eggs were very fresh and tasty. If there were enough eggs, the purchases would be made and the ladies would leave triumphantly. If not, I would have to send Joe to the orchard to see if there were any more while the ladies sat glowering at each other and me. Sometimes the chickens simply could not lay fast enough, which resulted in the two ladies not speaking to each other, or me.

Often, the Egg Ladies would give me instructions. "I need eggs next weekend. Keep them for me, please. Don't sell them to that Maria."

The next lady would arrive. "Keep a dozen for me next Saturday, I've got family staying. Don't sell them to that Teresa."

Egg orders had become complicated and my calendar was a hotch-potch of names, promises and reminders. Unwittingly, we had got ourselves into a situation that would be difficult to escape. Demand for eggs far outstripped our ability to supply. The only solution would be to add more chickens to our flock. And we couldn't do that because our plans to build on the orchard were progressing. Soon we would have to move the chickens out, so getting more now would only have exacerbated the problem.

Joe once suggested (only half jokingly) that we buy extra eggs from the supermarket to make up the shortfall. That way we wouldn't upset any of our Egg Ladies. And perhaps we could have eggs, too, as during that period we rarely tasted an egg ourselves. We never did resort to buying supermarket eggs, although it was tempting at the time.

Judith visited to view our progress with the house renovations and meet the chickens.

"Good Lord!" she said. "You've done wonders with this place! I hardly recognise it!"

We basked in her praise. We had chipped away at walls to expose the dry crumbling rocks beneath. We had cemented, smoothed, plastered and finally whitewashed. We had replaced doors, laid tiles, overhauled the electrics and plumbing. We were always exhausted, cut and bruised from our labours. A bit of praise from Judith was exactly what we needed to buck us up.

"Right!" said Judith, rubbing her hands together. "Now introduce me to those chickens!"

Off we trooped to the orchard, drinks in hand, and settled ourselves on the yellow sofa. Judith was enchanted by Ginger who perched on the arm, as usual, and told us all the latest gossip from the coop. The cicadas chirruped noisily, invisible in the bushes. Bugger and Fuck had uncovered an ants' nest and were pecking furiously, like woodpeckers beating tattoos on a tree trunk. Mala preened her snowy feathers.

I sighed. "We've really made problems for ourselves selling eggs in the village. We never seem to have enough. And if we give them to one customer, we upset another."

"Good heavens!" said Judith. "Don't you let those women bully you! Give 'em an inch and they take a mile. Hell's bells! First come, first served, I say... Or you could always get some more chickens."

"If only we could," said Joe, looking sadly round the orchard.

We explained our building plans for the orchard, and how, if we succeeded, the sale of the houses would leave us mortgage-free. It was a daunting project, one we would have preferred not to undertake. We loved the orchard and wished we weren't forced to lose it.

We sat for a while longer, until Judith drained her glass, stretched and stood up. "Must go, dears. Mother will be wondering where I am. She'll be fascinated when I tell her all the things you've done to the house. And your chickens are simply divine!"

We walked her to the orchard gate and exchanged kisses. Judith took a last look round the orchard. The girls were busily scratching in the dirt and carrying on with their chickeny business.

"Nothing quite like free range eggs," she said. "So fresh and tasty.

You haven't got a dozen you can spare, have you? Mother is very partial to a new laid egg."

Evidently dear Judith had become as Spanish as our customers.

For a while nothing changed. We kept selling the eggs we had, doing our best to keep the sales fair. Nothing changed except, sadly, I lost my favourite customer and friend.

Lovely Pepa, with all her naughty gossip, still popped in for eggs most weekends. It was very gradual, but I began to notice a change in her. She started to lose weight which suited her at first, but when her clothes began to hang off her, I was concerned. Her colour changed from healthy to sallow and the dyed red hair grew thinner revealing grey roots. Her visits became less frequent and I was shocked at her decline.

One day she rang the bell and asked for eggs as usual. Unfortunately, I didn't have any as I wasn't expecting her that day. She looked terrible, weakness forcing her to grip the door frame for support. The wicked, dancing expression in her eyes had gone, replaced by a haunted, frightened look that tore at my soul. She explained that she had to go into hospital for tests and that she wouldn't need any eggs for a while. Her eyes filled with tears and she admitted to me that she was scared. She was scared that she would never leave the hospital.

I never saw my friend Pepa again. She died in hospital. It's a silly thing, but I so wished that I had had eggs to give her that last time.

Her grave is in the village cemetery, a stone's throw from our house. The plaque says Josefina Maria Teresa Martinez Sanchez. But I will always know her as Pepa.

SALTED ALMONDS
ALMENDRAS

Carmen-Bethina often fried almonds in a frying pan with olive oil over an open flame. She then sprinkled them with salt and served them as nibbles to accompany Paco's wine.

Ingredients

- 4 cups blanched almonds
- 1 tbsp coarse sea salt
- 1 tsp paprika
- 2 tbsp extra virgin olive oil

Method

- Blanch the almonds by pouring boiling water over. Allow them to stand for 1 minute.
- Drain and dry with paper towels. The skins will now rub off easily.
- Grind the sea salt and paprika using a pestle and mortar. Mix well together.
- Preheat the oven to 180C (350F).
- Spread the almonds evenly on a baking sheet making sure they don't touch each other.
- Toast for 8 - 10 minutes or until golden brown.
- Transfer almonds to a bowl and drizzle enough oil over to

coat evenly.
- Add the paprika and salt mixture. Toss thoroughly and serve.

17

THE EQUATORS

Renovating the house took up all our time and we had to admit that some projects were beyond our capabilities. We could knock down walls, build new ones and tile the floors. Joe could carry out plumbing and sort the electrics. But that wasn't enough; we had set our hearts on creating two roof terraces. Old Spanish houses have no foundations and we had no idea if the dry crumbling walls would support the load of another floor. We needed expert advice and professionals to do the job. However, finding these proved to be no easy matter.

Paco's brother-in-law, Fausto, was a wealthy property developer, the owner of several apartment blocks on the coast and some resort hotels. He came to have a look, accompanied by Marisa, his five year old daughter, to help interpret. Little Marisa was exquisite. Perfect olive skin, rosebud lips and dark velvet eyes with sweeping lashes; she took our breath away. She was attending a school in Almería that concentrated on learning English early and her command of the language was already remarkable. We walked around the house and pointed out what we wanted.

"We'd like to make this window into a door, and build a terrace on that roof," Joe explained.

Fausto scratched his chin thoughtfully. Then he shook his head with regret, and delivered his verdict. His voice was very nasal and he scarcely moved his lips when he spoke which made understanding him very difficult. We looked at him blankly. Fausto repeated it, a little slower and a lot louder, but to no avail. Still looking at us, he nudged his daughter.

"My father, he say not possible," piped up Marisa, hopping from one foot to the other. "My father, he say all the house not strong. My father, he say better make house flat. Then make new one."

"Knock the house down and start again?" I echoed.

Little Marisa had found a hole in the wall and was poking at it, picking out little bits of masonry that tumbled to the floor. "Yes, my father he say house is rubbish."

Joe and I exchanged horrified glances. Nevertheless, we thanked Fausto for his advice and I fetched a juice for Marisa. But all was not lost. After encouragement from her proud father, Marisa made the visit worthwhile by launching into a rendition of 'Wheels on the Bus', all eleven verses of it, including actions. At the end of each verse she sucked noisily on her straw until her father prodded her, urging her to continue the song.

When they left, hand in hand, I phoned Judith.

"Builders?" she asked. "Are you sure? Bloody builders, more trouble than they're worth."

"Do you know any you could recommend?" I asked, ignoring the pessimism.

"Hang on, I'll ask Mother. Mother? MOTHER! Oh, there you are. Joe and Vicky want to know if we know of any good builders." The receiver was dropped, and I could hear their voices arguing in the distance, interspersed with the barking of dogs. I waited patiently.

"Vicky? Mother suggested Luis from the village. She's known him since he was in nappies, dear. Bloody good builder, Luis is. Just a tad unlucky, that's all."

"Unlucky? What do you mean, unlucky?"

"Well, dear, he was working on a house in the village here, and he didn't get the calculations quite right."

"So what happened?"

"Well, he was knocking some walls down. Unfortunately it affected the house next door. Luis went home thinking everything was ticketty-boo. When he came back next morning to start work again, the bloody house next door had collapsed. Damned bad luck, don't you know. Could have happened to anyone."

I agreed it was very bad luck and mentally struck Luis off our list.

We were given two more names by other people. One builder was so tattooed and pierced I was concerned he might spring a leak at any moment. The other was elderly and seemed far too frail to undertake anything much more than a little light decorating. Both took notes and promised to get back to us with prices. We never saw either again.

When we next visited Almería, we picked up 'The Messenger', an excellent free English newspaper. It was full of local news and events, but at the back were classified advertisements. We scoured the columns looking for a potential builder. There were two possible candidates under the heading 'Building Services'. The first was in the shape of a cartoon cement mixer bearing the legend 'NO BODGE JOBS!' with a name and telephone number. The second was reassuringly ordinary. *'Reliable and professional building work undertaken. Call Colin for a free quotation.'* We agreed to ignore the first and contact Colin.

Colin sounded fine on the phone and promised to come out the next week. He arrived, only six hours late, in a huge utility vehicle that absolutely suited his personality. With the physique of an American wrestler, he looked capable of completing the job single-handed. He was cheerful, enthusiastic, listened carefully to our requests and offered suggestions. We liked him immediately. He didn't think the terraces would be a problem, and we didn't tell him that Fausto thought the house ought to be demolished.

Colin said he thought our house had huge potential. "Why don't we build a metal staircase outside, from the garden up to the first terrace?" he said, flinging out an arm to demonstrate and knocking over a pot of geraniums. Colin was endearingly clumsy, like a boisterous bear cub.

"And this door," said Joe, pointing at the ancient, rotting back door, "needs changing. It's got a huge gap underneath. We get all sorts of insects marching in. And when the wind blows, all the leaves and dirt pile up inside."

Colin's huge fist closed around the door handle. He gave it a sharp wrench and the handle broke off in his hand. The door stayed where it was.

"Yes," he agreed. "This door needs replacing." He kicked the door open but it never closed properly again.

Not only did he trip over his own feet and Thief Cat's bowl, but his words tended to trip him up, too. They would tumble out of his mouth just slightly wrong.

"I've got an excellent team of Equators," he said. Equators? I assumed it was a technical term and didn't ask.

He admired the chickens, and told us about his own at home. Like us, he loved chickens ... definitely a point in his favour. "Why don't we do your garden at the same time?" he suggested. "We could build you a brilliant chicken coot."

"And an outside kitchen, and barbecue, and woodshed? And all paved?" My mouth was watering.

"Anything you want, just draw us a design."

We sat down in our overgrown garden to discuss the plans. Colin lowered his muscular bulk into a plastic garden chair. I couldn't help fretting that the chair might not take his weight, but my fears were unfounded, even when he leaned back to slip a flashy mobile phone out of his pocket.

"I'll just call the orifice and get some figures," he said.

"I'm afraid we don't get a mobile signal here..." I said, just as the mobile in Colin's hand burst into an Abba ring tone, making me out to be a total liar. Colin flicked his eyebrows questioningly and took the call.

"Well, we've never had a signal before," I muttered, and caught Joe sniggering.

Colin stayed another hour until the church-bells chimed fourteen, and by that time we had agreed a price. We wrote a deposit cheque and shook hands on the deal. We'd only planned to have the roof terraces done, but the wish list had grown. Roof terraces, new front and back doors, the entire garden done...

At first we were euphoric. We had finally found a builder we liked and who understood our needs. Then doubts crept in. Joe voiced them first.

"Do you realise we've just handed over one thousand euros to a complete stranger?" he said, anxiously scratching his groin.

"Yes, but we have a receipt," I said, waving the scrap of paper Colin had signed and dated. We both knew, deep down, that the receipt meant absolutely nothing and that Colin could be anybody. It was extremely worrying.

A month later, we were even more worried. Colin and his 'Equators' should have started on the first of April but no-one appeared. We tried phoning. No reply. We regretted not taking down his number plate but it hadn't occurred to us at the time.

However, on the 12th of April Colin's big utility vehicle drew up, followed by a truck full of building materials, and a car resembling a scrapmetal version of Chitty Chitty Bang Bang. Four lithe Ecuadorians got out and stood in a row, flashing white teeth and bling.

Each man was dressed identically in black tracksuit bottoms and orange T-shirts emblazoned with 'Colin's Careful Construction' across the chest. I was reminded of 1960's pop groups like The Drifters, who all dressed alike and moved in synch. The Equators looked ready to break into song.

Colin introduced them: William, Eduardo, Fernando, and Jesus.

"This is William," said Colin. "He's the chef." We shook hands.

"*Sí*, I am chief," said William, obviously used to his boss's malapropisms.

"Eduardo is the best tiler I've ever employed," said Colin, and a gold tooth glinted as Eduardo grinned. "He's a mestickulous worker, really autistic." Joe and I absorbed this information in silence.

"And this is Fernando, he's an excellent Jake-of-all-trades. I give him cart blank to get on with things." Fernando stepped forward and shook hands, his gold signet rings leaving impressions on our palms.

"And finally, this is Jesus. Jesus is Fernando's brother. He's just arrived in Spain and he's learning the trade. He's already a good welder."

Jesus was about seventeen and clearly shy. He had trouble making eye contact and shuffled his work boots uncomfortably.

We left the Equators to unload the truck and begin work. Colin departed after briefing William, by which time it was two o'clock, lunchtime. They had brought a little camping stove with them and began to cook a meal with ingredients packed in plastic boxes. Eduardo, the perfectionist, carefully emptied each box into the saucepan while Fernando stirred with a wooden spoon.

Eduardo peeled off the lid of the last plastic box. The contents appeared to be chopped vegetables, but he squawked in surprise and dropped the box as though it was red hot. Startled, Fernando stopped stirring and checked the box which had landed at his feet. A huge (plastic) spider sat there, its many legs partly buried in diced onions and peppers.

"That damn Jesus!" he growled, looking around for his young relative. Jesus was wisely out of their sight. I could see him crouched behind the car, his shoulders shaking in mirth. It became clear that Jesus, in spite of his shyness, was the practical joker.

William was a fine foreman, and the work progressed pretty smoothly. The team always brought their ghetto blaster which roared out popular Ecuadorian music while they worked. Unfortunately, the radio didn't work so they listened to CDs. Even more unfortunately, they only possessed three CDs in total, so the same songs were pumped out, day after day. It nearly drove us to distraction.

However, we loved watching them work. To watch professionals laying a brick wall is fascinating; I defy anyone to say otherwise. As for me, I had the added bonus of watching Eduardo who possessed buttocks like two golf balls in a sock. Joe cottoned on to what I was transfixed by and got very huffy with me, despite my insistence that I was just watching the work in progress.

Soon after catching me gazing at Eduardo, I noticed Joe was suddenly keen to show his strength. He began to help the men by carrying blocks, but this backfired as the Equators could carry six at a time while poor Joe huffed and puffed with just two.

Before long, the roof was prepared and ready to take the beam supports. The truck arrived delivering the concrete beams, each five metres in length, twenty beams in total. The weight of each was enormous and the Equators struggled and strained. Joe ran to help them and shouldered the beams, ignoring the fact that the Equators were half his age and possessed double his strength. The result? Joe's back seized and he was forced to rest in bed for several days. I consoled myself by watching Eduardo from behind, uninterrupted.

Jesus, as the apprentice, was given all the worst jobs. He fetched and carried for everybody. One day they ran out of sand for cement. Only a grotty mound of gritty sand remained, a relic from one of Alonso's projects many years ago. It was filthy and lumpy, unusable in its present state. William ordered Jesus to sieve it all, separating out stones and cat poo until it was fine enough to use.

But Jesus was incorrigible. You could see the cogs turning in his head as he plotted his next practical joke. I saw him furtively puncture tiny holes in Fernando's bottle of water. He used a small sharp nail, piercing the neck of the bottle, just below the top. Fernando suspected nothing, and was baffled by the fact that he dribbled water down his chin and T-shirt every time he drank. Jesus laughed so much he cried.

The roof terraces were finished and we were mightily pleased with them. They gave us a 360 degree view: the rolling mountains, the orchard, the sea in the distance over the village rooftops. The Equators cemented in a clothes drier and hanging out the washing became a pleasure for the first time in my life. What a treat to be encircled by such views and let the soft Mediterranean breezes blow the washing dry. We bought another table and chairs set, and at night, we sipped Paco's wine under the vast star-speckled sky.

It would have all gone smoothly, except for Colin. He proved to be the only fly in the ointment, although it was always unintentional.

BEEF IN FRUIT SAUCE (ECUADORIAN RECIPE)

CARNE CON SALSA DE FRUTAS

A quick glance at the ingredients that go into this dish will be enough to make you reach for your pan. Delicious!

Ingredients (serves 6)

- 3lbs (1.3 kilo) beef, cubed
- 1 large onion (chopped finely)
- 6 tablespoons vegetable oil
- 16 tablespoons beef stock
- 16 tablespoons dry white wine
- 16 tablespoons cream
- 2 peaches (peeled and chopped)
- 2 apples (peeled and chopped)
- 2 pears (peeled and chopped)
- 2 large tomatoes (peeled and chopped)
- Salt, freshly ground pepper
- Sugar to taste

Method

- Heat 4 tablespoons of oil in a frying pan and sauté onion.
- Transfer onion (use slotted spoon) to a casserole dish, and seal beef cubes quickly in remaining hot oil.

- Add to the casserole with the stock and wine.
- Season with salt and pepper.
- Cover, bring to the boil. Simmer on a low heat for approximately 2 hours, until meat is tender.
- Transfer beef (use slotted spoon) to a serving dish. (Keep warm.) Put stock aside.
- In a saucepan, heat remaining 2 tablespoons of oil. Add fruit, tomatoes and sugar. Cook for a few minutes, stirring continuously.
- Add enough of stock to just cover and simmer, stirring frequently.
- Allow to cool a little then blend, liquidise or sieve to a puree.
- Return the fruit puree to the saucepan. Add the cream and heat through. Do not allow to boil.
- Pour hot sauce over meat and serve with rice.

18

COLIN HELPS OUT

I painstakingly drew a detailed, to scale, plan of the garden and proposed chicken coop. However, every time I handed it to Colin, he lost it. Four times I reproduced that plan until finally I had the sense to hand it straight to William.

Colin meant well, but when he arrived to 'help', things invariably went wrong. He carefully took the measurements for our new front, kitchen and terrace doors to give to the joiner in town. Two weeks later he collected the doors and delivered them to us, leaving them with William. William checked them over. The kitchen door was fine, a good solid wood door that fitted well. Sadly, not so with the other two.

Both doors were typically Andalucían in design. Wood-panelled, with windows and shutters set in, Joe and I were initially very pleased with them. William looked grave, he had already spotted the problem.

"¡*Problema!*" he said, shaking his head and reaching for the tape measure to check. "These doors do not look right." Unfortunately the tape measure didn't budge and William's fingers fumbled as he tried to grasp it. It was glued it to the workbench.

"¡*Hombre!* That pest, Jesus!" William prised the tape measure off with a screwdriver. "*Sí*, it is as I thought. The terrace door has been made to fit the front door, and vice versa."

"Are the two sizes very different?" Joe asked.

"I will show you, no?"

William's brow was furrowed. He picked up a pencil and tried to make a mark on the door. The pencil wouldn't write. The point had been coated with glue which had dried. Muttering terrible threats to the absent Jesus, William picked off the layer of glue and tried again.

"That's not acceptable," said Joe. "How come the joiner got it wrong?"

William looked embarrassed. "I do not think it was the fault of the joiner," he said carefully. "I think, er, something else may have happened."

"You mean Colin gave the joiner the wrong measurements?" I knew Joe was annoyed, the narrowing of his eyes was a reliable indication.

William didn't reply immediately but his hesitation was answer enough.

"I'll phone Colin," he said at last. He reached into his pocket for his mobile phone, then patted all his pockets in disbelief.

"JESUS!" His voice echoed round the valley as he lunged outside. "Jesus! What have you done with my mobile phone? When I get hold of you - I am going to staple you to the damned workbench! Fernando? Where is that no good heathen brother of yours? Jesus? I know you are here somewhere… Jesus! Where are you, you scrawny little immigrant?"

Joe and I exchanged glances. If Jesus knew what was good for him, he would lie low for a while.

William must have caught up with Jesus judging by the colour of one of Jesus's ears, and the fact that Colin turned up in response to William's call. Colin's solution to the door problem was original and dramatic.

"Would you object if we widened your Porsche?" he asked.

"How do you mean?" Joe was doubtful. "How can you widen the porch?"

"Well, we knock this wall down here, rebuild it there, then widen the steps up to the front door. Then the door will fit."

We didn't really object, although it seemed a little drastic. It meant we lost a metre inside the living room, but gained a metre of porch. The terrace doorway could be narrowed quite easily to accommodate the other door.

Colin left William to oversee the project and drove away. Fernando and Eduardo set to work with sledgehammers, while Jesus removed the rubble as fast as he could. William continued rendering the new roof terrace walls up above but came down occasionally to see the progress, and to snarl at Jesus.

That evening, Joe and I leaned on the new roof terrace wall and looked down below, watching the Equators prepare to leave for the night.

Colin's Careful Construction team were already in the car, waiting for William. William climbed into the driver's seat and turned the key in the ignition. Pandemonium reigned and the Equators let out a unanimous yelp of fright. As William started the engine, the radio blasted at full volume, the hazard lights flashed, the windscreen wipers crashed back and forth and the car jerked violently forward before stalling.

There were a few seconds of complete silence, then William's door was thrown open. Before Jesus could escape, William had hauled him out of the car by the ear and thrown him unceremoniously to the roadside. Jesus protested but William accelerated the car away in a cloud of dust. Jesus picked himself up, and, still rubbing his painful ear, galloped after the fast disappearing car.

"¡Hombre! Wait! Stop! I am sorry, honestly!" But Jesus had gone too far. We watched the car shrink as it drove out of the valley followed by the tiny figure of Jesus waving his arms, imploring them to stop.

The chickens scratched and pecked in the orchard, oblivious to the fact that Colin's Careful Construction team were creating a chicken palace for them in our garden.

It was magnificent. I had designed it so that the chickens would have as many interesting diversions as possible. (In zoos, I believe it's called 'enrichment'.) I was trying to make up for the fact that their new coop would be far smaller than the orchard. Eduardo, meticulous as always, had embraced the project.

A third of the area was roofed with traditional terracotta tiles to provide shelter from sun and harsh weather. Inside the shelter was a wall of elevated nesting boxes which could be reached by a ramp. Another ramp led up to the roosting perch. Outside in the run, Eduardo and I built a water feature complete with waterfall cascading out of a terracotta pot. More ramps accessed platforms at different levels. I planted a small palm tree in the middle to provide shade and somewhere to escape when Attila the Hen was on the warpath.

Many years ago, in England, I had a small business designing and manufacturing stencils for the interior decorating market. Stencilling became unfashionable, and I stopped production, but still had plenty of stencils left. The new chicken coop was the perfect opportunity to use some. I painted all the walls white, then stencilled orange trees, butterflies and bees. Even the 'autistic' Eduardo approved of the result, although Paco and Carmen-Bethina fell silent when they saw the finished coop.

"It's very nice," said Carmen-Bethina at last, "but what is it for, exactly?"

"It's for the chickens. When the building begins up in the orchard, the chickens will move down here."

"¡*Madre mia!* You decorated it for chickens? All that painting on the walls?"

"Yes. Well, as it's in the garden, I thought I'd make it pretty."

"And the mirror?"

I had hung an old wardrobe mirror left by Alonso onto a wall. I figured that if budgerigars like mirrors, why shouldn't chickens? I didn't know the Spanish word for budgies so I didn't reply.

"And the waterfall?"

"Well, they can drink from it, or paddle, or whatever."

"It's, er, very unusual," said Carmen-Bethina.

Colin was colour blind as well as clumsy. I had asked for creamy, terracotta coloured slabs to be laid in the garden. When the delivery truck arrived, I nearly had a fit. The slabs were salmon pink. Joe and I watched them being unloaded.

"I never ordered pink slabs! I told Colin I wanted terracotta! I wanted a nice neutral colour!"

"Now, come on, Vicky," said Joe, scratching his nethers thoughtfully. "It doesn't matter. They're not that bad. It's only because they're new that they look so…"

"Awful?"

"No, I was going to say 'bright'," Joe said. "I'm sure you'll get used to them. You can't expect the men to take them all the way back down the mountain again."

Somehow I was persuaded to accept the dreadful pink slabs. Eduardo laid them beautifully, and if I was honest, after ageing and fading in the sun, (the slabs, not me) I did get used to them. Only when wet did they regress to that initial violent pink.

Slowly, steadily, the work was completed. Colin had promised to accompany his team on the last couple of days, so that all the final snags could be rectified. Joe and I were a little apprehensive as we knew things usually went wrong when Colin got involved. We would have preferred William to tie up the loose ends.

Colin set to work. Task One on the list was to put the glass into the doors. With the first one, he cracked the glass very slightly with the pins he was tapping in too enthusiastically. He cut himself glazing the second door and his blood seeped into the wood grain. The stain remains today.

Task Two was welding the final step in place on the wrought iron staircase. Jesus had welded the rest without mishap. Colin not only welded the step crooked, but also managed to bond a screwdriver to the step. It would have made a good Tate Modern exhibit.

Task Three was to fix chicken wire to the frame of the new coop. Borrowing our garden table and chairs to reach inaccessible places - he did an expert job. No mishaps, no problems. I admired his handiwork, then it dawned on me.

"Colin, we have a problem."

"What? It's a perfect job, you just said so."

"Colin, the table and chairs."

Colin stared, then clapped his hand to his forehead. He had

trapped the table and chairs inside the coop. Now he would have to undo all his good work to retrieve them.

At last all the jobs were completed to our satisfaction. We paid Colin and shook hands with each of the Equators.

"Thank you, William, you did a good job. You are an excellent foreman," said Joe. William beamed and puffed out his chest.

"Fernando, thank you for all you've done. The terraces are fantastic. We really appreciate your hard work." Joe allowed Fernando to crush his hand in his great paw.

"Thanks, Jesus, and we've got your mobile number in case we have any more little welding jobs. Now, behave yourself in future. No more pranks, eh?" Jesus blushed beetroot and looked sheepish.

"Eduardo," Joe said, "Colin was right. You are an artist, and we have the best chicken coop in Spain."

"And thank you for letting us watch you work, Eduardo," I added. "It's been a real pleasure." Joe was still glowering at me when the Equators drove away.

The wonderful new chicken coop in our garden remained empty because we had no need of it yet. Our building plans for the orchard needed to run a gauntlet of official permissions, bank perusals and the usual Spanish delays. However, this delay was good for the chickens who were able to enjoy the run of the orchard until the last possible moment.

What neither Joe, I nor the chickens knew was that a fiendish little individual was about to enter our lives and shatter our peace.

COLIN'S SPANISH OMELETTE
TORTILLA DE PATATAS

(Exactly as Colin dictated, hence the occasional rather surprising word… Nevertheless, delicious.)

Ingredients

- 8 or 9 eggs
- About half a kilo of spuds, peeled and sliced thinly
- A generous pinch of salt
- 50% olive, 50% vegetable oil
- possibly some lemon juice
- a proper non-stick 20 cm frying pan
- a circular dinner plate
- 45 - 60 minutes

And here's what you do:

- Half fill the pan with the oil. Heat it gently. Put the spuds in the oil, and stir to make sure they are all coated. The idea is to soften the spuds without browning them. It'll take about half an hour, and you need to give them a stir every now and again.
- When the potatoes are cooked, remove them from the oil. If you don't expect to eat the tortilla all in one go, you can sprinkle lemon juice on them - this'll stop them from going grey over the next few days (nothing wrong with the spuds

in your tortilla going grey - it just doesn't look very appetising).
- Break your eggs into a bowl, throw in the salt, and beat with a frisk or fork until the egg whites and yolks are thoroughly mixed.
- Add the spuds and stir.
- Drain most of the oil from the pan, leaving a thin coating. Turn up the heat a little (about 60% of full), and pour the egg and potato mixture in.
- When the mixture has begun to set, pull the edges away from the pan with a splatula - you're trying to get a rounded shape to the edge of the tortilla.
- Now comes the tricky bit - turning it over which can be pretty clumbersome. The Spanish do it by holding an oiled dinner plate against the top of the pan, and flopping them over. In Spain, you can buy a thing called a *vuelca de tortilla*, basically a plastic lid with a knob on one side for holding it.
- Once you have the tortilla on the plate, slide it back into the pan and carry on cooking and shaping the edge. Turn it two more times, so each side gets cooked twice, and when you have a nice golden colour on both sides, you're done.
- It's important not to overcook the tortilla. I prefer ones that still have a little bit of runniness in the centre, but more sensitive souls prefer them to be cooked solid.
- Let it cool for a bit, and then cut yourself a wodge and serve with a hank of crunchy baguette and a cafe con leche. Perfect!

19

COCKY

I was on my hands and knees laying floor tiles in the kitchen. I love tiling. To begin with, I love making up the tile cement: tipping in the powder, adding water, spinning with the whirly attachment on the drill until the mixture slaps around like a giant bucket of cake mix. I love the satisfying splats as I ladle out large dollops and they hit the floor.

Next, the pleasure of spreading it evenly with a serrated trowel that combs patterns like a newly ploughed field.

Then laying the tiles, each one straight and true, transforming dusty earth floors to cool, shiny surfaces that invite one to tread them.

Joe returned from collecting eggs in the orchard. "We're really low on grain," he said. "We'll have to go down to the chicken shop and get some more."

"Well, you'll have to go by yourself, I've only just made up all this tile cement."

I was so deeply absorbed with my project that it wasn't until some time later that a thought occurred to me. I had forgotten Joe is the most impulsive shopper I have ever known. Send him out for a carton of milk and he comes back with a crate of milk, beer, chocolate biscuits, a set of glasses and a cuddly toy. He loves buying things, even if we have them already or don't need whatever it is. It may have been a serious mistake sending him to the chicken shop alone.

I stripped off my rubber gloves quickly and grabbed the mobile phone.

"How r u getting on? Don't buy any more chickens!" I texted.

"Am on way home. Everything fine. C u soon," came the return text.

I wasn't fooled. "NO MORE CHICKENS! No space in new coop." I stabbed the keys as fast as I could.

"Ok, don't worry. Xxx"

But I did worry.

I cleared up my tiling mess, admired my handiwork and waited for Joe. I climbed the staircase to the roof terrace and watched for the returning jeep coming down the mountain into the village. At last it appeared and I shot outside to meet him.

Three large sacks of grain shared the back of the jeep with an ominous looking cardboard box.

"How did you get on with the tiling?" Joe asked, lifting out the box nonchalantly.

"Never mind the tiling. What's in the box? Please don't tell me you bought any more chickens…"

"No, I didn't. Honestly. I promise I didn't get any more chickens." But Joe's eyes refused to meet mine.

And then the box crowed.

"You're joking! You didn't buy a cock, did you? Tell me you haven't come back with a cockerel." I found my hands were on my hips in typical fishwife pose.

Joe looked a little rueful, then went on the defensive. "I couldn't resist him. He's very small, only a bantam. He was in a cage all by himself and he was crowing so…" The rest of his speech was drowned out by more crowing.

"But we discussed this! We agreed we didn't want any more chickens, especially not a cock! It said on the Internet cocks can be aggressive, and we haven't got the space!" I could hear the whine in my own voice.

"He won't be aggressive," said Joe. "He's very small."

Well, the deed was done and I blamed myself for sending Joe shopping alone. Now my dismay was replaced by curiosity. I wanted to see the little fellow, I wanted to know how our girls in the orchard would react to him.

Joe carried the box to the orchard, I pulled open the gate, and we stepped inside. As usual, the girls crowded to meet us. They eyed the box suspiciously. Joe set it down on the ground, pulled back the cardboard flaps and lifted out the newcomer. I gasped.

Only ten inches tall and about half the size of the other chickens, Cocky was exquisite. His feathers were an iridescence of colours, like an oil film on water. Mainly silver and lavender, they shimmered with different hues as the sun caught them, luminous and gleaming. His comb was crimson and exaggerated, as was his matching wattle. The tips of his wings touched the ground, slightly spread like the fingers of a hand. His tail was very upright and showy, while his feet were as bright as his comb.

It was difficult to say who was the most astounded by this flamboyant little creature, the chickens or I. Mala, Attila the Hen, Ginger, Bugger, Fuck and the others circled him warily. Fraidy gave off a nervous alarm call.

"He's amazing," I said, "but the girls are going to make mincemeat out of him. He's tiny!"

Joe stepped back and the chickens leaned forward to examine this extraordinary spectacle more closely. They towered over him. Cocky totally ignored his audience, stretched (not) very tall, pointed his beak to the sky and crowed.

The chickens were outraged! United in fury, they dived on him with shrieks of indignation, cutting him off in mid-crow. But Cocky was quick. He blasted out of the melee like a feathery cannonball and shot across the orchard into a leafy bush, sixteen angry chickens on his tail.

"They'll kill him!" I said, hand to my mouth. "Do you think we should rescue him?"

"Just wait," said Joe, but he sounded worried and was scratching himself down below, a sure sign of nerves. The bush shook, rattled and convulsed as the battle raged in its centre. Detached leaves flew off as the branches whipped and thrashed. Enraged squawks and screeches ripped the air.

Suddenly, without warning, Bugger catapulted out of the bush like a piece of soap in a shower. Then Fuck, Mala, Ginger and all the rest. Even Attila the Hen flapped out, righted herself and began to preen furiously in an attempt to regain her lost dignity.

Finally, out strutted Cocky, the unlikely champion. He rattled his feathers, flapped twice, stood on his tiptoes and crowed victoriously.

"Would you believe it?" said Joe. "He beat the lot of them!" He was indecently pleased by Cocky's victory, perhaps as he saw it as a coup for males in a female dominated world.

But the show was not over. Joe was about to be taught a lesson in stamina that may have left him feeling a shade inadequate.

Cocky sidled over to Bugger who was innocently pecking away at something microscopic. He executed a little side-stepping dance towards her, then quickly clambered aboard. No easy feat as Bugger was twice his size and not co-operative. However, he hung onto his object of desire by seizing the feathers on her head and then bucked like a jack hammer.

Bugger succeeded in shaking him off but Cocky's ardour was not cooled. He repeated his performance systematically with every chicken, and there were sixteen of them. When every chicken had been covered, Cocky just started again, jumping onto whoever was closest at the time.

"That little fiend certainly has stamina," said Joe. "He must be exhausted!" (Did I detect a tiny note of envy in his tone?)

From that day, the dynamics of the orchard changed dramatically. It seemed size didn't matter, after all. The girls adored their new leader, even though he was so small. Wherever he went, his harem followed. They allowed him to jump on their bones many times a day, and bore him no grudges. The tops of their heads became bald, like shaven monks, but still they endured his onslaughts and shadowed him like disciples. At dusk they clamoured to roost next to him and bickered amongst themselves to share his perch.

And the crowing! He never stopped. He crowed all day and often during the night, too.

Old Sancho still took his evening walks through the streets of the village, the black cat scampering at his heels. We heard the distinctive tapping of his stick accompanied by the usual fruity bursts of flatulence as he rounded the corner. So did Cocky, who would crow loudly. Old Sancho would approach the fence, lean on his stick and crow in reply. This infuriated Cocky who would crow louder and longer, standing on tiptoe for maximum effect. And there they would stand, the fence dividing them. Ten inches of feathered fury and the old man in his worn carpet slippers, each crowing at the other.

Eventually Old Sancho would get bored, smile benignly at Cocky and call to his cat. Off he shuffled, 'tap, tap, paaarp, tap, tap, paaarp', up the road. Cocky, satisfied that he had won the crowing contest yet again, strutted back to his adoring wives.

The villagers were fascinated by Cocky, or perhaps they just wanted to see the source of the endless crowing. There were a few cocks in the village at the time, but Cocky was easily the most handsome, the smallest and definitely the loudest. Our Egg Ladies brought their grandchildren to see him when they came to buy eggs. Cocky always obliged by crowing loudly but often disgraced himself by leaping onto a passing wife, regardless of his young audience.

"*Abuela*," asked the puzzled toddler, "Grandmother, what are they doing?"

"Oh, he's just pumping the other chicken up," I heard Teresa say. "Come on, let's go and get our eggs from the English." The child was dragged away by the hand, accepting this surprising piece of information as only a small child can.

Cocky had some endearing habits, too. Whenever he found some particularly delicious treats, like an ants' nest, he never ate them himself. Instead, he would emit an extended, high pitched chirrup, 'tkk, tkk, tkk, tkk', to call his wives. They would stop whatever they were doing and career over. Then they hoovered up his offering while he proudly stood by.

Although he was so much smaller than his wives, he had another trick that ensured his popularity. He would half fly, half jump to reach tasty fruit or new leaves. The prizes were pulled down and he would triumphantly call the girls, 'tkk, tkk, tkk, tkk'. His harem gobbled up the treats as he watched over them like a benevolent uncle.

It was Ginger who first alerted us to a growing problem. When we took our cups of coffee to drink in the orchard, Ginger usually perched on the arm of the old yellow sofa and chatted to us. This irritated Cocky no end. He was growing bolder by the day, and was clearly not happy to allow Ginger to consort with us. He resented our very presence and his body language left us in no doubt. Neck feathers bristling like a bottle brush, he faced us, hurling insults.

"What's the matter with him?" I asked. "Why is he always in such a bad temper?"

"Oh, he's just protecting his wives," said Joe. "He doesn't want Ginger to talk to us, that's all. He thinks we're after his women."

Maybe so, maybe Cocky was just following his instincts, but it was very uncomfortable. And his behaviour worsened as he grew in confidence. Collecting eggs and feeding became a problem and Joe took to carrying a stick to fend off the ten inches of feathered fury. We abandoned the yellow sofa and spent as little time as possible in the orchard. Chicken husbandry became a chore, not a pleasure.

"I think we should call him 'Quilp'," said Joe, "after Mr Quilp in Dickens's Old Curiosity Shop. He was a malevolent dwarf just like Cocky."

But Cocky's name had stuck although it was often preceded now by a choice word of Anglo Saxon origin.

It all came to a head one day when Teresa brought her husband with her when she came to purchase eggs.

"Miguel has seen an old box in your orchard," she said. "It's like an old packing case, *no*? Miguel likes old trunks. Do you want it, or can he take it?"

"Of course he can take it," I said. "Everything in the orchard is rubbish. The builders will be coming soon to start the new houses and they'll clear everything away. Help yourself to anything you want."

"Help yourself," agreed Joe. "You're very welcome to anything you want, but be careful of Cocky. He's really aggressive."

"What, that little thing?" laughed Miguel. "*¡Hombre!* He barely reaches my ankles!"

Joe and I exchanged knowing glances, but Miguel would not be put off. He strode off to the orchard before we could warn him further. Teresa, Joe and I carried on chatting about eggs, the rising price of bottled gas and who would be elected the next Mayor.

"What was that?" said Joe suddenly, holding his hand up for silence. Teresa and I stopped and listened. Then we heard it too. A distant cry of "¡*Ayúdeme!* Help! Help!" filtered down to us.

"Miguel!" said Joe, horrified, and galloped off up the street with Teresa and I hot on his heels.

CHICKPEA AND CHORIZO SOUP
GARBANZOS Y CHORIZO

This dish was inspired by the Moors who introduced the chickpea or *garbanzo*. It is best using the *picante* (hot) chorizo to give it a fiery little Moroccan kick.

Ingredients (serves 6)

- 175g (6oz) dried chickpeas
- 350g (12oz) chorizo, diced into cubes about the same size as the chickpeas
- 1 onion, finely chopped
- 1 clove garlic, chopped or crushed
- 2 tbs olive oil
- 750ml (1.3 pints) chicken stock
- 1 bay leaf
- Pinch of dried thyme
- 3 or 4 cloves
- 1 stick of cinnamon
- 1 tbs flat-leaf parsley

Method

- Cover the chickpeas with water in a bowl and leave to soak overnight.
- Drain and place in a large saucepan with the bay leaf, cloves and cinnamon stick.

- Add the stock and enough water to cover the peas completely.
- Bring to the boil then reduce the heat and simmer until the chickpeas are tender, approximately 1 hour. Do not allow to go soft or boil dry. Add more water if necessary.
- Drain and remove the herbs and spices.
- Meanwhile, medium heat the oil in a frying pan, add the chopped onion and cook gently until soft.
- Add the garlic and thyme and cook for about a minute.
- Turn up the heat a little and add the chorizo.
- Cook for about three minutes then add the chickpeas, mixing well. Cook for just long enough to heat it all through. The oil from the sausage will turn it all a red colour.
- Remove from the heat and stir in the parsley.
- Serve with crusty bread.

20

THE COMMUNE

Poor Miguel had never even reached the old trunk. No way was Cocky going to allow an intruder into his territory, a threat to his harem. He circled his human enemy, screaming insults, his neck feathers spiked out to twice their normal size. And where exactly was Miguel?

"*¡Madre Mia!*" gasped Teresa.

Our jaws dropped. Miguel had rolled himself up in a discarded cylinder of chicken wire. He stood upright, clutching the edge of the wire like a lady holding a towel around herself to shield her nakedness. Little trickles of blood dried on his legs where Cocky had managed to rake him.

Cocky was a whirling dervish. In perfect fighting-cock stance, his body was scythe shaped, airborne, with talons and spurs extended and sharp beak stabbing. Again and again he attacked, furious feathers bristling as he fought to rip his enemy to shreds. Thankfully, the roll of chicken wire protected Miguel from further injury.

We unwound and rescued the poor man and apologised profusely for Cocky's appalling behaviour. Teresa bathed the cuts on her husband's legs and I gave the couple a dozen eggs, refusing payment.

By now Miguel had recovered from the shock and was reflective.

"Well, you did warn me. ¡Madre mia! What a creature! Never have I met such a fierce little…" Words failed him.

The chest that Miguel had wanted was rotten and dotted with woodworm. It was the one that Joe had sawed an entrance into for the girls to lay their eggs. Unsurprisingly, Miguel refused it and left, still muttering and reliving the experience.

Joe and I sat down at the kitchen table for a conference.

"This can't go on," I said. "Cocky is a demon. What if a child wandered into the orchard? Cocky would rip a child to shreds."

"I agree. He's getting worse by the day. I don't see how we can keep him." Joe was depressed. Cocky may have had a filthy temper, but he was an awesome character.

"Who would take him?" I asked. "Who'd take a manic little cock who's convinced everybody wants to steal his wives? I know he's only acting on instinct, but he's positively dangerous."

"Phone Judith," said Joe. "She may have an idea."

I reached for the phone and dialled Judith's number. Somebody picked up the receiver and spoke, but it sounded as though they were talking through a cushion. I could hear several dogs barking so I was pretty sure I had dialled the right number.

"Hello, is that you? Judith? It's Vicky here. Are you okay? You sound really strange."

A short silence, then fumblings, then Judith's voice, loud and clear.

"Vicky? Hello, there. Yes, dear, of course I'm absolutely fine. Mother answered the phone and she's got a kiwi and porridge face pack on at the moment. Face is as stiff as a bloody board. Can't talk properly. Now, how can I help you?"

"I need some advice, please, Judith. It's Cocky."

"Cocky? Poor little chap, is he sick?"

"No, he's fighting fit. That's the problem." I described Cocky's dreadful behaviour and his latest battle with Miguel.

"…and so we'd like to re-home him, but we don't know anyone who would take him."

"Vicky! What utterly beastly behaviour! I can see the problem." There was a note of admiration in Judith's tone. Cocky had that effect on people; whatever ghastly crimes he committed, they were still in awe of the little devil. "Leave it with me, and I'll have a chat with Mother when she's scraped that gunk off her face. I'll phone you back later."

I thanked her and replaced the phone in its cradle. I could clearly picture the scene at Judith's house. Mother floating around in a silk negligee, with face mask, Judith in her tweeds and the dogs and cats generally creating havoc. A typical day at Casa Judith.

Later, as promised, the telephone rang.

"Vicky? It's Judith." Who else could it be with a voice that cultured and strident?

"Thanks for getting back to us, Judith."

"Well, dear, I think Mother has solved your problem."

"She has?"

"Yes, dear. Cauliflower."

"Sorry, Judith, it's a bad line. Did you say 'cauliflower'?"

Joe was listening and rolled his eyes at me. I turned away, trying to concentrate on Judith's words. I agreed with Joe. How could feeding Cocky cauliflower calm him?

"Mother knows someone who'll have him. Free range, don't you know. Oodles of space for Cocky to run about in."

"That's brilliant news! But what did you mean about the cauliflower?"

"That's his bloody name, dear. Cauliflower. He's a Brit, and Mother says he's always been called that, though most people call him 'Caul' for short."

"Oh, right. And how can I contact this, er, Caul?"

"Mother's already given him a tinkle on his mobile, dear. He's one of those New Age chappies. No electricity, no mains water. Lives in a commune in a valley near Lanjarón."

"So what do we do? Just turn up?"

"Yes, just turn up. Mother says he's very vague, very relaxed, don't you know. But I'm sure he'll be awfully thrilled with Cocky."

I scribbled down the directions Judith gave me and turned back to Joe. Joe raised his eyebrows, waiting for me to speak.

"Well," I said, "I think we may have found Cocky a new home. He's going to join a hippy commune."

"Hippy commune?" said Joe, "Aren't they laid-back peace-loving types? Can't see Cocky fitting in there."

"Well, at least if he misbehaves they won't eat him. They're all vegetarians, aren't they?"

Outside, Cocky crowed, oblivious to the fact that tomorrow he was to become a flower child and live with a man named Cauliflower.

As Joe and I drove towards Lanjarón, we could be forgiven for thinking that Andalucía was as close to paradise as is possible. The craggy mountains jutted against the sky, serving as a backdrop to the ancient whitewashed villages that appeared frozen in time, barely changed since Moorish times.

Rivers cut deep gorges through the countryside, and it was the sheer volume of water that surprised us. Waterfalls fed by snow-melt cascaded enthusiastically through crevices, sending up rainbows through the spray. The rocks were sculpted into fantastic shapes by the constant exuberance of the rushing water. It would have been an idyllic drive if Cocky hadn't crowed every few minutes from within his box.

"So how does Mother know this Cauliflower bloke?" asked Joe as we approached the reservoir below Lanjarón.

"Judith said Mother buys herbs from him."

We winced as Cocky crowed again, then marvelled at the expanse of water laid out before us. Lanjarón is famous for its bottled water. We trailed behind a convoy of lorries making their way towards the bottling plant.

Higher and higher we climbed into the mountains, until we were abreast of the giant windmills whose massive arms swept the sky.

"What if he doesn't like Cocky?"

"He will." I was confident. "And he's getting two of Cocky's wives. The No-Name Twins are great layers, he'll welcome the three of them with open arms."

The No-Name Twins were quiet and well behaved in their box. Unlike Cocky who crowed his dissatisfaction with tireless regularity.

Overlooking the town of Lanjarón is the ruin of a Moorish castle. Some say that the Moorish ruler at the time hurled himself to his death from the castle tower. The Christian army, led by King Fernando, was advancing and suicide must have seemed the better option. Death on the rocks was preferable to being conquered and converted to Catholicism.

Following Judith's directions, we swung off the main Lanjarón road and down a dirt track. Branches scraped the jeep's paintwork and bald rocks lay strewn in our path. A little stream bubbled in the centre of the track, leading the way down. Even Cocky fell silent as we bounced and jolted, Joe steering round obstacles designed to puncture our tyres or tip us over.

At last the track widened into a clearing. Parked in the shade of the trees was a jumble of extraordinary vehicles. London cabs, ambulances, vans and removal trucks sat axle-deep in vegetation, a cemetery of obsolete transport. There was even a red London bus. Saucer-eyed, we stopped and gaped.

The occasional old-style British number plate peeped out of the scrub. Peeling sign-writing proclaimed 'Fine Furnishings from Farnham' and 'Enjoy Real West Country Pork Pies' on the sides of ancient vans. Even more curious were doors cut into vehicle sides, and metal tube chimneys that erupted from roofs. Scattered around were dilapidated couches and chairs, encircling the blackened debris of past camp fires.

"What a place…" breathed Joe.

"How on earth did they manage to get all these vehicles down here?" I asked.

A tangle of puppies played under an antiquated dormobile, the only sign of life.

"What shall we do?" I asked. "Knock on a door?"

Joe got out of the jeep and stretched. A few more dogs lifted their heads out of the scrub, blinked and went back to sleep, unconcerned by Joe's arrival. Joe strode purposefully to the dormobile, and knocked on the door. Seconds passed. He was about to leave when a moth-eaten curtain twitched aside and a face appeared at the window.

"Hello," said Joe. "Can you direct me to where, er, Cauliflower lives, please?"

The face was immobile, a smudged pale shape blurred behind filthy glass. Then, very slowly, a hand appeared, forefinger pointing down the track.

"Thank you," Joe called, and the face hung there for a moment longer before melting back into the gloom.

"I suppose we'll have to carry on down," said Joe. "Talkative chap, wasn't he?"

The track did not improve, but we meandered down, tyres scrunching on scattered rocks. Another clearing opened, smaller this time. A battered minibus propped on bricks held centre stage, flanked by rusting carcasses of other aged vehicles. A tarpaulin awning shaded a seating area of threadbare cushions piled in dirty heaps. A figure reclined, oblivious to our arrival.

Cocky chose that moment to crow and the figure sat up slowly. Near him, a lethargic brown dog opened one eye, shook its head then flopped back down on the cushions.

"Hello? Are you Cauliflower?" called Joe.

The figure stood unhurriedly and faced us. He was of average height, middle-aged and round shouldered. I noticed his skin was the same colour as the cushions and his dog. Dry clumps of coarse hair sprouted from his scalp. A faded, tattered T-shirt that may have been green at some time clung to him. The lettering, once black, now faded powdery grey, proclaimed Bob Marley sings *No Woman, No Cry*.

He scuffed towards us, sandaled feet dragging in the dirt.

"Are you Caul?" Joe asked again. "I believe you're expecting us?"

"That's me," said Cauliflower after a long pause.

"We've brought you a little bantam cock and two chickens," I said, climbing out of the jeep. "I'm Vicky, and this is Joe."

I extended my hand then almost wished I hadn't when he clasped it weakly in his own dirt-ingrained one. His eyes were heavily hooded and expressionless.

"Mother said you were coming," he said at last.

I wondered fleetingly if anybody knew Mother's real name. Chatting obviously wasn't one of Caul's strong points, so Joe and I busied ourselves unloading the feeder, water container and boxes out of the jeep. Caul watched us, deep in thought.

We carried it all to the awning, where someone else had materialised. A woman, dressed in a sun bleached shapeless shift, leaned against the minibus, smoking a home-rolled cigarette. Stringy hair straggled down her back and her feet were bare. She swatted flies half-heartedly with a limp hand.

"Hello," I said, trying to behave as though everything was normal. "I'm Vicky."

No answer. She looked at me but made no reply.

"My woman, Nebula," said Caul. "She don't talk much." I resisted the urge to point out that neither of them were sparkling conversationalists.

"Right," said Joe. "Have you kept chickens before?"

Caul looked at Nebula. Nebula gazed back, impassive.

"Yeah," he said, a little shiftily. "Coupla years ago."

"Oh, that's good," I said, too brightly. "We've brought a supply of grain, but as you know, they'll find plenty to eat in the undergrowth as well."

"And the chickens are really good layers," said Joe. "You should have eggs every day."

"Eggs…" breathed Nebula. We all looked up. It was the first time she had spoken, but if we were expecting more, we were disappointed.

"Shall we let them out?" asked Joe. Cocky was scrabbling loudly in the box, claws scraping the cardboard sides.

Neither Cauliflower nor Nebula replied.

"Right," said Joe, taking the initiative. "Out you come..."

I held my breath, praying Cocky would behave. Joe first opened the box containing the No-Name Twins. Utterly unconcerned by their new surroundings, they made straight for the feeder and water. Joe opened the other box and lifted Cocky out. Cocky took in the scene with one glance, ignored us all and strutted over to the Twins.

"Hey, man!" said Caul, showing more interest in Cocky than we had seen him take in anything since our arrival.

The journey had affected Cocky not at all. Quickly he mounted one Twin, bucked, climbed off and then mounted the other.

"Hey, man!" said Caul.

The brown dog came sniffing up. The girls carried on pecking grain. Cocky rattled his lavender feathers, stood on tiptoe and crowed. The dog wisely decided not to investigate further and slouched away to slump on the cushions again.

"I don't think dogs will bother them, do you?" I said to nobody in particular. "Not with Cocky there on guard."

"What about foxes?" asked Joe.

"Foxes…" whispered Nebula.

"No foxes here, man," said Caul. "Too many dogs."

Cicadas clamoured in the trees. The brown dog twitched and snored. The chickens scratched happily in the dirt. There seemed nothing else to do, or say. We took our leave promising to call in a few days to see how Cocky and the girls had settled in. We left Cauliflower and his woman in the heat and dirt and navigated the track back up to the main road.

Driving home, we fell silent. I knew I would miss the troublesome little cock we had just given away, and I was sure Joe felt the same. I already missed the incessant crowing. We felt curiously unwilling to discuss the rather surreal visit.

"I'm pretty sure I know where Cauliflower got his name," said Joe eventually, breaking the silence.

"Really? So why d'you think he's called Cauliflower?"

"Did you get near enough to smell him?" asked Joe. He had a point.

"Another thing," I said. "Mother said she buys herbs from him. Did you see any cultivated areas there? Any kind of garden?"

Joe shook his head, then creased his brow in thought.

"No, but there were some very dodgy looking plants growing under the trees. I think Mother may have a little vice Judith doesn't know about."

"But Mother's eighty-five years old!"

"Well? Good luck to her," said Joe. "We won't grass on her."

It was a long drive home and we both felt a little depressed.

"Let's not go straight home," I said. "I hate thinking of the orchard with no Cocky in it."

"Okay, let's stop somewhere and have a coffee."

So, to distract ourselves, we stopped in the next small village. The square was very quiet and we were disappointed that it offered no bar for refreshments.

"Oh well," said Joe. "We can still take a stroll round the village. The church looks really old. Perhaps we could have a look inside."

It was a pretty church, constructed from local stone. The huge double doors looked firmly closed, but a faded, flapping notice was pinned up. I leaned forward to read it.

"What does it say?" asked Joe.

I translated it aloud:

'ALL SOULS' DAY MASS.
BEFORE THE SERVICE, PLEASE PLACE YOUR DONATION IN AN ENVELOPE TOGETHER WITH THE DECEASED PERSON YOU WANT REMEMBERED.'

That conjured up quite a picture and set us laughing. Joe composed himself and tried the handle of the church door.

"Well, I expect it's locked now," he said. "They probably only open it on special Holy days."

To our surprise, it was not locked, and the door creaked open.

SPANISH CAULIFLOWER AND PAPRIKA
AJOARRIERO

Serve as a vegetable accompaniment or in smaller portions as a *tapas* dish. Goes well with a full-bodied red wine.

Ingredients

- 1 large cauliflower, washed and broken into florets
- 6 cloves garlic
- Handful fresh parsley, roughly chopped
- 3 tablespoons olive oil (plus extra for frying)
- 2 teaspoons sweet smoked paprika (or hot paprika for more bite)
- Splash white wine vinegar
- 1 teaspoon sea salt

Method

- Cook the cauliflower in salted boiling water for 8 minutes or so until just tender.
- Drain, reserving a little of the water and set aside in a serving dish to keep warm.
- Meanwhile peel the garlic and crush 3 of the cloves, slicing the other three.
- In a small bowl or mortar, mix together the three crushed

cloves of garlic with the parsley and the salt and stir in the olive oil.
- In a frying pan, heat a little olive oil and sauté the three sliced cloves of garlic until they begin to turn gently golden.
- Turn down the heat and add the contents of the mortar.
- Add the reserved cooking water from the cauliflower, paprika and a splash of wine vinegar.
- Turn up the heat and bring to the boil, cooking for a couple of minutes.
- Pour the sauce over the cauliflower in the serving dish and serve straight away.

21

DEATHS AND PANCHO PINOCHET

Joe and I entered the church and peered into the silent darkness. They say the past whispers to those who listen, and I wondered how many generations had passed through those heavy doors to worship here. Joe ran his hand over the cool stone, searching unsuccessfully for a light switch.

The building had that slightly damp, mysterious atmosphere unique to old churches. Pale eerie shapes of statues beckoned from the shadows. Nothing stirred, no sound apart from our footsteps echoing on the flagstone floor.

We stood silently in the central aisle, trying to accustom our eyes to the dark, surrounded by ghosts of the past. On the altar, a couple of candles flickered, barely illuminating a bleeding Christ figure nailed to a wooden cross.

When Joe's mobile phone suddenly shrilled, we both sprang like startled rabbits. It was so unexpected, so loud, so inappropriate. Joe fumbled it out of his pocket and flipped it open. The strange bluish light illuminated his face and made it seem unearthly. He read the message and for a split second his eyes grew large before he visibly relaxed.

"Gosh, that gave me a fright," he said, passing me the phone and sinking onto a pew. "I nearly got down on my knees. I thought He was trying to tell me something."

Aloud, I read the words on the tiny screen, and instantly understood his shock.

"Jesus calling…"

I snapped the phone closed. It didn't seem the right time or place to accept the call. We could discuss welding jobs with our young Ecuadorian worker another time.

Chuckling, we left the church and headed home.

We met up with Judith and Mother a few days later. Of course Cauliflower and the commune were the main topic of interest.

"Frightful way to live, isn't it?" said Judith, shuddering. "But they seem happy enough. Bloody cold in winter, though. Colder than a witch's ti…"

"Judith!" said Mother. "Language!" Being in her sixties did not exempt Judith from her mother's scolding.

"Have you heard how Cocky and the chickens are?" I said quickly.

"Well, dear. I spoke to Cauliflower only yesterday. Seems it didn't take long for Cocky to settle in. Became a bit of a bloody nuisance, don't you know. But they've sorted all that out now."

Joe and I cringed. We knew exactly how bad Cocky could be.

"What happened?" I asked.

"Well, dear, Cauliflower and his cronies have a little hut in the woods where they spend a penny. That wretched Cocky of yours wouldn't let them near it."

"Oh no!"

Judith rubbed her hands together, relishing the story.

"Yes, but then they discovered that Cocky doesn't like this penguin they've got."

"Penguin?"

"Yes, dear, a stuffed penguin. A soft toy. Cocky hates the penguin. Probably sees it as competition, don't you know. So they've put this bloody penguin on the end of a pole. Whoever needs to spend a penny takes it with them. Works a treat, apparently."

All four of us erupted. The vision of the hippies fending Cocky off with a penguin on a stick every time they needed the toilet was too comical.

"Well, that's one thing we didn't try," said Joe, composing himself. "I'll phone Caul tomorrow, make sure everything's okay."

Judith and Mother told us the chickens were free to wander where they pleased. Of course Cocky guarded them closely, but the No-Name Twins were laying eggs and all seemed well.

The next day, Joe phoned Cauliflower as promised.

"Er, Caul? It's Joe. Just checking that Cocky and his wives are okay." He didn't mention the penguin.

"Hey, man, gotta bit o' bad news."

"Oh dear, what's the matter?"

"Sorry, man, 'fraid Cocky and the chickens didn't make it."

"They're dead?"

"Yeah, man."

"Oh no! What happened? Foxes?"

"No, man. A genet got 'em in the night."

"A genet? What's a genet?"

"Carnivore, man. Climbs trees. 'Bout the size of a cat. Bit their heads off." It was a long speech for Cauliflower.

"Oh, no! That's awful." Joe was shocked. "I've never heard of a genet before."

"Sorry, man."

"Oh well, nothing we can do about it. Pity."

"Yeah, man."

"One more thing, Caul. Those other chickens you had a couple of years before. What happened to them?"

"Genet had 'em too, man."

The memory of poor Cocky and the No-Name Twins had scarcely dimmed before our next trial appeared on the horizon. It began with another conversation with Kurt, and was to involve the Mayor and the coming elections.

"If you do not apply for *Residencia*, you vill become aliens," Kurt had said, his finger wagging in warning. That seemed a little alarming. Becoming aliens was not part of our life plan.

"Well, we wouldn't want that," said Joe. "How do you apply for *Residencia*?"

"It is easy, but you must make a lot of paper," said Kurt. "But do not vorry. My vife vill make all the paper for you."

Well, that was a relief. Kurt's solicitor wife Paula would complete all the paperwork, and submit the papers. Hopefully, that would take care of the *Residencia* issue and we'd be given Spanish ID cards. And it would also mean we'd be entitled to vote in the upcoming local elections.

"It vill not be a problem. Unless you are criminals." Kurt stared at us, unblinking.

"No, we're not criminals."

"Good. Paula vill need three passport photos. I vill instruct her to get the football rolling." He turned on his heel and strode away.

Weeks later, Marcia handed us an official brown envelope with our loaf of bread. It was the appointment we had been expecting. We were ordered to attend the *Oficina de Extranjeros* in the city at ten o'clock, on the 15th of March.

In spite of his military background, Joe's punctuality is lamentable. For this reason, I wrote lists and prepared everything ready for the trip to the city. I checked the petrol in the jeep and researched the location of the offices. I gathered up the necessary paperwork. I laid out our clothes and set the alarm clock.

That morning, all my plans went well. We drove into the city, parked, and made our way towards the address. Ten minutes to the hour, perfect timing. As we rounded the corner, we were forced to step off the kerb to avoid the huge queue of people lined on the pavement. Briskly, we overtook them and headed for the entrance gates.

A uniformed guard blocked our way.

"Show him the letter with our appointment," I said to Joe.

Joe smiled politely and offered the guard our paper. He didn't even look at it, or us. Gazing at nothing in particular, he waved us away, indicating the back of the queue.

"But our appointment is for ten o'clock," I said. The guard ignored me. The gates remained locked.

Agitated, we backtracked and joined the end of the queue. Now we had time to look at the waiting people. Mostly couples, every nationality was represented. There were dark North Africans, blonde Scandinavians, French, Germans, Dutch and many others. It reminded me of Noah's Ark, the animals went in two by two.

"Why are we in this bloody queue? Have you seen how many people are in front of us? We're going to miss our appointment!" Joe was seething.

He leaned forward and tapped the man's shoulder in front of us. The man turned.

"We've got an appointment for ten o'clock," said Joe. "How about you?" The clock on the office building struck ten.

The man didn't reply, but held up an identical sheet of paper for Joe to see. Joe checked the appointment time. Ten o'clock.

Another couple held up their sheet. Ten o'clock. In fact everybody's appointment was scheduled for ten o'clock. No wonder we received no preferential treatment. I had my work cut out soothing Joe and preventing him from storming off.

Every now and then, the guard unlocked the gates and parted them a crack, allowing another couple to slip through. It was going to be a long wait. Joe and I took it in turns to get coffee from the cafe opposite.

Three hours later, the guard allowed us in. Delighted, we slipped through and followed the arrows. The building was old, the steps worn by years of human traffic, but our progress was short-lived. We joined another queue.

Several more queues and an hour later, we reached the office, and it was our moment of glory. An official behind a desk beckoned us forward. He checked our passports and paperwork.

"Forefinger, right hand," he said, pushing forward a black ink pad.

We obliged and our fingerprints were taken. "Now you can commit a crime, but make sure you don't use that finger." It was clearly an attempt at humour, but the official's tone was flat, his face deadpan. I wondered how many times a day he repeated his joke.

At last it was finished and we departed. The Moroccan couple behind us took our places. As we descended the stairs, we heard the words, 'Now you can commit a crime, but make sure you don't use that finger...' echoing behind us.

In Britain, a kind of unwritten rule exists. Except in an emergency, or amongst family members, people rarely knock on each other's doors after nine o'clock at night. Not so in Spain. At half past ten one night our fridge-freezer was delivered. Also, our Egg Ladies often called late, sometimes near midnight. Our neighbour, Paco, frequently pounded on our front door well after midnight.

So one Sunday night, as the church-bells chimed 24 times, we were not especially surprised when a fist hammered on our door. What was surprising, however, was the fact that the fist belonged to Pancho the Mayor. Beside him stood his assistant, Felipe Frog.

Poor Felipe. The reason for our nickname was obvious. As our children would have said, God had touched (possibly thumped) him with the Ugly Stick. Squat, with a wide, pocked face and gaping mouth, he resembled a frog so closely I was convinced his children were tadpoles.

Pancho the Mayor, however, although short, was suave and sophisticated. Always smartly dressed, he exuded confidence, a true politician. His gaze never wavered and his hooked nose appeared capable of removing beer bottle tops. We all shook hands, and Joe invited them inside. I was a little embarrassed as I was wearing a bath robe, just about to go to bed. I felt Pancho's eyes slide down my body, and I pulled the robe closer about me.

Pancho spoke very good English, Felipe Frog none at all. We all stood politely smiling at each other, until Pancho collected himself and spoke.

"You must come to the Town Hall, tomorrow," he said. "It is urgent."

Felipe Frog nodded vigorously, as he always did every time Pancho spoke, whether in Spanish or English.

"Oh?" said Joe. "Is there a problem?"

"Yes, you must sign a paper. Then you can put a vote for me when it is time." Felipe Frog obviously understood the gist of his hero's statement and nodded furiously.

"Well, we don't have our *Residencia* cards yet," said Joe. "But I suppose we could bring the paperwork proving we've applied."

"That is good," said Pancho, his eyes never leaving me.

"Muy bien," said Felipe Frog, nodding enthusiastically.

There was an awkward silence. I was about to offer them a drink, really as an excuse to escape the Mayor's relentless gaze, when he spoke again.

"People are telling me you have chickens," said Pancho. Beside him, Felipe Frog nodded.

"Yes," I said. "We keep a few chickens."

"My wife likes fresh eggs."

"Oh, really?" I asked.

"Yes, she was saying this morning. She said eggs from the supermarket in town are not the same. She prefers eggs that are so fresh and tasty." His stare had become intense.

I took the hint and shot into the kitchen to bag up a dozen eggs. I was delighted to have a pretext to break free from Pancho's unflagging stare. I returned and presented him with the eggs.

"Very kind," said the Mayor, and, like royalty, handed the eggs to Felipe Frog to carry. "And now we will go. I will see you tomorrow at the Town Hall. Also, I have called a political meeting in the village square next month. I hope you will come." His tone left us in no doubt that he had issued an order.

Joe shook hands, and I extended mine for shaking. Pancho clasped my hand and raised it gallantly to his lips.

"Smarmy old git," said Joe, when they had gone.

I agreed with him but chose not to speak. It does a relationship no harm to remind one's partner one is still attractive to others.

The next morning, we drove to the Town Hall in Judith's village and signed the required papers. It was quite exciting to know that we now had a voting voice, one step closer to becoming part of the village. However, as usual, it was not going to be quite as straightforward as we had imagined.

SUMMER BAKED POTATOES
PATATA DE VERANO

These baked potatoes are great cooked on the barbecue and are full of Mediterranean flavours.

Ingredients

- 4 medium sized potatoes
- 4 cloves garlic
- Oregano
- Thyme
- Salt
- Olive oil

Method

- Wash the potatoes and cut in half, lengthways.
- Peel and crush the garlic and roughly chop the thyme and oregano (dried herbs are also good here).
- On one half of each potato, generously sprinkle the garlic and herbs, add a pinch of salt and a small drizzle of olive oil.
- Put the remaining half of the potato back on top, wrap in foil and cook in the BBQ embers for about 40 minutes, depending on size.
- You can also cook the potatoes in the oven.

22

SUPPORTING PANCHO

A month sped by, and the night of Pancho's campaign meeting in the square arrived. Posters had appeared both in Judith's village, and ours, advertising the event. I was furious with Joe who refused to come with me, preferring to watch football on TV instead. I walked the few steps to the village square and was greeted by Felipe Frog and a couple of helpers.

"*Buenas noches,*" said Felipe Frog, grinning broadly, and handed me a disposable cigarette lighter and a pen.

I thanked him and took the gifts which were printed with party slogans. There were plenty of people gathered around, so I looked for a familiar face to stand with. However, before I could head in any direction, a figure detached itself from a knot of people and strode towards me.

"Ah, the beautiful *señora* Twead," said the Mayor as he approached. He lifted my hand and brushed it with his lips. "I am most contented to see you here. And your husband?"

"Er, Joe's very sorry not to be here, he's busy tonight."

"*No pasa nada,*" he said, then leaned in close. "You, Veectoria, are a special guest, very special. And I have gifts for you." He felt in a pocket and drew out another party political lighter and pen. He pressed them into my hand and closed my fingers around them, one by one.

"Thank you very much," I said, thoroughly uncomfortable. "Er, please call me Vicky."

"Ah, Veeky… Such a beautiful name…" He had the Andalucían's usual problem with the letter 'v', so my name sounded more like 'Beaky'.

"Is that you, Vicky?" shouted a voice. Never had I been more pleased to hear Judith's stentorian voice.

"Judith, how lovely to see you here!" I meant it from the bottom of my heart. My relief was palpable.

"Pancho, you old devil!" roared Judith, joining us. "Put Vicky down, and tell me, how's that lovely wife of yours? And those strapping sons? Lord! How many grandchildren have you got now?"

The Mayor released my hand as though it had become red hot. He muttered something under his breath, turned on his heel and melted back into the crowd.

"Ghastly old sleaze bag, isn't he?" said Judith. "Now, come and stand over here with me and Mother."

Mother had clearly made a big effort for the occasion. She wore a floor length floral affair, topped by a jaunty hat trimmed with artificial flowers. She clutched a tiny silver handbag, her crimson fingernails like painted talons. As usual, a haze of Chanel No.5 surrounded her. I kissed her powdery cheek.

"Brought the old gal a folding chair to sit on, don't you know," said Judith. "Pancho's not renowned for short speeches, m'dear. Could be here a bloody long time."

"Are you going to vote for Pancho?" I asked, curious.

"Bless you, m'dear! Pancho Pinochet? Of course not! He's made a bloody pig's ear of his last term of office. Shan't be voting for him again. Mother won't either." Mother's artificial flowers nodded in agreement.

"Well, he seems to have a lot of supporters here tonight," I said, looking around at the milling crowd.

"Good Lord, dear. They're not here to support Pancho! They're here for the free food and drink. Bloody Spaniards can't resist a free meal, don't you know."

While we were speaking, Felipe Frog dragged up the customary wooden box and his master stepped up. Felipe Frog rapped on a table and gradually the crowd silenced and wheeled round to face the Mayor. Pancho cleared his throat and launched into his election speech. I understood very little of the meaning, but the tone and cadence were familiar. It could have been a political speech delivered anywhere in the world. The same rhetoric, the same repetitions, the same delivery. Felipe Frog's head bobbed up and down with each point made. I allowed Pancho's words to wash over me, just picking out a few key words now and then. Did I hear him mention that old promise of a proper sewage disposal plant? I noticed Mother had dozed off.

"Beaky? You understand what I am saying?" The Mayor had broken into English and was addressing me over the crowd.

I jumped, appalled that he was singling me out. One hundred heads swivelled in my direction. I nodded frantically, and Pancho continued with his speech, satisfied that I had appreciated the finer points of Sewage Management. I tried to shrink myself, but I was taller than most of the Spanish present.

"Beaky, you agree with my point?" Pancho's thunderous voice assailed me again. My face glowed crimson. Again, a hundred pairs of eyes turned and bored into me. Again, I nodded like a piston, willing him to leave me alone.

Judith saved me this time. In Spanish, she shouted, "Pancho, never mind all that! What about the swimming pool you promised us three years ago? Still waiting, you know!"

The resulting mumbles of assent deflected the crowd's interest away from me for just long enough. There were four ornamental trees planted in the square, and I slid behind the nearest. The crowd had settled down again, and Pancho relaunched, his voice echoing around the square. All too soon, I heard him break into English again.

"Beaky? BEAKY?" Alas, there was no escape. "Beaky, it is important to keep the roads into both villages mended, no?" I poked my burning face out from behind the tree and nodded furiously.

Mercifully, the speech ended soon after. Pancho gathered himself up and delivered his final punchline, a rousing question that I understood and rang in all the listeners' ears.

"So, would YOU trust the other Party to make these CRUCIAL decisions?" Silence. Then Uncle Felix's mule who was tethered nearby, lifted her head and brayed, perfectly on cue.

The crowd erupted, united in laughter. Pancho gave up and stepped off his box. The Smart Ladies took this as a signal and whisked off the covers from plates of tapas laid out on tables. Politics already forgotten, the villagers surged to the tables, chattering happily amongst themselves.

I took my leave of Judith and Mother and slipped away home. I would be attending no more political meetings.

Another official looking brown envelope arrived for us. We were being invited back to the *Oficina de Extranjeros* to collect our brand new *Residencia* cards. We had been accepted.

This time, we knew the route, and also knew the exact appointment time was not in the slightest bit important. The appointment was for 11 o'clock, but we weren't fooled. We could take our time. We had a café con leche at a nearby cafe. We didn't hurry ourselves and turned up the side street, heading for the building.

But where was the long queue of people waiting to be allowed through the gates? Nowhere. There was nobody waiting, not a soul in sight. Just the same stony-faced security guard on duty at the gate.

We approached him as before, and Joe showed him our letter. He glanced at the paper, then at the clock on the building.

"You are late," he said. "Nearly an hour late." Then he shrugged and unlocked the gates allowing us through.

The place was deserted. We found the office we needed and tapped on the door.

"Come in," said a flat, female voice.

We pushed the door open. Behind a large desk sat a dark, middle-aged lady filing her nails. She didn't look up, far too absorbed in her task.

"*Buenos dias,*" said Joe, and held out the letter. "We've come to collect our *Residencia* cards."

Reluctantly, she put the nail file down and took the proffered letter. Her eyes flicked from it to us.

"You are late," she said. "Nearly an hour late."

"But..." I started to protest, then subsided in the knowledge that my argument was futile.

The woman flicked through a bank of cards and located ours. She checked our photographs and handed the cards over. Her displeasure was obvious. It manifested itself by the way she slammed shut the filing cabinet drawer and kept her thin lips pressed tightly together. Her dark moustache bristled with annoyance.

We thanked her and turned for the door.

"Next time," she said through pursed lips, "make sure you arrive on time for official appointments."

The days running up to the Local Election were colourful and noisy. Colourful because so many posters had appeared. *'Vote for Pancho!'* they shouted silently. Pancho's eyes seemed to follow us wherever we went, his ever present face with hooked nose pasted on every available surface.

And noisy because of the frequent electioneering vehicles passing through the village. Small white vans with loudspeakers fixed to their roofs crawled through the streets blaring out their campaign messages. All three mayoral candidates' vehicles appeared daily, sometimes together, and the noise was awesome as they fought to gather support. Pancho waved to me as he passed our house, Felipe Frog barely visible over the steering wheel as he chauffeured his beloved master.

On Voting Day, Joe and I drove to Judith's village, eager to vote for the very first time in Spain. I still wasn't sure I wanted to vote for Pancho, or for Angelo Covas Sanchez who seemed a fairly promising candidate. I had decided to make up my mind at the voting booth. We parked, and climbed the steps of the Town Hall. Clutched in our hands were our shiny new *Residencia* cards.

On the doors of the Town Hall was pinned a long list of names. Apparently, these were the people eligible to place a vote. I ran my finger down the list, recognising many names from both our village and Judith's. We checked it twice. Then once more to be sure. Unbelievably, both Joe's and my name were missing.

Inside the Town Hall, everybody was very apologetic. It seemed that a few names had inadvertently been left off the electoral roll, ours included. Never mind, we could vote next time, they said.

So we drove home again, disappointed, not having had the chance to post a vote in any Spanish ballot box.

When the votes were counted, to everybody's surprise, Pancho and Angelo were dead level, even after a recount. We heard that they had decided to forget their differences. They would share the mayoral duties and work together.

However, we then heard on the village grapevine that an almighty row had exploded in Grumpy's bar. Chairs were thrown, parentage questioned. Felipe Frog needed several stitches. Angelo resigned. He relinquished all mayoral duties, refusing to work another day with 'that dictator - Pinochet'.

And so Pancho 'Pinochet' Marcos Martinez happily continued to reign as Mayor for another term, his fourth in a row.

In spite of the odd diversion provided by Mayors, meetings and officialdom we needed to concentrate on working on the house. It was hard work, day after day, week after week. Sometimes it was overwhelming and a change was needed. Then we'd abandon everything and take the jeep for a drive in the mountains. With the roof down, these trips never failed to blow away the cobwebs and cement dust and invigorate us. Refreshed, we would return home from our 'Away-Day' to continue with our toils.

Occasionally, if we were lucky, we'd see shy Spanish ibex, or mountain goats, negotiating sheer crags. We never had any success

more minutes until the mushrooms are soft. Place the vegetables onto a plate and keep warm.
- Add the pork to the pan and cook on high for a few minutes until browned all over then return the vegetables to the pan. Lower the heat and cook for 15 minutes or so until the pork is cooked through.
- Turn up the heat and add the brandy, cooking on high until almost all has been reduced, then add the cream.
- Lower the heat again and simmer gently for 5 minutes or so until the sauce has thickened.
- Serve with the parsley garnish and an extra sprinkle of paprika, with rice.

23

AWAY-DAYS AND ANIMALS

Early one morning Paco nearly beat down our door in his excitement.

"English! Come and see!"

We stepped out into the street and the sight that met our eyes filled us with horror. Strapped to the roof of his old white van was the carcass of a magnificent wild boar. It stretched the full length of the van, its blood still running in rivulets down the windscreen and dripping onto the road. Its eyes were open, glazed and sightless.

"Un animal magnífico, no?" said Paco, bursting with pride.

"It was," muttered Joe in English.

Much as we loved Paco, we could never agree with his attitude towards the unnecessary killing of animals. Neither could we share the Andalucían passion for bull fighting. We never attended a bullfight and switched the TV channel if one was shown. However, I'm ashamed to say we did eat some delicious steak that Carmen-Bethina cooked, only to be told that it came from a prize bull slaughtered in the bullring.

On our Away-Days, we were always on the lookout for snakes. Not because we were afraid of them. On the contrary, we were both fascinated by these ancient beguiling creatures. In fact there is only one 'dangerous' poisonous snake to be found in Spain - the viper. These snakes have instantly recognisable triangular heads and zigzags down the body, but they are so timid they are rarely seen.

Unfortunately, snakes have a silly habit of basking on the road, absorbing the heat from the tarmac. So we always drove carefully, not wishing to squash one inadvertently.

Snake sightings reminded me of the day we were having coffee with Carmen-Bethina and some of her female relatives. Paco came in from outside, carrying something. To our delight, it was a beautiful, three-foot long snake. It took a few seconds for the ladies round the table to realise what he was holding. Then they reacted. Ear-piercing shrieks tore the air. The ladies bolted into corners of the room, as far from Paco as possible. They crouched, hands to their faces, eyes enormous with horror. Paco grinned and held the snake up, allowing it to test the air with its forked tongue. The ladies became hysterical.

"¡Una serpiente!"

"Paco! Take it away!"

"Get that thing out!"

"¡Madre Mia!"

Paco clearly revelled in the reaction he was getting. He threw his head back and roared with laughter. Little Paco had no fear and stood beside his father, his face a mirror of his father's mischievousness. Joe and I approached to admire the snake. The snake wound itself tighter around Paco's arm.

"What a beautiful creature," I said, and extended fingertips to touch its shiny skin.

"Get it OUT!" screamed the women, clutching each other.

Paco had the devil in him that day. He took a few more steps into the room, stooped and held the snake out, as though he was going to place it on the floor. This was too much.

"Aaaaaaah!" screamed the women in one voice, and bolted en masse for the doorway.

The doorway was small, the ladies large and panic-stricken. Their terror resulted in a jumble of flailing arms, legs and bodies jammed in the doorway. At last they catapulted into the street, one by one in quick succession, like ping-pong balls spat out of a toy gun.

Tears of laughter ran down Paco's weather-beaten face. He passed the snake to Joe and plonked himself down in a chair, hands gripping the table edge, shoulders shaking with mirth. Joe and I, with Little Paco trailing along, took the snake outside. The street was deserted, no sign of any of the women. We headed for the wasteland behind the cemetery and admired the exquisite reptile one last time before we set it free. It slid away gracefully, invisible in seconds.

Later we saw Little Paco and his cousins searching for it again, but the snake had wisely vanished.

The Spanish had a very different attitude to animals than we were used to. In Britain it is normal practice to neuter or spay pet cats and dogs. In Spain, puppies and kittens abound. I suppose it was inevitable that villages were overrun by cats and dogs, and strays roamed the mountains.

In our village, many of the big new houses on the outskirts had a resident dog. Usually mean looking German Shepherds, these dogs guarded the houses and stayed alone when their owners returned to the city during the week. Often they would bark all day and night. It became a background noise we didn't even notice after a while.

By contrast, the Spanish adored and pampered their little house dogs, although dog obedience classes did not seem to exist. In our street, a neighbour had a Yorkshire Terrier named Lala. This little dog sat on their doorstep and yapped continuously. Small she may have been, but cowardly she was not; Lala considered any human ankle fair game. I took to finding alternative routes to avoid her attacks. Of course her owners always apologised when Lala nipped someone's foot. They'd smack her, then pat her and smile fondly. And so her delinquent behaviour continued, unchecked.

Dogs were allowed to bark, to bite, to roam in packs. Our Spanish friends were not concerned. Little songbirds were kept in tiny cages, chickens confined in wire prisons no bigger than shoe boxes.

Sometimes, however, the Spanish surprised us. This clipping from my favourite English language newspaper, 'The Messenger', both interested me and made me chuckle.

BUTCHER DEDICATES LOTTERY WIN TO HIS OXEN

A butcher from Pontevedra called Marcelino has won nearly a million and a half Euros in the Primitivia lottery. He says that he always played the lottery with the same numbers in a bar in his local town and now he knows exactly what to do with his money.

He's closing the butchers shop, giving away all his stock to his clients and will dedicate his time to looking after his two oxen which Marcelino says he loves as if they were his own children.

Often the mountain roads were deserted and half an hour might pass before we saw another vehicle. In the matter of road building, the Spanish are a ground-breaking people - literally. If they decide on a route, nothing stops them. Mere mountains do not stand in their way. Channels are blasted through the rock and brand new roads laid.

We were travelling along one such new road with banks of hewn rock touching the sky on either side, when something caught my eye. It was a movement. Something was hurtling down the steep slope at speed.

"Stop the car!" I said, pointing.

Joe braked. I thought it was a large rock falling, but as it descended, bouncing and tumbling, we saw that this was no boulder. It was a bird, a huge bird. As it descended, smaller stones dislodged and created a mini avalanche. We could hear the bird squawk in alarm. Finally, it hit the ground and came to an ungainly halt in the middle of the road in front of our jeep.

"What on earth...?" said Joe, climbing out of the car for a closer look.

The bird didn't move. It just sat there, stunned and silent, completely dazed by its fall.

"It's a bloody vulture!" said Joe, mouth hanging open.

There was no doubt about it, it was definitely a vulture, a young one. It sat hunched, but still waist high, its wings just grazing the ground. Its head and neck were characteristically bald and the beak was hooked and wicked looking. It ignored Joe, apparently still trying to gather its senses after its plunge down the rock face.

"Is it hurt?" I asked, joining him.

"I don't know," said Joe. "I'm not going any closer - have you seen that beak?"

"But we can't leave it there, it'll get hit by a car!"

"Well, what do you suggest we do?"

The vulture roused itself somewhat. Vision swam back into its dazed eyes and it shook itself slightly. At that moment, another car speeded towards us.

"STOP!" I shouted, waving my arms like a demented windmill.

The car pulled up and a couple got out. Their eyes grew round when they saw the problem. The vulture was obviously gathering its wits and feeling a bit better. It opened its razor-sharp beak and squawked again. We all stepped back.

"¡*Precioso!*" whispered the lady.

I agreed with her. The vulture was beautiful. Not in a conventional sense, but its sheer size, curved talons and aquiline beak inspired awe.

Meanwhile, her husband was busy on his mobile phone. Another car appeared.

"STOP!" we all shouted, and waved the car down.

The new arrivals gaped when they saw the cause of the delay. The vulture shifted from foot to foot, but made no effort to move away. More cars stopped. People craned their necks to see.

The husband's call on his mobile phone bore fruit. I could hear a distant siren increasing in volume as it neared, blue lights flashing.

As the police approached, the vulture was recovering. It spread its wings experimentally, drawing a gasp from the spectators. The wingspan must have been over six feet. The policemen marched up and sized up the situation quickly.

One of the policemen may have been a frustrated bullfighter. He quickly unbuttoned his jacket and stepped closer to the bird, holding the jacket matador style. With an expert flick of the wrist, he threw the jacket over the vulture's bald head. The crowd gasped again, then applauded. The vulture jumped in surprise, which dislodged the jacket a fraction. It slipped down the vulture's neck and caught on its hunched shoulders, rather like a scarf. No longer blinded, the vulture twisted its neck and looked left and right. Then it spread and flapped its vast wings. At first it barely cleared the road surface, then it gathered momentum and soared up, taking the policeman's jacket with it.

The audience held its breath. Shading their eyes from the glare of the sun, they watched vulture and jacket rise.

The jacket soon fell off, catching on an outcrop high above us. The vulture continued on its way, evidently fully recovered. The policemen dispersed the crowd and ordered us all to resume our journeys. I assumed they scaled the rock face to retrieve the jacket when the onlookers had disbanded.

We had no idea why the vulture tumbled down the rock face. Perhaps it tried to perch and lost its foothold.

Back at the village, I practised my Spanish by telling our neighbours all about our eventful Away-Day.

"*Tenia una aventura,*" I began. "I had an adventure."

Carmen-Bethina's eyebrows shot up in surprise, as did Paco's. Then they both giggled, and finally laughed unrestrainedly. I was totally bewildered. What had I said that was so funny?

I told Joe about the laughter and he suggested I call Judith. I lost no time.

"Judith, why did Paco and Carmen-Bethina laugh when I said, '*Tenia una aventura*'?" I asked, when the barking dogs had subsided enough for Judith to hear me clearly.

"Lord, dear! Is that what you said? No wonder they laughed!"

"Why?" I was baffled.

"Bloody Spanish language, dear! Strictly speaking it's correct, but it can also mean, 'I've had an affair.'"

I never used the word *'aventura'* again, and we named that stretch of road 'Vulture Gulch'.

In the heat of summer, we often escaped for a day on the beach. Early in the season we frequently encountered jellyfish. Experts agreed that numbers were increasing steadily due to climate change. Usually, they were not difficult to spot as they floated like discarded plastic bags near the surface.

"The beach?" said Judith one day. "Mmm, quite fancy that meself! Let me know next time you plan to go, dears. Mother won't come, stays out of the sun, don't you know. But I'll join you."

Judith a beach babe? I couldn't quite picture that. And I knew with absolute certainty that a day on the beach with Judith would be eventful.

GAZPACHO (COLD TOMATO SOUP) FROM ANDALUCÍA

GAZPACHO ANDALUZ

Hollow out some lengths of cucumber to form 'glasses' to serve this popular Spanish summer starter. Spectacular!

Ingredients (serves 4)

- 2 or 3 slices of white bread
- 4 large tomatoes
- 1 small cucumber peeled
- 1 clove of garlic (finely chopped)
- half a small onion
- 1 small red pepper
- 3 tablespoons of olive oil
- 2 tablespoons of white wine vinegar
- salt and pepper to taste
- water
- ice cubes to serve

Method

- Pull the bread to pieces and soak in a cup of water.
- Roughly chop the tomatoes, pepper, onion and cucumber.
- Place in a food processor and blend to a smooth paste.
- Squeeze the bread to remove excess water, add the oil,

vinegar and seasoning.
- Blend for a second time, adding water little by little until you achieve the desired consistency.
- Refrigerate until well chilled.
- Serve in tall glasses with crushed ice, or hollow out cucumber as shown in the free Photo Book 1.

24

JELLYFISH AND CHICKENS

The next time we went to the beach, we did as Judith asked.

"Beach tomorrow? Spiffing, dear! I'll be ready, just pick me up on your way down the mountain."

The next day, we stopped at her house and knocked on the door.

Judith was fully prepared. A day at the beach was obviously an event to be taken seriously. Joe loaded her stuff into the jeep. Items included a parasol, rugs, folding chair, wicker picnic hamper, binoculars, several towels and a choice of reading matter. And she looked the part. Resplendent in a cotton shift the size of a Boy Scout's tent, she'd topped it off with a giant sombrero. Sunglasses obscured her face. Off we went, Judith holding on to her sombrero all the way down the mountain.

We always avoided the heavily populated tourist beach and instead chose the stretch the Spanish preferred. There were no souvenir shops or amusements, but we could park the jeep on the sand and enjoy seclusion. We always brought our own drinks and picnic, but there was a shack on the beach that served as a cafe, should we need it.

It took a while to unpack the car and get settled, and we were hot and perspiring. Both Joe and I were anxious to get in the water and cool off.

"Coming in for a swim?" I asked Judith.

"Not yet, dear. I'll read me paper and get lunch organised. Brought enough for all of us, don't you know."

Joe and I swam for a while then rejoined Judith. She'd been busy in our absence. Spread on a white cloth was a feast. Triangular crustless sandwiches, home-made sausage rolls, scotch eggs, bowls of fruit; it was like a piece of England.

"Bottoms up!" said Judith, handing us long-stemmed glasses of Pimm's.

After lunch, contented and full, Joe and I stretched out on the sand to sunbathe.

"Damned hot!" said Judith. "Think I'll put me bathing costume on and go for a dip."

"Do you need any help?" I asked.

"No, m'dear, I can manage."

Joe politely averted his eyes while Judith wrestled with changing. She disappeared from view completely under an enormous towel. We heard her grunting, and the flailing under the towel made me think of wildcats fighting in a sack. At last the towel dropped and she was ready. Smelling faintly of mothballs, Judith's swimming attire was serviceable, but definitely not designer. It was black and large with built-in pleated skirt, reminiscent of the nineteen-fifties.

"Look out for jellyfish," said Joe as Judith made her way to the water's edge. Famous last words.

Minutes later, an almighty yell woke us from our doze. Judith, sombrero awry, was exiting the water at a rate of knots. Joe and I jumped to our feet.

"Jellyfish! Bloody critter got me..." spluttered Judith, wincing and holding her leg. "Hurts like hell!"

The rash on her leg was already swelling and angry looking. She sat heavily on the sand, her face creased in pain.

"What can we do?" I asked.

I looked around, but there was nobody on the beach apart from a family some distance away. Judith was suffering; she was writhing and clutching at her leg. Jellyfish stings are notoriously painful.

And then I had an inspiration. I love TV survival programmes, the kind where they show you how to rub two elephant beetles together to make a fire, and a bit of trivia I had absorbed suddenly surfaced.

"Quick, Joe! Pee on her!"

"What?" Joe was aghast.

"Pee on her leg! It'll take the sting away!"

"Don't be ridiculous! I can't just pee on Judith!"

"You have to! I can't do it, it has to be male pee."

"But..."

"Good Lord," said Judith, extending her leg. "If it'll take the pain away, just bloody DO it!"

"Well, I could ... but you'll both have to look away." Joe was crimson with embarrassment, and scratching his groin in consternation.

"Okay," I said, "just get *on* with it!"

For a long moment he just stood there in horror. Then, realising that both Judith and I were deadly serious, he eased his trunks aside, took aim, and began urinating on Judith's leg.

He was still in midstream when a shadow fell across us. We became aware we were not alone. The man from the distant family group had joined us, presumably having noticed Judith's predicament. Politely, he held out a tube of ointment.

"¿Medusa?" he asked quietly. "Jellyfish? This ointment will take away the sting immediately."

Joe swung away, tucking himself back into his trunks as fast as he could. The Spanish man avoided looking at Joe, didn't comment on his bizarre behaviour. Instead, he splashed water on Judith's leg, then gently applied the ointment. The relief, according to Judith, was instantaneous.

"Vinegar also works well," said the man, now looking pointedly at Joe, then nodding towards the cafe up the beach.

The kind Spanish man departed and Judith's rash subsided. All was well again. However, I couldn't help but notice the Spanish women from the family group give Joe frequent sidelong glances. Was it disbelief at his strange behaviour? Or perhaps, as Joe asserts, admiration for his equipment. We will never know.

It was a happy period of our lives. Plenty of Away-Days and leisure time to break the monotony of working on the house. However, yet again it took just one phone call to upset our equilibrium.

"This is Kurt."

"Oh, hello, Kurt. How are you?"

"I am vell. All the papers are now ready. The builders vill arrive today, this afternoon."

"Today? But the chickens are still in the orchard! We need to…"

But Kurt had already hung up.

When we first planned to build two houses on our orchard, we knew our less than perfect command of Spanish would be a hurdle. Negotiating with the bank, council permission, building regulations and architects' plans were all beyond our linguistic capabilities. We needed someone to act as Project Manager, and Kurt was the obvious choice. And Kurt's business partner, Marco, being on the town council would be very useful.

We'd waited months for the paper groundwork to be completed, and now it was all finally kicking off.

"Joe? Joe!"

"What?"

"Kurt just phoned. He said the workmen are coming this afternoon to start work on the orchard."

"For goodness sake! He could have given us a bit of warning!"

By choice, we would have moved the chickens at night. We would have waited until they were roosting, then plucked them from their perch one by one. But we didn't have time for that luxury. Past experience told us that catching them was not an option either.

"We'll have to herd them," I said. "Herd them down the street, round the corner and through the garden gate. Then up the steps in the garden and into the new coop."

Joe rolled his eyes. What choice did we have? It was as good a plan as any. Being a week day, the village was almost deserted. The only inhabitants were Marcia and Old Sancho at the shop, Geronimo and Uncle Felix.

I sacrificed an iceberg lettuce from the fridge to the cause. I figured that should lure them in the right direction.

"Right," Joe said. "I'll get behind them and drive them out into the street. You show them the lettuce and they should follow you."

"Like the Pied Piper?"

"Yes, like the Pied Piper."

It started well. Joe herded them out of the gate, and I began walking backwards, waving the lettuce enticingly. Ginger and Attila the Hen led the way, the rest of the flock following. Bugger and Fuck tried to turn right instead of left, but Joe quickly cut them off. I kept walking backwards, rewarding them with a few lettuce shreds to keep them focused. I was concentrating so hard, I was unaware of what was happening behind me.

Geronimo and his three dogs had rounded the corner.

A fairly orderly, organised scene suddenly became a cacophony of confusion. Excited barks rent the air. Twelve canine feet galloped past me, intent on chicken chasing. Joe shouted. Geronimo shouted. Chaos reigned.

Fourteen chickens scattered in all directions, squawking in panic. Some shot back into the orchard. Bugger and Fuck dived between Joe's legs and careered up the street. Ginger and a few others flapped onto a sagging telephone cable. Fraidy cowered, terrified, in the middle of the road. I spun round.

"*Lo siento*, señora," said Geronimo, shrugging, palms upward. "I'm sorry."

Fraidy collected herself, and flapped up intending to join Ginger on the telephone wire. Geronimo, beer bottle still in hand, leaped. Like the goal keeper of his beloved Real Madrid, he caught Fraidy in mid air. He handed her to Joe.

"Well saved," muttered Joe in English, "that's one. Only thirteen to go."

Geronimo snapped his fingers, and his three moth-eaten dogs slunk back to his heels. A crestfallen Geronimo took a swig of beer to compose himself.

"I'll shut the dogs in *mi casa*," he said. "Then I'll come back and help you catch the hens, *no?*"

It took another two hours to find and herd the missing chickens. Bugger and Fuck were the hardest to locate, but we eventually found them in the cemetery, pecking happily between the headstones.

"Would you like a drink?" I asked Geronimo when the last chicken had been put into the new coop. "A coffee? Or perhaps something stronger?"

"*Café solo,*" said Geronimo. "Just black coffee. It is still early."

I put a full bottle of brandy on the table as well as the coffee. I knew Geronimo well.

"Perhaps just a little drop, *señora,*" said Geronimo, and sloshed a generous measure of brandy into his coffee.

We talked about the village, the chickens, the new houses, but mostly we talked about Real Madrid. Geronimo stayed until only two fingers of brandy remained in the bottle and his speech was too slurred to comprehend. As he staggered away, the phone rang.

"This is Kurt."

"Oh, hello, Kurt."

"The workmen vill come tomorrow morning. Now you haf more time to remove the hens."

"But we've moved them already! They're in our garden now, in their new…"

But Kurt had already replaced the receiver.

By now it was early evening. Joe and I stood on our roof terrace saying a last goodbye to the orchard opposite. It was strange to see no chickens scratching. And after tomorrow, the orchard would never look the same again; it would become a building site.

A familiar sound caught our attention. 'Tap, tap, paaaarp! Tap, tap, paaaarp!' Old Sancho was taking his evening stroll, the black cat at his heels. We watched as he neared the orchard fence, his usual smile replaced by a look of bewilderment. He'd got accustomed to Cocky's absence a while ago. But no chickens? For a long moment he peered into the orchard. Then he shook his head, called his cat and shuffled away. I felt very sad, it was the end of an era.

The team of workmen arrived next morning. Their first job was to rip out all the fencing, then dig out the remaining trees. Heavy machinery was brought in and the old ruin was flattened. Huge clouds of dust billowed into the air. We watched the progress in fascination, as did the villagers. At the weekends, dozens of villagers paraded past to see how things were going. Only Old Sancho avoided the scene.

When we first bought the plot, Alonso showed us how he irrigated the orchard. He had built an enormous underground tank, the size of a swimming pool. It was made from concrete and filled by a combination of rain and mains water. Kurt explained that every village house was charged each quarter for a certain amount of water, whether they used it or not. Alonso regularly read the meter and kept meticulous records of his household's consumption. Then, at the end of each quarter, he filled the reservoir with any leftover water from his quota. We knew that just below ground level, there was an awesome amount of water.

The builders carried on gouging and levelling. They were aware of Alonso's reservoir, expecting to break through it at any moment. We stood watching from our roof terrace, holding our breath. And then they hit it.

The JCB's bucket smashed into the structure. Whooosh! A huge plume of water shot into the air like a geyser, spurting countless gallons into the sky.

"How big was that reservoir?" marvelled Joe, as the water fountained. "Big," I said. "Massive! That's a lot of water."

The driver of the JCB wisely backed off. The other workmen scattered to higher ground and leaned on their pick axes, watching the water-show in wonder. The geyser died down, but water continued to gush from the smashed side of the reservoir. It swamped the orchard, and searched out the quickest path downhill. It surged, gathering momentum, then started to gush down the street.

Joe looked worried and scratched his groin, eyes fixed on the torrent.

"Oh my God!" I said. "It's going to flood the cemetery!"

MARINATED ANCHOVY TAPA
TAPA DE ANCHOAS

Bought fresh, these appetising little fish can be cleaned and marinated in sherry vinegar with garlic and olive oil. They are so small they don't need cooking and are a real favourite in the summer months.

Ingredients

- 8 - 10 fresh anchovies
- 150ml (5 fl oz) sherry vinegar
- Juice 1 lemon
- 1 garlic clove (crushed)
- Handful broadleaf parsley
- 100ml (3 ½ fl oz) extra virgin olive oil

Method

- Remove the heads from the fish, split down the middle, remove the spine and rinse the fillets.
- Lay the fillets skin side up in a dish and pour sherry vinegar over, after 20 minutes the fish will turn pale.
- Remove the fish from the vinegar and place into another dish. Mix up the remaining ingredients and add to the fish.
- Marinade in the fridge for 1 - 2 hours, then serve on crusty bread.

25

THE NEW HOUSES

The water flowed unchecked. I pictured wreaths floating in water, graves submerged. But we were lucky. There was just enough camber in the road to direct the flow past the cemetery gates.

Geronimo, however, was not so lucky. He'd been standing in the street, watching, when he suddenly realised that the water was gathering momentum and heading straight for him. His dogs yelped and bolted, leaving their master to face the deluge alone.

Holding tight to his beer bottle, Geronimo hopped onto a milestone. He sat there with his feet tucked up, perched like a pixie on a toadstool.

I'd never understood the purpose of that particular milestone. On it was engraved the legend:

El Hoyo
0 Km

But it rescued Geronimo that day. The torrent poured past him, ever downward. It flowed down the street to the next corner, then carried straight on to collect in the olive grove below. The baked soil drank it greedily.

That Saturday, I saw the weekend farmer surveying his olive trees and scratching his head. We hadn't had a drop of rain for weeks, but his trees were well watered, the earth still moist. On either side, his neighbours' land was dry and thirsty. Only his plot was wet.

"*Un milagro,*" he muttered, shaking his head in disbelief. "A miracle."

We didn't enlighten him.

Over the next months, work in the orchard progressed quite well. We kept a low profile, leaving Kurt and Marco to direct proceedings. Sometimes the builders didn't turn up for a couple of weeks, then they'd appear again and carry on as though they'd never been away. In our experience, this was a mysterious trait common to builders all over the world, so we didn't worry.

When the foundations were laid, Paco paced the plot with us.

"Pah!" he said, his boot kicking at the idle cement mixer. "*Fatal, fatal!*"

It seemed he objected to the mix of the cement used, the less than perfect straight lines and the depths dug. Whether it be football or building, it's strange how every amateur has opinions on how a job *should* be done. We mentioned Paco's concerns to Kurt.

"The job is good," he said. "Your neighbour got out of the bed with the wrong leg today."

Kurt may have been right. As the houses grew, Paco admitted that they were excellent, his earlier condemnation forgotten.

The two houses were taking shape when the Gin Twins came for another visit. Because the orchard was at a higher level than our house, the growing buildings were soon the same height as our roof terrace, although on the other side of the street.

Juliet and Sue nursed their gin and tonics and watched the men at work.

"Ah, this is the life," said Juliet, sipping from her glass.

"All we need is music," said Sue. "Then it would be perfect."

Juliet jumped up and came back carrying our portable stereo and a stack of CDs. A flick of a switch and loud music blared around the valley. Of course, just listening to the music was not enough. Before long, gin-fuelled, Juliet and Sue started to dance. The workmen smiled, and called out encouragement. Then they put down their tools and were dancing, too. Not much work was done the rest of that day, but it didn't matter.

The second time work stopped I was more concerned. Our daughter was visiting and desperate to take a tan back to England. The builders had stopped for lunch, and would not start work again until three o'clock. Karly snatched at the opportunity to sunbathe nude. With her iPod plugged into her ears, she lost track of time and dozed off.

I looked at the clock at three-thirty and wondered why the cement mixer hadn't restarted. Idly, I stepped onto the roof terrace and looked over to the building site. Seven builders, leaning on a half finished wall, were enjoying the view. Some smoked, some had opened bottles of beer. All eyes were trained on Karly spread-eagled on the sun-bed.

"Karly!" I hissed.

Karly woke, sat up, rubbed her eyes and saw her appreciative audience.

"Oh my God!" she squeaked, grabbed her towel and fled inside.

The builders went back to work, grumbling.

And sometimes things went wrong. Like the day the builders severed the cable that supplied electricity to the entire village. In our kitchen, the washing machine stopped, alerting us to the power cut.

"I'll check the fuse box," said Joe, and did so. "No, everything's okay here. It's not only our house."

We stepped outside. The builders' cement mixer had stopped and they were standing around. We walked down to the square. Marcia stood with her hands on her hips on the doorstep of her shop.

"¡Madre mia! No electricity again!" she said, shaking her head, hairpins glinting in the sun. "Come with me and look."

She beckoned us to follow her inside. We walked through the shop and into the kitchen beyond. On a chair in the middle of the room sat Old Sancho. He was staring straight ahead, hands on his knees. His black cat dozed on another chair, one yellow eye slightly open to watch our entrance.

Slowly Old Sancho turned his head to regard us. And it was then that we noticed. On one side of his skull little tufts of snowy hair sprouted. On the other side, the hair had been clipped neatly, the shorn clumps lying on the floor. Old Sancho smiled in his childlike way, unaware how odd he looked.

"Today is the first time I have used them," said Marcia, waving a shiny new pair of electric hair clippers at us. "I thought it was a good idea. I thought it would save our sons trouble. They usually take their father down to the barber in the city."

I couldn't help it, I started giggling. Joe tried to control himself but failed, and started laughing too. The black cat opened both yellow eyes wide with surprise. Old Sancho beamed, sharing the humour even though he had no idea why we were laughing. Marcia shook her head and frowned, lips pressed together, but not for long. Then her ancient face crumpled too, and her laughter joined ours. A couple of hairpins tinkled to the floor.

The black cat had had enough. It jumped off the chair and stalked out of the room, head held high, tail waving disdainfully.

"¡Madre Mia!" said Marcia again, as the clippers in her hand buzzed back into life. We left them to it, and returned home.

The builders had patched the cable, a temporary measure until the Electricity Board arrived to make a proper repair. Our washing machine was churning again, and we assumed Marcia was putting the final touches to Old Sancho's haircut.

Kurt had told us that the build would take approximately eight months to complete. It didn't. It was nearly a year and a half before the two houses were ready to move into.

Everyone in the village admired them. Everyone said they would sell quickly. Everyone wanted a guided tour. The ship's bell by our garden gate rang constantly at the weekends. We had no choice, we were forced to become estate agents. Again and again we showed people around the new houses, reciting our sales pitch.

'¡Precioso!' they all said. "Beautiful!"

And the houses were a credit to Kurt, Marco, the architect and the builders. The first one sold speedily to a member of Paco's extended family. The second one remained vacant for longer.

One weekday, someone clanged the ship's bell.

"You get it," said Joe. "I'm fed up showing people round that house. I'm going out to chop firewood. Winter will be here again before we know it."

I opened the garden gate to a smart, smiling young man.

"*Buenos dias.* Can I view the house?" he asked. "I saw it advertised on the Internet."

So yet again I traipsed round the house, pointing out the stunning views, showing off the sparkling new bathrooms, the security system and discussing the fact that the garden was big enough for a pool. Perhaps I overstepped the mark when I drew attention to the fact that the neighbours below were very quiet - this house overlooked the cemetery. He had the good grace to smile.

I wasn't hopeful. This young man seemed too young, and more of a city type than someone who would enjoy living in a village house.

"Will you take an offer?" he said, when the tour was complete.

I was surprised. Perhaps he was a genuine buyer.

"Of course," I said and invited him into our house.

We spent a happy half hour bargaining and getting to know each other. Roberto spoke a little English, and I could get by in Spanish. With the help of a calculator we finally agreed on a price. It was the same as the first house had sold for, so I was delighted. We shook hands.

"Are you married?" I asked, curious about our new neighbour.

"No, I do not have a wife," he said, amused. He left, promising to contact Kurt to sort out the details.

Joe came in from chopping wood.

"Any news?" he asked.

"Only that I think I've sold the house," I said. "But I suppose we should wait until Kurt confirms it before we celebrate."

True to his word, Roberto contacted Kurt and paid a deposit on the house. Now we could celebrate. If we could have seen into the future, we would have celebrated even harder. We didn't know that house prices were about to plummet and banks collapse as the world was gripped in the 'Credit Crunch'. We had sold the house just in time.

And I was hatching a plan. Young, single, good looking; surely Roberto would make a perfect partner for Sofía? I couldn't wait to tell our neighbours.

"He's very nice," I told them. "I think Sofía would really like him." Sofía was trying not to look interested, but I could tell she was listening intently.

"Pah!" roared Paco, thumping his knee with his fist. "There will be something wrong with him! Too fat, too thin … supports the wrong football team. Sofía will find something wrong with him."

"What does he look like?" asked Sofía, too casually.

"He's quite handsome. And he must be doing well to be able to afford the house."

"We'll see," said Carmen-Bethina. "Time will tell."

Kurt popped in some time later that month to get our signatures.

"Roberto is coming now here to sign papers," he said. "And he is bringing his vife."

"His wife?" I asked, puzzled. "He told me he didn't have a *'mujer'* (woman, wife)."

Kurt rarely smiled, but this time his face threatened to crack into something closely resembling a grin.

"*Ja*, I believe they haf just got married. They are, how you say, newly-veds. It was a special ceremony."

"Oh, that's nice!" I was pleased for Roberto, but disappointed my match-making plans for Sofía had been dashed. "What's his new bride's name?"

"Roberto's new vife is a chap named Federico."

"What?"

"Ah, here they are now."

Roberto and Federico came up the garden path holding hands. They smiled into each other's eyes, and then at us. Joe's jaw had dropped, but he quickly collected himself, remembered his manners and shook hands.

Roberto and Federico soon became part of the village. When they moved in, I took them some eggs as a welcoming present, following the example set by our neighbours. Spanish people are extraordinarily generous. From the first day we moved into El Hoyo, we were showered with gifts, albeit sometimes unwanted ones.

SPANISH MEATBALLS
ALBÓNDIGAS

Spanish meatballs appear on every restaurant menu in Spain, and it's obvious why. They are heavenly!

Ingredients (serves 4)

- 400g (14oz) minced chicken
- 100g (4oz) minced bacon
- 2 medium onions (one grated, one sliced)
- 1 carrot (grated)
- I large tomato (chopped)
- 2 cloves garlic (chopped finely)
- 3 dessertspoons brown or white bread crumbs
- 1 glass white wine
- 1 bay leaf
- Tomato puree
- Half a stock cube
- 3 dessertspoons soy sauce
- Handful of frozen peas
- 1 teaspoon fresh parsley (chopped)
- I teaspoon oregano

MEATBALLS:

- Mix the minced chicken with the bacon.
- Add the grated onion, half the chopped garlic, soy sauce,

oregano and breadcrumbs.
- Mix well and roll the mixture into small balls.
- Roll these in the flour until coated, then set aside.

Sauce:

- Heat a little olive oil in a frying pan and add the sliced onion, chopped garlic, parsley and pinch of salt and pepper.
- Fry gently for about 10 minutes until soft, then add the chopped tomato.
- Then grate and add the carrot.
- Dissolve the stock cube in a little water.
- Add this, the white wine, peas, a squirt of tomato puree and the bay leaf to the sauce.
- Stir well and allow to carry on simmering very gently.
- In another frying pan, heat enough oil to cover the bottom.
- Fry the meatballs until brown all over, keeping the meatballs moving and the heat low.
- As each batch of meatballs is cooked, add to the pan containing the sauce.
- When all the meatballs are fried and added, allow to simmer gently for half an hour.
- Serve hot with salad and crusty bread.

26

GIFTS

Our house was a hovel when we first moved into it and it seemed that the villagers felt sorry for us. Carmen-Bethina frequently popped round with plates of food, aware that we had no kitchen in the early days. We dreaded these gifts, these bowls of brown sludge with suspicious looking objects bobbing balefully just under the surface. The floaters were probably just Spanish sausage, but they looked much worse.

Two of our Egg Ladies shared the name Isabel, so we nicknamed them Isabel *Arriba* and Isabel *Abajo* (above and below) because of where they lived in the village.

Isabel Arriba presented us with a cloth she had embroidered herself. We were touched by the gift but unsure what to do with it. The house was thick with brick dust from our labours, so we just folded the cloth neatly and set it aside for the moment.

The other Isabel, Isabel Abajo, took one look at the chaos we were living in and beckoned us to follow her down the street. She unlocked a garage and pointed with a flourish to something lurking in a dark corner.

We peered at it. Impatiently, Isabel brushed its surface with her hand, sending up clouds of ancient dust.

"It is a table and four chairs," she said. "You must take them, then you can sit down."

Joe tried the 'grateful-but-no-thank-you' approach. "Thank you," he said. "But we haven't built the dining room yet. Perhaps later, when we've finished the house."

But Isabel was already dragging the furniture out for our inspection. Joe jumped to help her which only succeeded in convincing her that we were just being polite by declining.

"You must have somewhere to sit," she said. "And this is a very good table, and very good chairs."

One of the chairs only had three legs and the table rocked drunkenly. Someone had used it as a workbench at some time and its surface was furrowed with dents and gouges. Woodworm holes peppered the legs in crazy random patterns.

"We already have furniture…" I tried, but was swept aside.

"You can fix it up easily," said Isabel. "A bit of varnish and it will be like new."

Helpfully, she stacked two chairs and handed them to me. Joe gave up the fight. He picked up the table and carried it outside. Isabel followed with the remaining two chairs. She was delighted, whether by her act of charity, or because she'd successfully cleared a corner of her garage, I couldn't say.

The unwanted table set was a constant annoyance. It cluttered up the house and we were at a loss at what to do with it. We couldn't put it on the village skip in case she saw it, and we didn't want to offend her.

"Let's burn it," said Joe one cold evening. "I'll chop it up into pieces so it fits in the stove."

We burnt most of it that night, just a few chair legs remained in the log basket.

I suppose it was inevitable that Isabel Abajo called for eggs the next day. The bell clanged and I went down the garden path to answer it.

"¡*Hola* Isabel!" I said very loudly, praying that Joe would hear me and act quickly.

"*Buenas tardes*," said Isabel, following me back to the house. "I'd like a dozen eggs, please. They're always so fresh and tasty."

Judging by Joe's guilty expression, he had picked up my hint and acted quickly. I stole a glance at the log basket hoping he had removed all incriminating evidence from Isabel's view. To my horror, he had picked up the nearest thing to hand and thrown it over the firewood in an effort to conceal the chair legs.

"That is a beautiful cloth," said Isabel. "Isn't it the one the other Isabel embroidered for you?" There was reproach in her voice. The question 'why put such a beautiful cloth over a log basket?' hung unspoken in the air.

But we had got away with it. She didn't see the chair legs waiting for that night's fire, and went away thinking the English had even stranger customs than she had imagined.

Often, when we visited Marcia and Old Sancho's shop, we were given presents. Marcia would hand us a plastic carrier bag containing almonds, tomatoes, peppers or melons. Sometimes she presented us with a plate of rice pudding. On Old Sancho's eighty-third birthday we were given slices of cake.

The first time they gave us a sack of stale bread we thanked them politely, but were puzzled.

"A gift from my son," said Marcia, pushing a hairpin back into her bun. "It is stale bread from the bakery."

Marcia and Old Sancho's sons owned the bakery in the next village. Okay, so now we knew where the bread came from, but we still didn't understand why it was being given to us.

Sometimes bags of stale bread would be hung on our gate, or left on our doorstep. It was a mystery.

I popped next door to ask Paco.

"For the chickens!" he said. "Soak the bread in hot water and give it to the chickens. And give your eggshells to the chickens, too. Eggshells will make the next eggs strong."

It seemed an almost cannibalistic practice, giving back the eggshells the girls had produced, but we followed his advice. The girls liked the eggshells and enthusiastically hoovered up the soggy bread. So now we accepted our gifts of stale bread gratefully, and the mystery was solved.

There was one gift that always made me smile, even though it wasn't presented to us. On Little Paco's birthday, I popped next door to give him his present and a card. Birthday cards are difficult to buy in Spain so I gave him a homemade one. He opened both card and present and thanked me politely.

"Did you get lots of presents?" I asked.

Little Paco nodded his head, but his eyes were downcast. He was obviously upset.

"He has games for his Playstation, toys, footballs, all sorts of things," said his mother, drying her hands on her apron.

"What's the matter, then?" I asked him. "You don't seem very happy. Didn't you like your presents?"

Carmen-Bethina tossed her head impatiently. Little Paco hung his head. His bottom lip trembled and his dark eyes filled.

"What I really want," he quavered, "is a puppy…"

Carmen-Bethina snorted. "A puppy?" she said. "I've told you over and over again, no puppy! I do not want a dog in the house, do I make myself clear? Puppies are messy, and they need looking after. And who will end up looking after it? Me! You are not having a puppy, and that's final!"

Paco came into the house and caught the tail end of his wife's rant.

"Pah! We already have two dogs," he said, meaning the hunting dogs that were kept outside. A fat teardrop trickled down Little Paco's cheek. "Your mother is right, we do not need any more. Now, that is enough! You are not getting a puppy and I do not want to hear another word about it."

"*Claro,*" said Carmen-Bethina firmly.

Next weekend, Paco's Range Rover screeched to a halt outside as usual. Out climbed Paco, Carmen-Bethina, Sofía and Little Paco. Thunderous knocking on our door. I opened up and they all came inside. Paco was looking rueful, Sofía was smiling and Carmen-

Bethina shrugged with a helpless gesture. Little Paco's head was bowed low over something he cupped in his hands, something snuggled under his chin.

"What have you got there?" I asked, but I already knew.

Little Paco lifted his head and revealed his treasure. A tiny puppy slept, oblivious to its surroundings.

"This is Bianca," whispered Little Paco. "She is English."

"Don't know where he got that name," grunted Paco. "What is wrong with 'Blanca'? That is a proper name for a dog."

"She is beautiful, *no?*" said Carmen-Bethina, her previous reluctance at puppy ownership forgotten. Paco rolled his eyes heavenward but extended a few fingers to stroke the silky ears. So Bianca, the brown and white Cocker Spaniel, entered all our lives and wriggled her way into our affections.

During the first month, Bianca was not well. Little Paco's big sister, Sofía, appointed herself as Chief Nurse. We were told she stopped going out in the evenings, staying in to watch over the sick puppy instead. She fed Bianca by hand, tempting her with tasty nutritious morsels.

"She even missed the big *Fiesta* in Almería," said Paco wonderingly. "She is staying up with that puppy every night and still goes to work early."

Sofía's devotion paid off. Bianca began to thrive and grow. We noticed the difference because we saw the family and puppy only at weekends and Bianca's growth spurt and increase in energy were obvious. At first, she was too small to climb our doorstep. Soon, she could put her front paws on the doorstep but needed a push from behind. Later, she bounded over the doorstep with ease.

I've never owned a dog so I have no personal experience of dog behaviour. However, whether it was the breed, or Bianca's unique nature, I found her to be utterly charming. Such enthusiasm, such joyfulness! Every time we saw her she treated us to huge welcomes. Her laughing face and excitement was infectious. Not just her stumpy little tail, but her whole body wagged in delight. The wag started at her wet black nose, travelled down her neck and body, over her back and round tummy, past the hind quarters and finished with the delirious twitching of her tail.

There were down sides, of course, but aren't there always? She would charge into our house, hurl herself ecstatically at us and pee on the floor, or on our feet, in excitement. I took to leaving a mop and bucket of water with disinfectant handy in anticipation of Bianca's flying visits.

Bianca grew so quickly that even she did not realise how big she'd become. She still thought she was small enough to sleep on the back of Carmen-Bethina's sofa. This was fine until she started dreaming and twitching. Inevitably, she would fall off, landing on her back, wedged between sofa and wall. There she would lie, panting, tongue lolling, until someone rescued her.

We couldn't walk past Paco's house to collect our bread from Marcia without Bianca. Even if we tiptoed, she would torpedo out, ears streaming behind her, bouncing around us with excitement like a giant furry rubber ball.

"Bianca! Bianca!" came the shout from inside Paco's house. "Bianca? Come back here!"

"Bianca, go home," Joe and I chorused, but to no avail.

So all three of us would go to the shop, two walking, one dancing. Geronimo, sitting outside, would tighten his grip on his beer bottle in anticipation of Bianca's exuberant greeting. His three dogs rolled their eyes at the youngster's undisciplined behaviour. Old Sancho smiled at her cavorting. His black cat narrowed her eyes and arched her back, ready to spit if Bianca came too close. But Bianca was oblivious to hostility - everyone was her very best friend. Despite receiving a scratch on her nose from the cat's lightning paw, Bianca still greeted the cat like a long-lost friend.

I wondered if Bianca's diary would read something like this:

Extract from Bianca's Diary

Saturday

07.00 - Wake up. Hooray! My favourite thing!

08.00 - Breakfast. Hooray! My favourite thing!

10.00 - Get under Carmen-Bethina's feet. Hooray! My favourite thing!

12.00 - Help the English fetch their bread. Hooray! My favourite thing!

13.00 - Chew Sofía's best shoes. Hooray! My favourite thing!

14.00 - Play with Little Paco. Hooray! My favourite thing!

17.00 - Get scolded by Paco. Hooray! My favourite thing!

18.00 - Dinner time. Hooray! My favourite thing!

22.00 - Bed time. Hooray! My favourite thing!

We collected the bread and mail from Marcia, delivered Bianca back home and squeezed our front door closed before she could follow. Until next time.

Perhaps the most unusual gift we ever received came from the sky. Well, not exactly, but it was thrown over the twelve-foot high wall to land in our garden.

TUNA WITH A SPICY SAUCE
ATÚN CON SALSA

There are so many ways to cook tuna, but this recipe with hot paprika and garlic is a big hit with us.

Ingredients

- 2 large fresh tuna steaks or 4 small ones
- 6 garlic cloves
- 3 tablespoons olive oil
- 1 teaspoon hot paprika
- Salt and pepper

Method

- Grill the unpeeled garlic until they become soft.
- Allow to cool a little, then cut the end off each garlic clove and squeeze the garlic flesh into a bowl.
- Add the paprika, olive oil, salt and pepper to the bowl and mix well.
- Place the tuna steaks into a shallow dish, pour over the above sauce and leave to marinade for about half an hour.
- Cook on a barbecue or grill for about 5-6 minutes each side.
- Serve with a salad and boiled potatoes.

27

AND MORE GIFTS

We were inside the house drinking coffee, when we heard a strange noise coming from the garden. It was a flapping, scrabbling, metallic noise. Joe stepped out to see what had caused it. I watched him, framed in the doorway. He stood looking around, turned on his heel, then bent over, obviously peering intently at something on the ground beyond my line of vision.

"Hello…" he said, using the voice he reserves for small children. "Where did you come from?"

My curiosity got the better of me. I went out to join him.

"What is it?" I asked.

There, looking up at us, not flustered in the least, was a chicken. A rather ugly chicken, if I'm perfectly honest. She was very dark brown and tattered, with ragged tail and feathers that stuck out at all angles. She was very young as her comb was barely visible. Her beak was short and blunt where it had been singed off over-zealously by somebody. (Singeing chicks' beaks is a nasty practice still carried out by some who believe it will stop chickens pecking at their own eggs.)

But perhaps the most remarkable thing about this chicken was her boldness. She was not frightened in the least. On the contrary, she took several steps forward and looked up at us quizzically with her head on one side.

"Who are you?" I asked her. "And what are you doing in our garden?"

Chickens can fly quite well, but reluctantly. They only take to the air as a last resort if chased or in a rush to get somewhere, like at feeding time. They never fly high. Therefore we concluded that she did not soar over our twelve-foot wall; she must have been thrown. The noise we had heard was her flapping and her claws trying to grasp the metal staircase that ran up the inside of the wall. Anyway, she landed unharmed and quite unfazed by the experience.

Joe opened the garden gate and looked up and down the street. Nobody there.

"I'll get her something to eat and drink," I said, "while we decide what to do with her."

I walked back into the house, and to my astonishment, she followed me. Usually, chickens head straight for the flower beds, intent on horticultural demolition. But this chicken stayed glued to my heels like an obedient sheepdog. I tested her by changing direction. Still she shadowed me. Wherever I went, she was one chicken step behind.

"Well, you're an odd chicken," I told her. "We'll call you Regalo because you were a present, a gift."

We only had one chicken coop so there was no other option; we were forced to put her in with The Mafia and the others. They were clearly not impressed with Regalo. Attila the Hen led a ferocious attack which sent poor Regalo scuttling up the ramps to the top level.

Meanwhile, Joe and I walked to the shop to collect our bread. Geronimo and Old Sancho sat outside, Geronimo's three dogs slumped at his feet like piles of old carpet.

"*¿Qué tal?*" we asked.

"*Mal,*" Geronimo said, shaking his head grimly.

We entered the shop and Marcia handed us our loaf of bread.

"Marcia, somebody threw a chicken over our garden wall this morning," I said.

"*¿Sí?* I have your post here. To me it looks like a lot of bills. Another loaf of bread tomorrow as usual?"

"Yes, please. Do you know who it belongs to? The chicken, I mean," I persisted.

Marcia shook her head, and the inevitable hairpin flew out. "I saw a chicken walking past the shop this morning," she said. "Wait, I will ask Sancho." She went outside.

"Sancho, the English say today someone threw a chicken over their wall."

Old Sancho listened carefully, a grave expression on his face. He pondered, forehead screwed in concentration. Then he smiled and spoke. Marcia bent low to catch his reply, ear close to his lips, then straightened.

"He says today he saw a chicken walking up the street," she said.

Geronimo then looked up and set his beer bottle down on the bench thoughtfully.

"Was it a brown one?" he asked. "I saw a brown chicken today. It was going in that direction." He waved his Real Madrid scarf in the general direction of our house.

Clearly we were getting nowhere. Everyone had noticed Regalo walking the village streets, but nobody seemed to have lost her. And nobody had seen who threw her over our wall. We thanked them all for their help and returned home to see how Regalo was faring. Not very well, as it turned out. Attila the Hen was determined not to allow her down from the top level. Whenever Regalo ventured back down the ramps, Attila and her hench-hens launched at her, sending her in a flurry back to the top mezzanine.

And there Regalo stayed for six weeks. She became a familiar figure, claws gripping the edge of the platform, head craned down to watch the activity below, body rocking slightly in an effort not to fall over the edge. I put food and water for her on her solitary platform or she may have starved. Even at night she slept up there, whatever the weather. When I went to feed the chickens in the evening, she would wait for the coop gate to open, then hurl herself through the gap. I got used to opening the door and standing back as she flapped into the garden.

Regalo was the only chicken allowed to walk free in the garden, simply because she did not behave like a chicken. She never gobbled my carefully tended flowers and she was never difficult to catch. Instead, she just wanted to be wherever we were. If I was watering the garden, she was at my feet every step of the way. If we sat at the table, she sat beside us, either under the table or on a chair, as though she wanted to join our conversation.

Back in the 19th century, an amateur biologist named Douglas Spalding reported that domestic chickens would 'imprint on' the first suitable moving stimuli they saw thirty-six hours after hatching. The chicks would follow the stimuli (usually a human) imagining it to be their mother. We were convinced that explained Regalo's behaviour. She was imprinted on and considered herself human. Part chicken, part human, she entertained us hugely.

After about six weeks, Attila, Ginger and the others became bored with bullying her. They allowed her down into the coop for short intervals, then for longer periods until she finally integrated into the flock. She still wanted to join us in the garden but she had settled in at last.

To understand how we fell foul of another gift, I must provide a snippet of background history.

In 1868, the archeologist Antonio Gongorra Martinez made an important discovery. In the north of the province of Almería, he came upon some ancient caves. Remarkable bronze and stone age artefacts were unearthed.

One cave was decorated with archaic symbols, figures of archers, mountain goats and deer. But the most common and recurring theme was that of a man holding a rainbow. It is thought that the 'Indalo' or 'Rainbow Man' most likely represented a Shaman or God figure.

In the 1870's, local villagers took to daubing the symbol on their houses as a good luck charm, hoping to ward off evil.

After an earthquake had destroyed the villages of Mojácar and Vera, the surviving inhabitants were understandably nervous. They took to imitating their northern Almerían neighbours whose villages had escaped lightly, believing the Indalo must have protected them.

They copied the practice and made sure the remaining and rebuilt houses of Mojácar and Vera displayed Rainbow Men, too.

And so the Rainbow Men marched across Almería. The prehistoric symbol was adopted as the logo for Almería, and a bringer of good luck. Today you will see the Indalo on car bumpers, statues, T-shirts, key-rings, shop fronts, everywhere.

However, the good luck is conditional. The superstition decrees that the charm will only work if you are given the Indalo as a gift. It's simple - if you are presented with an Indalo, you will enjoy good luck. But beware - an Indalo purchased and carried by yourself will only bring bad luck.

The Rainbow Man figure is curiously attractive. We had several around the house and garden, presented to us at various times.

We were shopping one day when a little Indalo caught my eye. It was about the size of the palm of my hand and cast in some heavy kind of metal. It had sharp, angular lines apart from the lovely sweep of the rainbow. We were leaving the shop but I was strangely drawn back to the little figure.

"Buy it, if you want," said Joe. "You don't believe that superstitious rubbish, do you?"

"Of course not," I said, and purchased the little Indalo.

I slipped it into my jacket pocket with my purse. The weight of it was comforting as it bumped against me as I walked.

We were in the Post Office when I unzipped my pocket and felt for my purse.

"My purse! It's gone!" I said, desperately checking and rechecking the pocket.

The Indalo was still there, but the purse had vanished. Close scrutiny revealed that the sharp angles of the Indalo had torn the pocket lining as I walked, allowing the purse to fall out. The Indalo had caught on the frayed fabric and was safe.

"What a bloody nuisance," said Joe, as we retraced our steps looking for the purse.

"Not a nuisance," I said. "That was the curse of the Indalo! It's because we bought it for ourselves. I don't want it any more. I'm going to throw it away."

"Don't be ridiculous," said Joe. "Here, give it to me."

I handed it over and he put it in the back pocket of his shorts. We didn't find the purse but it hadn't contained much, so its loss wasn't disastrous, just annoying.

We walked back to the car park, heavily laden with shopping. Suddenly, without warning, a car reversed out of its parking space causing Joe to jump back. He stumbled and landed heavily on his backside. The Spanish driver didn't even notice and drove away without a backward glance.

Joe's face was a grimace of pain as I helped him back on his feet. "Did you hurt your back again?" I asked, concerned.

"No, I sat on that bloody Indalo! It really hurt!"

It had to go. We gave the little Indalo to a puzzled passing shopper who thought it was part of a promotion.

"*Regalo, regalo* (a gift)," we insisted, pressing it into her hand. She was bemused, but quite pleased with the present.

Back at home, Joe was still rubbing his backside ruefully. He pulled his shorts aside and we both jumped at the sight. Emblazoned on his left buttock was the perfect imprint of a Rainbow Man, branded in fiery red.

And we were to discover that the Indalo would bide its time - it hadn't finished its mischief yet.

SCRAMBLED EGGS WITH HAM
HUEVOS REVUELTOS CON JAMÓN

Scrambled eggs are a traditional *tapa* in Spain. This recipe uses serrano ham but you can use all kinds of ingredients. Try it with bacon, chorizo, asparagus, mushrooms or onions.

Ingredients

- 50g (2oz) *jamón serrano* or other ham
- 1 tbsp olive oil (for frying)
- 4 eggs
- 2 tbsp milk (optional)
- salt and pepper

Method

- Cut the *jamón* into small pieces.
- Beat the eggs together with the milk (if desired) and season with salt and pepper.
- Stir in the chopped *jamón* and pour into a frying pan. As the egg is cooking, gently stir it until it is cooked through but still very soft. Keep a close eye on it, if you leave it too long it will go like rubber…
- Once it's ready, get it on your plate straight away and serve with crusty bread. Tapas recipes don't come much simpler than this!

28

THE JEEP

When we bought the jeep in England, we were very proud of it. We kept it in our garage and always made sure it was clean and shiny. It had hardly any miles on the clock and was like a new car when we started our life in Spain.

Within a few weeks, things changed. Even though we kept it under cover, the all-pervading Spanish dust swept from the Sahara and into every crevice, inside and out. The paintwork no longer gleamed. The zips on the soft top became temperamental. The upholstery was gritty, and the windscreen was permanently coated beige.

The years in Spain hadn't been kind to the jeep. And it didn't help that we used it to transport bags of cement, firewood, sacks of chicken grain and giant satellite dishes. Gradually it became scratched and dented, well used. The suspension suffered carrying heavy wood-burning stoves and an oil leak appeared. It was our work-horse, no longer pretty but essential.

"I think we ought to get the car serviced," said Joe. "Imagine trying to live up here without a car. It'd be impossible. We really don't want to risk it breaking down."

"What a thought! You're right."

"And we really don't want to be forced to buy a Spanish car, do we? When the five years is up, we'd be stuck with a Spanish car to take back to England." Had more than three years already passed in our Five Year Plan? It was hard to believe.

"Okay, I'll book it in at a garage down below." I searched the Yellow Pages and phoned a garage to make an appointment.

"They want to keep the car for the whole day," I told Joe. "What are we going to do while they work on it?"

"Dunno, take books to read? Or take our swimming stuff and find a public pool?"

"Good idea. Okay, we'll do that. The appointment is for Thursday."

We found the garage without too many problems and left the jeep. The swimming pool was within walking distance and we spent a leisurely day there.

"It's a nice pool, isn't it?" said Joe, climbing out. "And those statues over there are really realistic."

"What statues?"

"There ... on the other side of the fence."

Without my glasses I couldn't see clearly, so I walked over to take a closer look.

"Joe! They're not statues, they're real!"

Over the fence in the park were two ostriches, very much alive. The outsize birds seemed perfectly at home and stood watching the swimmers impassively. The swimmers barely glanced at the ostriches which were evidently a permanent fixture. Time passed quickly as we swam, read our books and watched the ostriches. At six o'clock we walked back to the garage.

"*Lo siento,*" said the mechanic, "I'm sorry, but your car is not ready. We need to keep it for another day."

"But how do we get home? What's wrong with the car? Can't we take it anyway and bring it back tomorrow?" Joe was very annoyed.

"*Lo siento,*" said the mechanic again. "I am sorry but the car is in pieces. You cannot drive it today. I will call you a taxi, *no?*"

We had no choice. Joe grumbled and growled until the taxi drew up and we got in. The driver spoke no English and it took a while for him to understand our destination. The village of El Hoyo was very small and remote. The driver set off, hunched over the wheel, occasionally popping peppermints into his mouth. He turned the radio up high and sang tunelessly to the music.

All went well until we left the city and started climbing the mountain roads. Perhaps the driver was on a promise from his wife. Or perhaps he had played too many arcade games. He took the bends at such speed that we were thrown from one side of the taxi to the other. I gripped onto the hanging strap desperately and tried not to look down the sheer drops.

"Tell him to slow down," I muttered.

Joe leaned forward. "Driver, would you mind slowing down a little, please?"

"¿Qué?"

"Could you please slow down?"

"¿Qué?"

"It's no good, Vicky, he doesn't understand my Spanish. Or he can't hear me over the music."

"Try again."

"Driver! ¡Mas lentemente!"

The driver reached forward and picked up the peppermints. Smiling, he offered the bag to us behind, now steering with one hand, fingertips drumming the wheel in time to the music. He hardly watched the road. I shuddered and closed my eyes, convinced we were about to sail off the road to a chasm below. Joe tried one last tactic. Tapping the driver on the shoulder, he spoke in English, a forced smile stretched over clenched teeth.

"Driver, if you don't slow down I may have to kill you."

The driver looked most alarmed at Joe's manic expression and speeded up. I didn't open my eyes for the rest of the journey.

The garage receptionist phoned the next day. They were sorry, but the jeep needed new parts which they would have to order. We couldn't collect the car for another week.

"What are we going to do?" Joe asked. "No car for a week? We need a car! We can't manage without one."

"I suppose we could hire a car? Let's ask Paco to give us a lift down, then hire a car for a week."

"That'll be expensive."

"Well, why don't we take some time off from working on the house, go and explore the countryside a bit? We could do with an Away-Day, and a rest might cure that cough of yours."

Paco dropped us off at the car hire place, and we chose a Ford Ka. The assistant waved us good-bye, and we set off with our newly purchased map. We headed off up into the mountains for a day of sight-seeing. On the way home, we drove into the town of Almerimar. Neither of us liked the look of it much, too many hotels and high rises. However, as we were exploring, it seemed churlish not at least to take a peek at the beach.

In spite of his military background, Joe has a healthy disregard of rules, almost an allergy. If Joe were to see a red button marked 'Do Not Press Under Any Circumstances', he'd press it before I could even squeak. I am the complete opposite. I need to read the instructions, ponder, research it, think some more, make a list, and even then I wouldn't press the button. So, of course Joe ignored the large signs that ordered us in Spanish, English, French, German, Mongolian, etc. not to drive on the beach. Instead, he revved up the engine.

"I hope you're not going to drive on the beach," I said. "Look at all those warning signs."

"Hey! Tyre tracks," he said. "People obviously drive on the beach all the time."

"Those aren't car tracks, they're tractor tyre marks," I pointed out, but too late.

The little Ford Ka had the heart of a powerful 4-wheel drive, but unfortunately only the build and engine size of a ... well ... Ford Ka. It was willing, even enthusiastic, but as we drove towards the gloriously setting sun, it struggled, sank, then shuddered to a halt.

"We're stuck!" I hissed, furious.

"No problem, I'll sort it," said Joe, trying to open the car door. The Ka, in its eagerness to please had buried itself neatly and solidly in the soft sand. So deep were we that even opening the doors was impossible.

"Now what?" I asked.

Joe ignored me. Military responses had presumably kicked in. He squirmed out of the open window and landed headfirst in an undignified heap beside the car, spitting sand and swearing.

"Have we got a shovel?" he asked. That didn't deserve a reply. Who takes a shovel with them when they're going for a drive?

"Okay, Plan B," he muttered and began to dig away at the sand with the Andalucían roadmap until he opened the door enough for me to get out, too. We both worked feverishly at clearing sand away from the wheels, but we were going nowhere.

The beach was almost deserted. A lone horseman cantered away in the distance silhouetted against the setting sun. Waves lapped gently. The half-buried car waited patiently. As the sun dipped and the beach grew dark, we waited. And waited.

A figure materialised out of the twilight, walking in our direction ... salvation! Not exactly a knight in shining armour, but a smart, elderly Spaniard taking a constitutional and walking his dog. Judging by his clothes, he was dressed for a night out. Joe galloped wildly across the sand to intercept him, gesturing and gibbering like a lunatic.

"Excuse me, can you help us, please?"

"¿Qué pasa?"

"Over there..." Joe pointed at our stranded car then dissolved in a coughing fit.

One glance was enough for the man to sum up the situation. "¡Madre mia!" He generously only pointed out the warning sign briefly then shrugged. Rolling his eyes heavenward, he carefully removed and folded his smart jacket. Then he joined Joe at the back of the car. Such a nice man.

"Vicky! Accelerate now!"

I pressed my foot down on the pedal as they pushed. In the wing mirror I could see the man straining until the veins stood out on his temples.

"Faster! Accelerate harder!"

The little car lurched forward bravely but its wheels spun and a great arc of sand plumed out. The poor man was covered from coiffured hair to polished shoes. It was as though someone had dumped a bucket of sand over him. There was sand in his pockets, sand in his trouser turn-ups, probably sand in places he wouldn't discover for days. Even his dog looked sympathetic.

Our new best friend snorted in disgust. Picking up his folded jacket, he stomped away into the gloom, muttering something that sounded suspiciously like *"gente Inglesa idiota"* (stupid English people). His dog followed without a backward glance. Perhaps we would still be there if it hadn't been for an English couple taking a late walk. They went home, collected their monster 4-wheel drive and kindly pulled us out. Joe and I drove back home barely speaking. Only Joe's coughs punctured the silence.

The answer-phone's red light was flashing when we got back. I lifted the receiver, hoping it was good news from the garage. Instead it was Judith on the end of the line.

SPINACH AND MACKEREL TOASTS

A lovely, colourful, slightly unusual, tasty dish for summer days. Great for an aperitif, buffet, *tapas* party dish, or whatever takes your fancy.

Ingredients (makes about 10)

- 2 small tins mackerel fillets in olive oil
- 1 french style baguette cut into rounds (make the cut diagonally to get bigger rounds)
- Bunch fresh spinach
- 2 cloves garlic

Method

- Wash and drain the spinach, peel and finely chop the garlic.
- Drain the oil from the mackerel, place onto a plate and roughly break up the fillets with a fork.
- Heat a little olive oil in a pan and gently cook the garlic until it begins to soften.
- Add the spinach and cook covered for a minute or so.
- Turn the spinach over to get a good coating of oil, put the lid back on and cook for a further minute.
- Remove from the pan and drain away any excess liquid.
- Toast the bread lightly on each side and arrange onto a large plate.
- Place a small amount of spinach onto each piece of toast and

then top with the mackerel.

29

DOCTOR'S ORDERS

"Vicky? Joe? Dammit, I loathe these infernal machines. Vicky, would you be an absolute angel and pop round tomorrow? Mother's under the weather again and we've had the quack out. He's given her a prescription and I wondered if you'd be kind enough to pick it up for her tomorrow? Only if you're going down the mountain, of course, don't you know…Tyson, I do wish you'd stop that! Good Lord, Curly…Buster! That's an antique! Now, where was I? Oh, yes, the bloody prescription. Might see you tomorrow then, toodley pip!"

Next day, we knocked on Judith's door, setting off the hounds baying within. Judith opened the door, fighting back the pack.

"Vicky! Joe! Frightfully good of you," she said, letting us in.

"How's Mother?" I asked.

"Well, dear," she said in a stage whisper. "Quite honestly, I'd say she's fine today. But when she heard the doctor was dropping in this morning, she took herself straight back to bed."

"That's odd," I said. "Why do you think…" I stopped as a man came into the hall.

"Vicky, Joe, I don't think you've met *Dottore* Esteban, have you?" said Judith. The doctor was young and easy on the eyes. Crisp, dark hair curled over his collar, and he had a decisive handshake.

"How do you do, Madam, Sir? I am, ah, very pleased to meet you." The doctor's English was excellent, if formal.

"The good doctor has just finished upstairs, dears. He says Mother just needs a tonic and she'll be right as rain."

"Oh, that's good news," I said. "We'll pick up the prescription for her today."

"Excuse me, Sir. That is a nasty cough you have," said the doctor, turning to Joe. "Ah, perhaps Sir will permit me a quick examination?"

"Well, I…"

"That's a good idea!" I said. "Joe hates going to the doctor and he's had that cough for ages."

"Well…"

"Good!" said the doctor briskly. "I have my stethoscope here. If you'd kindly open your shirt…"

Joe had no choice, and obeyed without further protest.

"Hmm… Cough now… Ah, I think you have a little chest infection. A course of antibiotics will be the best thing. I will write for you a prescription. I believe you live in El Hoyo? Ah, next week I will be visiting El Hoyo. I am seeing Sancho Lopez."

"Old Sancho at the shop?"

"That is correct. And now I must go. Ah, one last thing… I believe you have chickens?"

"Er, yes, one or two."

"Fresh eggs, ah, delicious. So tasty. I will see you next Wednesday."

We got the hint. I mentally crossed scrambled eggs off our menu for the week. The doctor left and we went upstairs to pay our respects to Mother. The scent of Chanel No.5 assailed our nostrils even before we entered her bedroom.

Mother was sitting bolt upright in bed, propped up by enormous, frilly pillows. I was expecting to see a frail old lady, but she looked wonderful, and as sprightly as ever. Her almost transparent negligee was topped by a saucy bed-jacket. Her face was fully made-up, and ringlets of silver hair cascaded around her shoulders. There was a dent in the bed where the doctor had sat.

"Has the doctor gone?" murmured Mother, smoothing the satin sheet with her manicured hand. "Most awfully handsome, isn't he?"

"Mother! You're old enough to be his bloody great-grandmother!" Judith's outraged voice floated in from behind us.

Mother smiled, fluttered her false eyelashes and sipped from her wine glass. I noticed another one, empty, on her bedside table. Joe and I took our leave, went downstairs and waded through dogs to reach the front door.

"Well, that was lucky, wasn't it?" I said as we drove away. "That doctor might sort out your cough. And you wouldn't get a doctor calling on you at home like that in England, would you? Better than the National Health, if you ask me."

"Huh, we'll see."

We collected the prescriptions and delivered Mother's to Judith. At home, we picked up another answer-phone message. The garage had called to say the jeep was ready. So the next day we drove yet again to the city, collected the jeep and returned the hire car. The assistant at the car hire place didn't notice the sand in every nook and cranny, and we didn't point it out.

The repairs to the jeep and the service were not cheap, but we felt the money was justified. Unfortunately, the oil leak soon reappeared but we couldn't face taking it back to the garage.

"How do you complain effectively in Spanish?" despaired Joe. "Now, if this was England…"

I cut him short. I didn't want to hear. I hated hearing anything that might help Joe decide we should leave Spain at the end of our five years.

Wednesday came round quickly and the doctor called.

"Hmm…" he said after examining Joe. "Your cough is no better. Ah, I think we need a more direct course of antibiotics. I think we will put you on a course of regular injections. I can, ah, give you a choice."

"A choice? What sort of a choice?"

"Ah, well, you can drive down to the Centro Medico for the injections. Or one of the ladies in the village can give you the injection. Ah, she's very experienced."

Joe looked at me and made up his mind. "Okay, I'll go to the lady in the village. That'll save me driving down the mountain every time."

"Good, then I will give Marcia the medication. Ah, you know

Marcia Lopez at the shop? Good, your first injection will be on, ah, Monday, next week. Now, I must go, and, ah, thank you very much for the eggs."

"Marcia?" spluttered Joe when I returned from seeing the doctor out. "I didn't know she was a nurse! I'm not sure I like the sound of this!"

I kept quiet. I didn't think Marcia was a nurse either, just a wise and experienced old lady. And I didn't accompany him for his first visit that Monday. He returned grim-faced and flopped into a chair.

"How did you get on?" I asked.

A long pause. "It was awful. Awful."

"Why? Why was it awful?"

"When I got there, Marcia was behind the counter as usual. She told me to come into the kitchen because she'd got my stuff all ready there. So I follow her into the kitchen, and all her family are sitting there."

"Old Sancho?"

"Yes, Old Sancho, and those sons of theirs, and their wives. Oh, and a couple of teenagers - and some little ones. There were loads of people sitting round that huge table of theirs."

"So what happened?"

"Well, you know how polite everybody is... They all stood up and offered to leave the room while she did the injection. But I said, don't worry, stay where you are... I didn't want to disturb them."

"Did they leave the room?"

"No, I absolutely insisted they stay. So they all sat down again. I pushed my sleeve up for the injection but Marcia kept shaking her head like mad. You know how she is - hairpins flying everywhere. Anyway, she was pointing at my trousers..."

"Oh!"

"Vicky, I had to pull my trousers down so that she could inject me in the backside. In front of all those people."

"Oh, you poor thi..." Stopping myself laughing was difficult.

"That's not all. As if that wasn't bad enough! When Marcia gave me the injection, she said '¡Madre mia!' and pointed to my bottom, then prattled away to her relatives. I couldn't see them because they were all behind me. Anyway, they all went quiet then started laughing."

"Why? Why would they do that?" I asked, trying hard to compose myself.

"Well, I've only just realised myself… It was that bloody Indalo branded on my backside, wasn't it? That's what was amusing them."

I couldn't speak.

"You can laugh, but how would you have liked it? I tell you, give me the National Health any day."

I stopped laughing. My hopes for staying permanently in Spain were looking decidedly shaky.

Five short years. Five years nearly gone, and I was still desperate to stay in beautiful Spain. The thought of leaving was devastating but a deal was a deal. If Joe wanted to return to England, then I'd promised to agree.

I couldn't bear to bring up the subject. I couldn't bear to think of selling our house, giving the chickens away and turning our backs on the village and our friends for ever. It was Joe who finally brought the subject up.

"Five years are almost up," he said. "I think we should go on holiday."

"But we're on holiday every day already!" I kept my voice lighter than I felt.

"Vicky, we always said this was a Five Year Plan. I want to go somewhere totally different, somewhere neutral. Not England, not Spain. I want to enjoy a holiday away from everything and think about the future."

So there was still hope. I knew Joe wasn't exactly unhappy, but how much did he want to go back to England? Was I being selfish wanting him to stay? Just how much did he miss the National Health, English food, English friends and the familiar English way of life?

"Okay, that's a good idea. Where do you fancy going?"

"I want to go somewhere exotic. Are we still members of that home exchange site?"

"Yep, is that what you'd like to do? Swap houses again?"

"Why not? This house is finished now. And I think we should go for quite a long time - perhaps a couple of months. Then I'll have time to think, and decide if we should go back to Britain."

HomeExchange.com was a fabulous site. We'd discovered it in England a few years before. We'd posted up our details, then had the pleasure of having people from all over the world contact us wanting to exchange homes for a holiday. That first time, we'd agreed to swap with a retired American couple.

What a holiday we had! We swapped everything: house, car, computer and friends - for a blissful month. For four weeks we stayed in a mansion on a private island in South Carolina. We drove their Mercedes, played pool in their billiard room and drove their golf cart down to the private beach. The island was a nature reserve, and wild deer came right up to the house.

In return, Chuck and Barb stayed in our modest suburban house, drove our little jeep and went sightseeing in West Sussex. We felt it was an uneven swap but they assured us they were delighted.

"We sure enjoyed visiting your castles," Barb had drawled. "And we went to see where your Battle of Hastings took place. Britain sure does have a whole lot of history."

"And your cute jeep was awful good fun!" said Chuck. "He raised his silver eyebrows and paused, "Have to say we found your roundabouts a bit testing, though."

This time we had a quirky house in a tiny, remote mountain village to offer. Would anyone want to sample Spanish village life? We needn't have worried. As before, plenty of people contacted us, but it was Ken and Glennys' email that stood out.

From: G&KFlagstaff@gotalk.net.au
Subject: Possible Exchange
1 attachment: home.jpg

G'day!

Wondered if you'd be interested in exchanging with us sometime around Sep/Oct/Nov? We have a large house overlooking the golf course with private swimming pool. Close to shopping, beaches and hinterland. Pleasant 4 hr drive to Barrier Reef. We'd love the opportunity to improve our Spanish and experience real village life.

Hope to hear from you,

Cheers,

Ken and Glennys Flagstaff.

Queensland, Australia? Private swimming pool? Of course we were interested! We replied immediately and so began our cyber friendship. Over the next few months we corresponded, the level of excitement in our emails rising as the exchange date drew closer.

Paco and Carmen-Bethina were totally bewildered by the concept.

"¡Madre mia!" said Carmen-Bethina. "And you have never met these people? How do you know they will not ruin your house? They could steal everything!"

"We've been writing to each other for ages. We've seen their photos, we know about their two grown-up children, Rob and Amy. They don't seem like strangers."

"Pah!" said Paco, setting the wine bottle down with a thump. "What is wrong with El Hoyo? El Hoyo is the best place in the world! Carmen and I have never been out of Andalucía..." he leaned forward, eyes bulging, "...and we don't want to!"

"¡Claro!" Carmen-Bethina nodded her head in agreement.

After a frenzy of lists and preparation, the day came to collect Ken and Glennys from the airport. I recognised them easily from the photographs; it was like meeting old friends. We managed to squeeze their luggage into the jeep and set off back to the village. We had 24 hours together before they would take us back to the airport to catch a plane to Australia.

There was a lot to show and tell. We had just enough time to point out the quirks of the house and car, and introduce the chickens. Then Joe and I were in the sky, looking down on Andalucía, heading to Australia. From now on, the only contact we'd have with our Spanish life was via email.

WARMING WINTER'S BRUNCH
DESAYUNO

This is a very traditional Andalucían breakfast, typically eaten by farmers, shepherds and workers during the winter months.

Ingredients

- 5 - 6 cloves garlic
- 1 red pepper
- 1 jar white beans (or chickpeas, or baked beans)
- 3 or 4 sweet or spicy chorizos
- Olive oil

Method

- Peel and roughly chop the garlic.
- Remove the top and seeds from the pepper, chop into bite-sized chunks.
- In a large frying pan, heat the olive oil and add the garlic and peppers and fry until slightly coloured.
- Chop up the chorizo also into bite-sized chunks and add to the pan, cook for a few minutes on a high heat.
- Add the beans and than lower the heat, cover and cook gently for 20 mins.
- Serve with thick slices of fresh bread.

30

HOUSE SWAP

From: G&KFlagstaff@gotalk.net.au
Subject: Welcome to Aus!!

Hi Joe and Vicky,
Hope that by the time you open this you will have had a good rest to help you get over your long and tiring trip. How was the journey? Hope that you are settling in at our home and that everything is ok for you? Did Rob pick you up ok?
We made it back to El Hoyo after dropping you off at the airport - no problems....no wrong turns or anything. Ventured into the city yesterday to do some shopping but everywhere was closed...must have been a public holiday or something. Ken fiddled with the zip on the jeep and got it working ok...so don't worry about it. Everything here is good, so just relax and enjoy yourselves.
Talk later
Glennys
PS Who is that old man who wonders round the village in the evenings? He's always got a black cat following him.

From: G&KFlagstaff@gotalk.net.au
Subject: Greetings from El Hoyo!

Hi Joe and Vicky,
Very glad you love our home and Rob picked you up from the airport ok. He's pretty reliable. Have you met Amy yet? Did she leave the house nice and tidy for you? Surprised you've never seen a vacuum system like ours before. Very handy just plugging the tube into the wall.
Went shopping again - more successful this time. Well armed with the dictionary of course!! Couldn't find a number of things, but maybe they're not available here. Anyway, had a good time and think that we're set up for the next month!!
Having a try of the sticky pudding recipe today to see if it works…if it is a disaster I think I will leave town before the fiesta!!
The mouse has to be docked in the dock in order to charge, but you sometimes have to wriggle it until the green light flashes. Ask Rob if you can't get it working.
Somebody called Judith phoned. Couldn't hear properly because of dogs barking, but I think she just called in case we needed anything.
Very kind of her.
Hope you enjoy the pool today…the weather here is perfect.
Till later
G & K
PS Don't forget to ask Amy or Rob if you have any questions. Isn't that what kids are for? Telephone numbers on the fridge.

From: G&KFlagstaff@gotalk.net.au
Subject: Fiesta - wow!!!!!!!!!!!

'Hola' to you both,
Sorry we haven't written for a few days, but it's been the fiesta and you obviously know what that's like!!!!!!!!
Rob phoned and said you've had thunderstorms. It's always like that in

Q'land this time of year. Hope that you've been able to get some swimming in between storms.

Fiesta ends today and I'll be glad to have an end to all the rocket blasts that I'm sure are undermining the foundations of the house! The noise has frightened off the cats and dogs and put the chooks off their laying...apart from deafening me and Ken!!!

Pudding contest went well and I managed to pull off first prize!!! I think the fact that the mayor was being kind to visitors (and I think he likes blonde ladies) may have had a lot to do with it. Very nice of them all though. You said that they liked sweet and sticky and that's what they got. Had lots of nice comments about it from the women...not that I could understand them except for their gestures. Everyone's been very helpful and kind to us. Last night we went and joined in a bit of the dancing...not as much as we we would have liked, but we had to be careful not to overtax Ken's knees. The band was very good and the singer excellent.

For my prize they gave me a very nice 24 piece crockery set, which is lovely, but weighs a ton and there's no way that we can pack it in our suitcase. So I'll leave it here in the hopes that you can use it or give it to someone else. Everything here is going well, we plan to investigate some of the other little towns around here once the Fiesta is over and we recover.

Till later -

Glennys and Ken

PS Took lots of photos of the Fiesta and competition. Too tired to do anything more today, but will get Ken to send them tomorrow.

PPS Weather is beautiful. Will write out the Sticky Toffee recipe for you.

From: G&KFlagstaff@gotalk.net.au
Subject: Lazy chooks?

Hello again,

So glad that you're enjoying yourselves and that Rob got you tickets to the Indy too. Yes, I agree - deafening and smelly but VERY exciting. Those cars go so fast!!

The chooks are not behaving at all....we've only had 2 eggs since the Fiesta.......Ken has talked to them, sung to them and is now threatening them with the pot........all to no avail I'm afraid. He's checked all around and there are none hidden and no evidence that they are eating them...so don't know what we can do?
Really enjoying sitting on the roof terrace, but I think there are even more Spanish flies than Aussie ones! How do you put up with them?
Getting the hang of the bread, fruit and fish vans that come to the village now. Bit different to our shopping malls back home!
Cheers from
Glennys and Ken
PS Hope you like the photos! (See free Photobook 1)

From: G&KFlagstaff@gotalk.net.au
Subject: Gas fire

Hi again,
Just a quick question...can you help us by explaining again how to light the gas heater? The weather has gone a lot colder recently and we realize that as it may get even colder in the next month we thought we should know how to light the heater. Ken had a look and is not keen to press buttons until he knows what they do...we would hate to blow up the house!
Had a visit from the village kids last night doing trick or treat. (It was 1'clock in the morning!!!) Paco was with them and came in and chatted to us for a while. He asked us to say Hi. We managed a conversation in spite of our poor Spanish.
Seems that Marcia's husband is poorly and they are staying with family down below. Obviously the shop is closed now too but we met a really nice villager called Geronimo. He's got long curly hair and always wears a football scarf and he's really friendly. Do you know who I mean? He brings us our bread sometimes if we don't hear the van. Often stays for a drink. Can't half put it away!
Seems that Paco is very happy with his grapes for his wine this year too.

Enjoy your trip to Hervey Bay. Hope the whales perform for you. You may see some calves, too.
Bye for now,
Glennys

From: *G&KFlagstaff@gotalk.net.au*
Subject: *Wildlife*

Yes, do go ahead and feed the lorikeets - they're the cute rainbow coloured little ones. And feed the kookaburras if you want, but DON'T feed the cockatoos!! They've got vicious beaks and will tear the fly screens to shreds to find food.
Glennys

From: *G&KFlagstaff@gotalk.net.au*
Subject: *Malo Suerte*

Hello Vicky and Joe,
Ken here. Sorry we haven't been in touch for a while. I'm afraid we've had a bit of a mishap.
Glennys and I were taking a nice walk outside the village towards the little white shrine when Glennys slipped on the gravel pathway. We thought she'd just sprained her ankle but it blew up like a balloon and she couldn't walk. I had to get the jeep and put the old girl in the car without moving the ankle - then drive down the mountain to the hospital.
Anyway, we found the hospital after asking for directions and it turns out she has a spiral fracture of the fibula. She's going to need surgery - pins and screws. We've got travel insurance so after long talks they arranged for her to be transferred to a private hospital in Almería. Got to say, I didn't realise that was an hour away, and I had to follow the Ambo - siren, flashing blue lights, everything. Your poor little jeep had to follow in the dark, at breakneck speeds of 130-140kmph. It was horrendous - through red lights and overtaking all in

sight, while being honked at and abused by other motorists who must have wondered what the hell I was doing. I knew I couldn't afford to lose the Ambo otherwise I wouldn't know where I was. Miraculously we all arrived together at the hospital and the treatment the old girl is receiving is excellent.
Anyway, she's comfortable now and I'll keep you posted.
Hope you are well and still enjoying QLD.
Best wishes,
Ken

From: G&KFlagstaff@gotalk.net.au
Subject: Back in the village

Hola both of you,
Well, I'm back in the village, and Ken and I can't believe the villagers' kindness. Geronimo brings me handpicked roses, Carmen next door is supplying enough food for us each weekend to last most of the week (some of which we don't recognize...probably a good job too!!) and we've had other visits from previously unknown villagers who were no doubt eager to view the latest curiosity!
Of course I can't get round the house much on crutches on the tiles (too scary!) so I miss the daily visits to the roof terrace. Don't miss the flies though!
Don't know who, (Geronimo maybe?) has arranged for the doctor to call each week. Seems to produce a flurry of great excitement as people we've never seen before call to announce the imminent arrival of the doctor. Obviously I'm honoured to received such a highly esteemed visitor!
Funny though, the only bruise I got as a result of the daily injection to prevent blood clots came from this revered doctor. Ken manages every other day without pain or bruising to me. Maybe Ken's missed his calling!
Anyway, don't worry, we're coping.
Hope you're still having fun in Aus.
Glennys
PS Have been doing a lot of reading.

From: G&KFlagstaff@gotalk.net.au
Subject: Wrapping up

Hi again,
Just making final arrangements. Ken's cleaned the house ready for your return and I hope you'll find everything in order. The chooks are fine, but still refusing to lay - sorry!
Paco offered to take us to the airport amid much chest thumping and insisting, but the insurance company have laid on a taxi. Felt that we were personally offending him by refusing and felt really bad. Hope he understood.
The taxi is coming at 6.00 a.m. so Ken will have to stand in the square with a torch and wait for him, then guide him here. If anybody's awake and sees him they'll be even more convinced that Australian people are very odd!!
Anyway, in spite of the accident - this has been an amazing holiday. We've house swapped ten times before, but this holiday has been unique. I don't think we'll ever forget the kindness, friendliness and hospitality of El Hoyo.
Thank you.
Do keep in touch,
All the very best,
Glennys and Kenneth
PS Nearly forgot- sad news- the old man (Sancho?) husband of Marcia at the shop died last week. Thought you'd want to know.

Joe had still said not one single word about leaving or staying, and I hadn't dared broach the subject. It was too painful. I would just have to wait.

I peered down at Andalucía as the plane began its descent. It was midwinter, but the Spanish sun still bathed the mountains, shadows throwing the cultivated terraces into sharp relief. Little whitewashed villages glinted, connected by brown meandering roads. I could even see the sparkle of mountain streams and a shepherd surrounded by his sheep. I drank it all in. My hands gripped the arm-rests; we'd be back in El Hoyo in a couple of hours...

Joe leaned over me and gazed down at the view. He said something, but the aeroplane engine noise as it prepared for landing drowned out his words.

"Pardon? What did you say?" I strained to hear him.

Joe squeezed my hand and tried again, louder this time.

"It's wonderful to be home, isn't it?" he said.

STICKY TOFFEE PUDDING A LA GLENNYS
FIESTA WINNING RECIPE!

This is the recipe that won the Pudding Contest at the village fiesta.

Ingredients

PUDDING:

- 1 ¼ cups chopped dates
- 1 ¼ cups water
- 1 teaspoon bicarbonate of soda
- 60g (2oz) butter
- ¼ cup castor sugar
- 2 eggs
- 1 cup self-raising flour

SAUCE:

- 200g (8oz) brown sugar, firmly packed
- 1 cup fresh cream
- 20g (1oz) butter

Method

- Grease a deep round cake tin. Line the base with paper. Grease both the pan and the paper.
- Combine dates and water in a saucepan and bring to the

boil. Remove from heat, add soda and stand 5 mins.
- Blend or process until smooth.
- Cream butter and sugar in a small bowl with a mixer until combined.
- Beat in eggs one at a time.
- Fold in the flour, then date mixture.
- Bake in moderate oven for about 50 mins or until cooked through.
- Allow to cool slightly and then turn onto a rack over an oven tray.
- Pour ¼ cup of sauce over the pudding and return to the oven.
- Bake uncovered for 5 mins more.
- Serve with sauce and whipped cream.

Toffee sauce:

- Combine sugar, cream and butter in a saucepan and stir over heat without boiling until sugar is dissolved.
- Simmer for 3 mins stirring all the time.

> "This is the recipe that I used……however I had to improvise in Spain as the ingredients seemed a little different and we needed a larger amount. I added some chocolate powder to the cake mix, and I baked it in a large dish, not a tin, without turning out and over. I just poured some extra sauce over the top and then cooked it for a few extra minutes and served direct from the large dish."

Glennys, Australian Home Exchanger

31

EPILOGUE

I found That List the other day. It was pushed into the back of a drawer, yellowed and forgotten. I unfolded it and checked it off mentally.

Sunny weather - *True. No argument there.*
Cheap houses - *Well, yes, but we're not selling ours anyway.*
Live in the country - *Yes, we do.*
Ridiculously low council tax - *Still true.*
Friendly people - *True. And not just friendly, but generous, kind, quirky, welcoming…in short, just wonderful.*
Less crime - *True. (Apart from being burgled at that hotel when we were house hunting.)*
No heating bills - *NOT true! Nights are freezing during winter.*
Cheap petrol - *Cheaper than Britain, yes, but rising all the time.*
Wonderful Spanish food - *Absolutely no argument with that…*
Cheap wine and beer - *Oh, yes!*
Could get satellite TV so you won't miss football - *We did, and Joe's only missed one match. That was due to a magpie flying into the dish. Both magpie and dish survived.*

Much more laid-back life style - *Absolutely!*
Could afford house big enough for family and visitors to stay - *That one's backfired a bit. We get too many visitors...*
No TV licence - *True.*
Only short flight to UK - *True, but we rarely go.*
Might live longer because Mediterranean diet is healthiest in the world - *Don't know yet, time will tell.*

I could clearly see where Joe's pen had gone through the paper when he'd added to the list so long ago.

CAN'T SPEAK SPANISH! - *Well, still got a long way to go but we can chat in Spanish quite easily now.*
TOO MANY FLIES! - *He was dead right about that! Our record stands at 72 flies swatted in one sitting.*
MOVING HOUSE IS THE PITS! - *Yes, it is, but as we aren't moving again, who cares?*

We are still in contact with Glennys and Ken. They send frequent emails describing their latest house swaps: other parts of Australia, New Zealand, Vietnam... Rob, their son, is touring Australia with his family in a motorhome. It seems travelling is in the family blood.

Judith remains a good friend of ours. She has another dog she's named 'Invisible'. So now she has nine and a 'Half' and one that's 'Invisible'. She always said she'd never have ten.

Mother celebrated her ninetieth birthday recently. She is frail, but still fashion-conscious and feisty. The aroma of Chanel No.5 and herbal cigarettes linger wherever she goes.

Old Sancho is sadly missed. His walking stick still leans in a corner of the shop, gathering cobwebs. His black cat now follows Marcia all the time. She scolds it when it winds around her feet and trips her up, but she never pushes it away. Last spring the cat had a liason with a battle-scarred old tom in the village. Marcia gave us one of the resulting kittens, and we've named him 'Sancho'. Marcia approves. Little Sancho is the bane of Thief Cat's life, pestering the poor old thing when she wants to sleep, but he's a source of constant delight to us.

On very quiet evenings, I sometimes hear a strange but familiar sound. Soft footsteps are shuffling up the street. Little Sancho hears it, too. He stops chasing Thief Cat's tail and pricks up his ears. It sounds like 'tap, tap, paaarp, tap, tap, paaarp' approaching. I smile. Old Sancho is taking his evening stroll.

Sometimes the ship's bell rings, but there is no-one there. I know it is Pepa, coming for eggs and to tell me the latest village gossip.

Kurt drops by occasionally. *"Ja,* this is a good house," he says, looking round. "You haf done good verk."

The Gin Twins visit every year, sometimes twice. They bring welcome gifts of Marmite, English books and news from our former life. Gin sales at the city supermarket always soar at this time.

Geronimo continues to be employed by the council. He's also been appointed as a kind of village police officer. It's probably fortunate that El Hoyo isn't a crime hotspot. He has a brand new Real Madrid scarf, and has tied the old one to his television aerial. It unfurls in the wind, flapping above the village roofs, a banner and reminder of his beloved football team.

Uncle Felix visits us every February to supervise the pruning of our vine. He's a little more bent every year and has lost his last two remaining teeth, but his mule still adores him.

Great Aunt Elsa has pride of place above the mantlepiece. She continues to watch over us and is much admired by the villagers.

We only have six chickens now. As before, we rarely eat eggs as they get given away faster than the chickens can lay them.

El Hoyo continues to thrive. Some more new houses have sprung up and there are fresh faces in the village. EEC money has paid for a better road down the mountain to the city, cutting the journey by half.

Paco and Carmen-Bethina still live next door. Paco's face is a little more lined and leathery, and Carmen-Bethina is rounder, but they never really change. Joe and I are always welcome, but still referred to as 'The English'. Little Paco has grown tall and attends the High School. His favourite subject is football. Sofía has a boyfriend, but assures her parents he isn't 'The One'.

But Paco and Carmen-Bethina now have their dearest wish; at last they have become proud grandparents. The wife of Diego, their eldest son, recently gave birth to a little girl. This baby, together with others born to village families ensure the future of El Hoyo.

And so life goes on...

A REQUEST...

We authors absolutely rely on our readers' reviews. We love them even more than a glass of chilled wine on a summer's night beneath the stars.

Even more than chocolate.

If you enjoyed this book, I'd be so grateful if you left a review, even if it's simply one sentence.

THANK YOU!

SO WHAT HAPPENED NEXT?
A PREVIEW OF THE NEXT BOOK IN THE SERIES

Two Old Fools ~ Olé!

Never believe that life in a tiny Spanish mountain village is predictable. Vicky and Joe have finished fixing up their house and look forward to peaceful days enjoying their retirement. Then the fish van arrives, and instead of delivering fresh fish, disgorges the Ufarte family. The peace of El Hoyo is shattered.

Chapter 1
The Fish Van

Joe and I were in the kitchen, drinking coffee and feeling deliciously smug. It was a Monday morning in April and we were remembering what Mondays used to bring, back in the grey old days, before we moved to Spain.

"We're so lucky, aren't we?" I said. "In England, we would've been getting ready to go to work. You'd have been stressing about getting your uniform sorted, or paperwork prepared. And I'd be planning my lessons and worrying about getting reports done, or staff meetings, or whatever."

Joe nodded. "Yep! Instead, we're sitting here, listening to the cuckoo in the valley and Geronimo's donkey singing to his girlfriend in the next village. I might even start writing my book soon."

I was unconvinced. Not a word of Joe's masterpiece had been committed to either paper or word-processor as yet. His book was a bit of a standing joke.

One of the chickens launched into her Egg Song, the triumphant announcement that another egg had just been introduced into the world.

"And new-laid eggs for breakfast," I said.

I sighed, the self-satisfied sigh of the truly content. Five years had passed since we'd left England behind and set up home in El Hoyo. Five years of living in a crazy, tiny mountain village, miles away from the nearest big town.

I stole a glance at Joe across the kitchen table. When you've been living with somebody for a long time, you can sense when something is bothering him. Joe was deep in thoughts of his own.

"You are glad we decided to stay in Spain, aren't you?" I asked, after a pause.

"Of course I am! It's a wonderful life here."

"Then what are you thinking about?"

"Nothing. It's just that sometimes I..."

"Sometimes you what?"

Joe held his hand up, a signal for me to remain silent. "Shh, Vicky... Is that the fish van?" he asked, a puzzled expression creasing his brow.

I stopped and listened. I could hear birds, the chickens scratching outside and, yes, the distant familiar hoot of the fish van.

"That's odd," I said. "The fish van doesn't usually come on a Monday in April. There aren't enough people in the village to buy fish. Let's take our coffee up to the roof terrace and look."

"You're so nosy," said Joe, but he followed me just the same, and picked up the binoculars on the way.

On the far side of the valley, we could see the white fish van wending its way down the twisting mountain road, horn beeping to announce its arrival as it always did. But it was not alone, it headed a procession. The convoy consisted of three vehicles. First the fish van, then a largish truck with canvas sides and finally a black minibus. Any traffic in the village during the week was unusual, but a convoy?

"What is that writing on the side of the truck?" I asked.

Joe focused the binoculars and concentrated. "Er, I think it says, 'Ufarte' and 'Almería'."

We digested this gem of information in silence.

"Ufarte?" I repeated at last. "Are you sure?"

"Yep, quite sure. Ufarte."

As the three vehicles entered the village, all three drivers leaned on their horns and wound down their windows allowing three different sets of music to blare out into the valley.

Joe and I exchanged glances. Who were these people? What were they doing in our village? We had a bird's eye view from our roof terrace and we froze in horror as the raucous convoy thundered past the village square, turned into our street, and parked below, right outside our house...

READ MORE

BOOKCLUB DISCUSSION QUESTIONS
23 TALKING POINTS

1. If you had to explain to somebody what 'Chickens' was about in one sentence, what would you say?
2. Do you feel you grew to know the author's character through the book? Could you identify with her? When?
3. Choose some keywords that describe the author, and some to describe Joe.
4. Were there situations you could identify with? If so, which and how?
5. How important is the setting of the book? If you know rural Spain, do you think the author paints a true picture? If you've never been to rural Spain, can you imagine it now?
6. Would you ever like to visit El Hoyo? Can you see yourself living there and being part of village life? Would you take part in the fiesta activities and compete in the pudding contest?
7. Have you ever considered moving abroad? If so, does this book put you off, or does it make you want to start planning?
8. How realistic was the characterisation? Would you want to meet any of the characters? Did you like them? Are there any you would want to avoid? Which was your favourite and least favourite?
9. Did the stories make you laugh? If so, which ones, and why did you find them funny?
10. Did any events in the book make you feel sad? The author shed tears as she wrote one part, can you guess which it was?
11. There are lots of animals in the book (chickens, Cocky, a mule, cats, dogs). Did they add to your enjoyment of the book or not? Were they well described? Which were your favourite?

12. Does this book make you want to keep chickens?
13. The author received many emails from US readers complaining about two of the chickens' names. Did those names spoil the book for you?
14. Was there a passage from the book that stood out for you? Why?
15. The author set out to capture the colour and spirit of Spain through the descriptive passages and characters. Did she succeed?
16. Did you have to force yourself to read the book, or did you find yourself engrossed and turning the pages? At what point in the book did you decide whether you liked it or not? What helped make this decision?
17. Did you like the inclusion of Spanish recipes or not? Will you ever try any of the recipes? Which ones?
18. Did the book end the way you expected? Did you feel all the ends were tied up?
19. Did you learn anything from the book that you didn't know before?
20. If you could change something about the book, what would it be and why?
21. 'Chickens' is the first of a series. Did you like the book enough to want to read the sequels?
22. Would you recommend this book to other readers? To your close friend? Mother?
23. Have you read memoirs before? If not, did 'Chickens' make you want to try some more?

THE OLD FOOLS SERIES

Book #1

Chickens, Mules and Two Old Fools

If Joe and Vicky had known what relocating to a tiny Spanish mountain village would REALLY be like, they might have hesitated...

Book #2

Two Old Fools - Olé!

Vicky and Joe have finished fixing up their house and look forward to peaceful days enjoying their retirement. Then the fish van arrives, and instead of delivering fresh fish, disgorges the Ufarte family.

Book #3

Two Old Fools on a Camel

Reluctantly, Vicky and Joe leave Spain to work for a year in the Middle East. Incredibly, the Arab revolution erupted, throwing them into violent events that made world headlines.

New York Times bestseller three times

Book #4

Two Old Fools in Spain Again

Life refuses to stand still in tiny El Hoyo. Lola Ufarte's behaviour surprises nobody, but when a millionaire becomes a neighbour, the village turns into a battleground.

Book #5

Two Old Fools in Turmoil

When dark, sinister clouds loom, Victoria and Joe find themselves facing life-changing decisions. Happily, silver linings also abound. A fresh new face joins the cast of well-known characters but the return of a bad penny may be more than some can handle.

Book #6

Two Old Fools Down Under

When Vicky and Joe wave goodbye to their beloved Spanish village, they face their future in Australia with some trepidation. Now they must build a new life amongst strangers, snakes and spiders the size of saucers. Accompanied by their enthusiastic new puppy, Lola, adventures abound, both heartwarming and terrifying.

One Young Fool in Dorset (Prequel)

This light and charming story is the delightful prequel to Victoria Twead's Old Fools series. Her childhood memories are vividly portrayed, leaving the reader chuckling and enjoying a warm sense of comfortable nostalgia.

One Young Fool in South Africa (Prequel)

Who is Joe Twead? What happened before Joe met Victoria and they moved to a crazy Spanish mountain village? Joe vividly paints his childhood memories despite constant heckling from Victoria at his elbow.

Two Old Fools in the Kitchen, Part 1 (Cookbook)

The *Old Fools' Kitchen* cookbooks were created in response to frequent requests from readers of the *Old Fools series* asking to see all the recipes collected together in one place.

THE SIXPENNY CROSS SERIES
SHORT FICTION, INSPIRED BY LIFE

A is for Abigail

Abigail Martin has everything: beauty, money, a loving husband, and a fabulous house in the village of Sixpenny Cross. But Abigail is denied the one thing she craves... A baby.

B is for Bella

When two babies are born within weeks of each other in the village of Sixpenny Cross, one would expect the pair to become friends as they grow up. But nothing could be further from the truth.

C is for the Captain

Everyone knows ageing bachelors, the Captain and Sixpence, are inseparable. But when new barmaid, Babs, begins work at the Dew Drop Inn, will she enhance their twilight years, or will the consequences be catastrophic?

The Sixpenny Cross Collection: Books 1-3

D is for Dexter - coming soon

MORE BOOKS BY VICTORIA TWEAD...

How to Write a Bestselling Memoir
How does one write, publish and promote a memoir? How does one become a bestselling author?

Dear Fran, Love Dulcie (letters collated by Victoria Twead)
A glimpse of life and death in the hills and hollows of bygone Australia through the letters of two newly-weds.

Morgan and the Martians - A COMEDY PLAY FOR KIDS
Morgan is a bad boy. A VERY bad boy. When a bunch of Martians gives him a Shimmer Suit that makes him invisible, he wastes no time in wearing it to school and creating havoc. Well, wouldn't you?

Two Old Fools in the Kitchen, Part 1 (COOKBOOK)
The *Old Fools' Kitchen* cookbooks were created in response to frequent requests from readers of the *Old Fools series* asking to see all the recipes collected together in one place.

ABOUT THE AUTHOR

Victoria Twead is the New York Times bestselling author of *Chickens, Mules and Two Old Fools* and the subsequent books in the Old Fools series.

After living in a remote mountain village in Spain for eleven years, and owning probably the most dangerous cockerel in Europe, Victoria and Joe retired to Australia.

Another joyous life-chapter has begun.

For photographs and additional unpublished material to accompany this book, download the
Free Photo Book
from
www.victoriatwead.com/free-stuff

CONTACTS AND LINKS
CONNECT WITH VICTORIA

Email: TopHen@VictoriaTwead.com (emails welcome)

Website: www.VictoriaTwead.com

Old Fools' Updates Signup: www.VictoriaTwead.com

This includes the latest Old Fools' news, free books, book recommendations, and recipe. Guaranteed spam-free and sent out every few months.

Free Stuff: http://www.victoriatwead.com/Free-Stuff/

Facebook: https://www.facebook.com/VictoriaTwead (friend requests welcome)

Instagram: @victoria.twead

Twitter: @VictoriaTwead

Behind-the-scenes glimpses and memoir writing help:

https://www.patreon.com/VictoriaTwead

Ant Press publishing: www.antpress.org

We Love Memoirs

Join me and other memoir authors and readers in the We Love Memoirs Facebook group, the friendliest group on Facebook.

www.facebook.com/groups/welovememoirs/

ACKNOWLEDGMENTS

I owe a huge debt of gratitude to many people who have helped me along the way. Without them, this book would never have taken shape. So, sincere thanks must go to the following:

Caroline and Nicholas for Spanish wildlife advice and kindly reviewing the manuscript without taking offence when they read about themselves.

Ken and Glennys, for allowing me to relate their stories and reproduce their photographs (see free Photo Book) and emails.

My son, **Shealan**, for his invaluable help answering all my computing questions.

My daughter, **Karly**, for allowing her stories and photographs to be used, ('Mum! If I'd known, I'd have washed my hair!') and for her constant encouragement.

Joe, for putting up with me during my highs and lows, for his ideas and patience checking everything during the writing process.

My English friends, **B and L**, for their friendship and anecdotes.

Gwenda, who was the first 'stranger' to see my writing and gave me all the confidence I needed to carry on. Her support throughout has been invaluable and she is a stranger no more.

And last but certainly not least, my friends **Tweek and Al** for their generosity and unfailing support for everything I have done in the last 30 years.

Some of the people and place names have been changed.

If I have made mistakes in any of the recipes, please forgive me. I am no chef or mathematician. Similarly, please overlook any Spanish language errors; I still have much to learn.

This memoir reflects my recollections of experiences over a period of time. In order to preserve the anonymity of the wonderful people I write about, some names have been changed, including the name of the village. Certain individuals are composites and dialogue and events have been recreated from memory and, in some cases, compressed to facilitate a natural narrative.

ANT PRESS BOOKS
AWESOME AUTHORS ~ AWESOME BOOKS

If you enjoyed this book, you may also enjoy these Ant Press titles:

MEMOIRS

Dear Fran, Love Dulcie: The Hills and Hollows of Life in Bygone Australia Letters collated by Victoria Twead

Chickens, Mules and Two Old Fools by Victoria Twead (Wall Street Journal Top 10 bestseller)
Two Old Fools ~ Olé! by Victoria Twead
Two Old Fools on a Camel by Victoria Twead (thrice New York Times bestseller)
Two Old Fools in Spain Again by Victoria Twead
Two Old Fools in Turmoil by Victoria Twead
Two Old Fools Down Under by Victoria Twead
One Young Fool in Dorset (Prequel) by Victoria Twead
One Young Fool in South Africa (Prequel) by Joe and Victoria Twead
Two Old Fools Boxset, Books 1-3 by Victoria Twead

Fat Dogs and French Estates ~ Part I by Beth Haslam
Fat Dogs and French Estates ~ Part II by Beth Haslam
Fat Dogs and French Estates ~ Part III by Beth Haslam
Fat Dogs and French Estates ~ Part IV by Beth Haslam
Fat Dogs and French Estates ~ Part V by Beth Haslam
Fat Dogs and French Estates ~ Boxset, Parts 1-3 by Beth Haslam

From Moulin Rouge to Gaudi's City by EJ Bauer
From Gaudi's City to Granada's Red Palace by EJ Bauer

Dear Fran, Love Dulcie: The Hills and Hollows of Life in Bygone Australia collated by Victoria Twead

South to Barcelona: A New Life in Spain by Vernon Lacey

Simon Ships Out: How One Brave, Stray Cat Became a Worldwide Hero by Jacky Donovan
Smoky: How a Tiny Yorkshire Terrier Became a World War II American Army Hero, Therapy Dog and Hollywood Star by Jacky Donovan
Smart as a Whip: A Madcap Journey of Laughter, Love, Disasters and Triumphs by Jacky Donovan

Midwife: A Calling by Peggy Vincent
Midwife: A Journey by Peggy Vincent
Midwife: An Adventure by Peggy Vincent

Heartprints of Africa: A Family's Story of Faith, Love, Adventure, and Turmoil by Cinda Adams Brooks
How not to be a Soldier: My Antics in the British Army by Lorna McCann
Moment of Surrender: My Journey Through Prescription Drug Addiction to Hope and Renewal by Pj Laube

One of its Legs are Both the Same by Mike Cavanagh
A Pocket Full of Days, Part 1 by Mike Cavanagh
A Pocket Full of Days, Part 2 by Mike Cavanagh

Horizon Fever 1 by A E Filby
Horizon Fever 2 by A E Filby

Completely Cats - Stories with Cattitude by Beth Haslam and Zoe Marr

Fresh Eggs and Dog Beds: Living the Dream in Rural Ireland by Nick Albert

Fresh Eggs and Dog Beds 2: Still Living the Dream in Rural Ireland by Nick Albert
Fresh Eggs and Dog Beds 3: More Living the Dream in Rural Ireland by Nick Albert
Fresh Eggs and Dog Beds 4: More Living the Dream in Rural Ireland by Nick Albert

Don't Do It Like This: How NOT to move to Spain by Joe Cawley, Victoria Twead and Alan Parks

Longing for Africa: Journeys Inspired by the Life of Jane Goodall. Part One: Ethiopia by Annie Schrank
Longing for Africa: Journeys Inspired by the Life of Jane Goodall. Part Two: Kenya by Annie Schrank

A Kiss Behind the Castanets: My Love Affair with Spain by Jean Roberts
Life Beyond the Castanets: My Love Affair with Spain by Jean Roberts

The Sunny Side of the Alps: From Scotland to Slovenia on a Shoestring by Roy Clark

FICTION

Parched by Andrew C Branham

A is for Abigail by Victoria Twead (Sixpenny Cross 1)
B is for Bella by Victoria Twead (Sixpenny Cross 2)
C is for the Captain by Victoria Twead (Sixpenny Cross 3)
D is for Dexter by Victoria Twead
The Sixpenny Cross Collection, Vols 1-3 by Victoria Twead

NON FICTION

How to Write a Bestselling Memoir by Victoria Twead
Two Old Fools in the Kitchen, Part 1 by Victoria Twead

CHILDREN'S BOOKS

Seacat Simon: The Little Cat Who Became a Big Hero by Jacky Donovan
Morgan and the Martians by Victoria Twead

LARGE PRINT BOOKS

Chickens, Mules and Two Old Fools by Victoria Twead (Wall Street Journal Top 10 bestseller)
Two Old Fools ~ Olé! by Victoria Twead
Two Old Fools on a Camel by Victoria Twead (thrice New York Times bestseller)
Two Old Fools in Spain Again by Victoria Twead
Two Old Fools in Turmoil by Victoria Twead
Two Old Fools Down Under by Victoria Twead
One Young Fool in Dorset (The Prequel) by Victoria Twead
One Young Fool in South Africa (The Prequel) by Joe and Victoria Twead

Fat Dogs and French Estates ~ Part I by Beth Haslam
Fat Dogs and French Estates ~ Part II by Beth Haslam
Fat Dogs and French Estates ~ Part III by Beth Haslam
Fat Dogs and French Estates ~ Part IV by Beth Haslam
Fat Dogs and French Estates ~ Part V by Beth Haslam

A Kiss Behind the Castanets: My Love Affair with Spain by Jean Roberts

Dear Fran, Love Dulcie: The Hills and Hollows of Life in Bygone Australia Letters collated by Victoria Twead

A is for Abigail by Victoria Twead (Sixpenny Cross 1)
B is for Bella by Victoria Twead (Sixpenny Cross 2)
C is for the Captain by Victoria Twead (Sixpenny Cross 3)
D is for Dexter (Sixpenny Cross 4) by Victoria Twead

ANT PRESS ONLINE

Why not check out Ant Press's online presence and follow our social media accounts for news of forthcoming books and special offers?

Website: www.antpress.org
Email: admin@antpress.org
Facebook: www.facebook.com/AntPress
Instagram: www.instagram.com/publishwithantpress
Twitter: www.twitter.com/Ant_Press

HAVE YOU WRITTEN A BOOK?

Would you love to see your book published? Ant Press can help! Take a look at www.antpress.org or contact Victoria directly.

Email: TopHen@VictoriaTwead.com